TRANSPORT SOCIOLOGY

Social Aspects of Transport Planning

TRANSPORT SOCIOLOGY

Social Aspects
of Transport Planning

Edited by

Enne de BOER

PERGAMON PRESS

OXFORD · NEW YORK · BEIJING · FRANKFURT
SÃO PAULO · SYDNEY · TOKYO · TORONTO

UK	Pergamon Press, Headington Hill Hall, Oxford OX3 0BW, England
U.S.A.	Pergamon Press, Maxwell House, Fairview Park, Elmsford, New York 10523, U.S.A.
PEOPLE'S REPUBLIC OF CHINA	Pergamon Press, Qianmen Hotel, Beijing, People's Republic of China
FEDERAL REPUBLIC OF GERMANY	Pergamon Press, Hammerweg 6, D-6242 Kronberg, Federal Republic of Germany
BRAZIL	Pergamon Editora, Rua Eçạ de Queiros, 346, CEP 04011, São Paulo, Brazil
AUSTRALIA	Pergamon Press Auststralia, P.O. Box 544, Potts Point, N.S.W. 2011, Australia
JAPAN	Pergamon Press, 8th Floor, Matsuoka Central Building, 1-7-1 Nishishinjuku, Shinjuku-ku, Tokyo 160, Japan
CANADA	Pergamon Press Canada, Suite 104, 150 Consumers Road, Willowdale, Ontario M2J 1P9, Canada

First edition 1986

Library of Congress Cataloging in Publication Data
Main entry under title:
Transport sociology.
Includes bibliographies.
1. Urban transportation—Social aspects—Addresses, essays, lectures. 2. Urban transportation—Environmental aspects—Addresses, essays, lectures. 3. Urban transportation—Planning—Addresses, essays, lectures
I. Boer, E. de
HE305.T74   1986   388.4   85–28410

British Library Cataloguing in Publication Data
Transport sociology: social aspects of transport planning.—
(Urban and regional planning series)
1. Transportation—Planning—Social aspects
I. Boer, E. de II. Series
380.5   HE193
ISBN 0–08–023686–3

Printed in Great Britain by A. Wheaton & Co., Exeter

Acknowledgements

This book is the result of continued efforts to provide students in transport planning with relevant materials on the social side of transport. Without these often unwilling victims I would never have collected such a variety of papers in a field so uncommon and inaccessible to the sociologist.

Professor Andreas Faludi inspired me to compose from it a reader for publication. Paul Smeele was always willing to make helpful comments. Professor Frank, Mr. De Jong and Professor Schmidt-Relenberg were so kind as to correct thoroughly the English translation of their respective papers. Desmond Sweeny and Walt Massie rid the manuscript of "Dutchisms". It was typed by Mrs. P. van den Berg and Mrs. H. Willemsen. Mrs. Jongedyk-Hruzova redrew the illustrations. However, this reader never would have been completed without my wife's constant encouragement and if she had not taken Bauke and Truusje skating alone.

Contents

Biographical Notes

(The order follows that of the articles in the reader.)

1. Gordon FELLMAN is Associate Professor of Sociology at Brandeis University. He was a founder of the second advocacy planning organization in the United States, Urban Planning Aid, operating in metropolitan Boston. The study from which "Neighborhood protest of an urban highway" stemmed is reported more fully in "The deceived majority, politics and protest in Middle America" (1971 in association with Barbara Brandt).

2. Marvin G. CLINE was, at the time of writing his contribution, a research associate of the Washington Center for Metropolitan Studies and Assistant Professor of Psychology at the University of Maryland.

3. Donald APPLEYARD was Professor of Urban Design in the Departments of City Planning and Landscape Architecture of the University of California at Berkeley. Among his many publications are several in the field of street-environments like *The view from the road* (with Kevin Lynch and J. R. Myer) 1963 and *Livable Streets* (1981).

4. Rudolf DE JONG is a staff-member of the International Institute of Social History in Amsterdam. He is an expert on Spain, Latin America and Anarchism.

5. Donald APPLEYARD see 3.

   Mark LINTELL is an architect and city planner who received degrees in Cambridge (UK) and at Berkeley. He has international professional experience and co-operated with Appleyard in the San Francisco Urban Design Study.

6. Norbert SCHMIDT-RELENBERG is Professor of Sociology at the University of Giessen (GFR). He has published several books on urban sociology, family and sexuality. Presently he is especially interested in social problems of developing countries (Selbstorganisation der Armen, ein Bericht aus Venezuela (1980) — Selforganization of the poor, a report from Venezuela).

7. Torsten HÄGERSTRAND, Emeritus Professor of Social and Economic Geography at the University of Lund, Sweden, has since the

1940s been conducting research on internal migration, spatial diffusion of innovations, geo-coding, urbanization and regional development.

Since the beginning of the 1970s his scientific preoccupation has been to develop a new conceptual construct, called "time-geography", which is a strongly process-oriented perspective, trying to grasp the interplay between society's place-, time- and thing-use.

8. Mayer HILLMAN is a social scientist who has been engaged for the last 16 years at the Policy Studies Institute (formerly Political and Economic Planning) in London on research into the social aspects of transport planning. In addition to writing articles and reading papers at many major conferences on his research, he is co-author of the following books:

> *Personal Mobility and Transport Policy* (1973)
> *Transport Realities and Planning Policy* (1976)
> *Walking is Transport* (1979)
> *The Social Consequences of Rail Closures* (1980)
> *Danger on the Road: the needless scourge* (1984).

9. K. C. KOUTSOPOULOS is Professor of Geography at the National Technical University of Athens. His research interests involve analysing the spatial impacts of transportation and the influence of urban form and structure on human mobility. His latest book is on the impact of new urban highways on the mobility of the transportation disadvantaged (the carless, the poor, the elderly and the young).

C. G. SCHMIDT is Professor of Geography at the University of Colorado, Denver. He is the author of publications focusing on commercial and industrial location processes and socio-economic problems of inner city residents.

10. Mayer HILLMAN and his colleagues at the Policy Studies Institute have for more than a decade been engaged in research into the social aspects of transport planning, producing reports on mobility in general (1973, 1976), access for sport and recreation (1972) walking (1979) and rail closures (1980).

11. Delbert A. TAEBEL and James V. CORNEHLS are Professors of Urban Affairs at the Institute of Urban Studies, University of Texas at Arlington. They published a book on *The political economy of urban transportation* (1977). Professor Cornehls (Urban Affairs and Economics) has additionally published on Urban economics, economic development and Latin American Economics. Professor Taebel (Urban Affairs and Political Science) has published numerous articles on urban government and administration.

12. Harmut FRANK is Professor of Urban and Building Economics of the Academy for Creative Arts (Hochschule für Bildende Künste) in

Hamburg. His research activities have been in the field of infrastructural planning and the profession of architects and town planners. More recently, planning in developing countries and problems of state intervention on housing have occupied his interest.

Biographical note on the editor

Enne DE BOER is Senior Lecturer at Delft University of Technology (The Netherlands). He a.o. is teaching on transport sociology and civil engineering, science and society. His publications are predominantly on social problems in transport and on airport planning. He is conducting research on social impact of transport withdrawal, severance effects of motorways, and acceptability of noise barriers.

General Introduction

Summary

E. DE BOER

A few years ago, a large international conference was held in Rotterdam on the theme of "Transport planning in an age of uncertainty". One critic noted that the factual content of the conference almost entirely neglected the element of uncertainty, which he regretted: there is no clear way ahead for transport planning[1]. Ours is an "era of transition", but where to?[2]

We have discovered in the USA, perhaps somewhat earlier than in Western Europe, that the increasing motorized traffic once thought to be beneficial for our mobility and freedom has had a devastating influence on residential streets and thus on essential conditions for social integration and individual development. New infrastructure, built to relieve existing over-loaded streets and roads and to improve accessibility, acts like a barrier, frequently destroying the existing social fabric by carving a corridor through built-up areas. Moreover, increased accessibility is counter-weighted by consequent changes in land use: people and institutions are operating on a larger scale, because of and dependent on this new access. For car-users the net effect may be positive (but this remains to be seen). For people without access to a car it is without doubt negative: local facilities are disappearing without the opportunity to replace them by using public transport or non-motorized means of transport, because land use patterns have adapted to the automobile. For such people (especially the young, the old and the handicapped) the local community is extremely important: for them there is no community without propinquity to paraphrase the title of a paper by Melvin Webber[3].

There is no new technology to help us out: no electric transport system surpassing the automobile and also bringing advantages to those deprived of mobility. Belief in the technical and socio-economic feasibility of such systems has virtually disappeared in the second half of the seventies, because of energy shortages. In the USA public transport has declined more than in Europe, where land use is generally more controlled, but neither here nor there can we have the illusion of providing public transport to give automobility to those left behind. Only upon first sight did the economic crisis promise a counter trend: a decline in car-use and car sales does not imply a return to public transport. This counter trend can only be expected where public transport is already a reasonable alternative for the car: on main routes during rush hours. Growing patronage at such

3

times immediately demands a growing capacity which is used for only a few hours. This in its turn requires growing subsidies. Alas, economic decline does not permit unlimited support of transport operators; instead there is a tendency to withdraw subsidies. In Britain rural transport has already declined considerably. The Netherlands still has an elaborate system of rural and urban public transport, but the axe is about to be applied[4]. Thus there seems to be neither a way ahead nor a way back: transport is in social crisis, especially since the general public has discovered that government often enhances a dubious public good without due respect for their interests. Public projects irrespective of their goals (ranging from highway construction to traffic restraint) meet with mounting resistance of local interests which cannot be easily surmounted by efficient procedures but require patient consideration of local problems and locally proposed solutions. As the 1977 Leitch-report bluntly states: "The Department will just have to grin and bear it."[5] The substance of this reader is thus indicated and explained: it is about problematic social aspects in transport planning, both important and frustrating for urban and transport planners.

If we want to go ahead with transport planning in a sensible and successful way we will have to devote more attention to social aspects than in the past. This is especially true (though not exclusively) for the themes covered by this reader: the social impact of infrastructure, the street, mobility (or rather immobility) ideology. Traditional topics like traffic safety and modal choice, both concerned with the efficiency of the transport system, might gain from an analysis in which not only individual deviant and choice behaviour is highlighted (by psychologists) but attention is paid as well to what is collectively regarded as normal (or simply reasonable) and to positional or role constraints upon choice: to social and cultural determinants of behaviour. In some of the included papers information concerning these topics can be found: constraints on modal choice are akin to constraints on mobility. Schmidt-Relenberg's "On the sociology of individual . . ." deals explicitly with determinants of driver-behaviour, but it has been included (under "the street") for his treatment of structural principles of road-systems.

This reader then is less oriented to inefficiencies of the present transport system than to its purposes and to the paradoxes it has created: access and severance, mobility and transport-deprivation, social integration on a regional or even larger scale and disintegration at the local level. There is hardly a tradition of studying the social aspect of transport. Literature on the subject is therefore dispersed over numerous periodicals. The purpose of this reader is to give an introduction and an overview to students and practitioners in urban planning, transport planning and sociology.

There are 4 parts altogether. The order might be called inductive: working upwards from tangible, controversial problems to more abstract questions of mobility and ideology, about which discussion is often much more academic.

The social impacts of infrastructure (Part I) attracts by far the most public attention and shows in fact the whole range of problems treated in subsequent parts. It makes clear how pervasive and complicated is the process of change set off by adapting infrastructure. *The street (Part II)* has been changed considerably in the past century, not only by traffic but also by socio-economic development and town planning. Yet if traffic is restrained, the street can continue to have a number of essential functions now often suppressed. The victims of this suppression are predominantly the transport-disadvantaged, more or less synonymous with people having little or no access to the car. In Part III on *mobility*, not only the disadvantaged categories are depicted. The multifarious nature of constraints upon mobility and access is analysed along with the consequences of immobility highlighting the value of transport in individual life. *Ideology* (Part IV), coherent ideas concerning problems, their causes and solutions, has hardly ever played an explicit role in transport planning which was regarded as an apolitical and thus technical matter. The ideologies implicit in or to be interpreted from planning and those developed during the controversies of the late sixties and seventies (by Marxists for instance) can nevertheless clarify our present state and the choices to be made.

The introductions to these parts each contain a short systematic treatise on their subject, summaries of the incorporated papers and a list of selected literature as an aid to further reading.

The papers — largely unknown but sometimes famous though inaccessible (like Hägerstrand's "What about people . . .") were selected from different countries with different perspectives on transport problems. The selections are varied in character: empirical, theoretical and practical. This mixture, which admittedly did not quite succeed for every part, was chosen so as to offer vivid, systematic and useful treatment. Though the subject matter is social, the analysis is mostly not explicitly sociological. Academic sociology has neglected transport, evidently because it did not perceive its social importance, nor the problems it created. Sociology crystallized around other more conspicuous societal problems. Yet Saint-Simon, one of the acknowledged predecessors of sociology (his pupil Comte coined the term) developed an influential ideology, "Saint-Simonism", for building a new society after the French revolution in which infrastructure was assigned a central role[6]. One of the American fathers of sociology, Charles Horton Cooley, published *The theory of transportation* in 1894[7]. William Ogburn remembered for instance for the theory of "social and cultural lag" (slow societal reactions to technological development) in 1946 tried to predict *The social effects of aviation* in book-form[8].

An introductory paper by the editor, "Transport sociology", traces the development of this sociological sub-discipline, indicating its relevance for both sociology and transport planning and in fact summarizing the substance of this reader. The concluding paragraphs attempt to outline what remains to be done in transport sociology, both academically and practically, to arrive at a truly social transport planning.

Notes

1. Martin Richards (1978) in *Transportation*, **7**, No. 3, p. 344, reviewing E. J. Visser (ed.) (1978). *Transport decisions in an age of uncertainty*, Proceedings of the Third World Conference on Transport Research, 1977, Nijhoff, The Hague.
2. G. R. M. Jansen, P. Nijkamp and C. J. Ruijgrok (eds.) (1985) *Transportation and mobility in an era of transition*, Proceedings of an international conference at Zandvoort (NL), North Holland, Amsterdam.
3. Order in diversity, community without propinquity, pp. 23–56 in L. Wingo (ed.) (1963). *Cities and space, the future use of urban land*, Johns Hopkins, Baltimore.
4. In 1981 a modest withdrawal of rural services took place, concerning about 6000 passengers a week in the provinces of Friesland and Groningen alone. Its impact on former users was investigated by the editor in a before and after study commissioned by the governments of these provinces (interim reports: *The social function of rural transport threatened*, 1981 and *Missing the bus*, 1982). Fares moreover are rising sharply since government subsidies are to be cut by 20 per cent in 5 years. It has resulted in a declining patronage and consequent withdrawal of services.
5. Report of the Advisory Committee on Trunk Road Assessment (1977) (Chairman: Sir George Leitch), HMSO, London, p. 138.
6. Pp 58, 59 in A. Vidler *The scenes of the street*; pp 27–112 in S. Anderson (ed.) *On streets* (1978), MIT Press, Cambridge (Mass.).
7. Ch. H. Cooley (1894) *The theory of transportation*, Publications of the American Economic Association, **IX**, No. 3, pp 226–374.
8. W. Ogburn (1946) *The Social effects of aviation*, Houghton Mifflin, Boston.

Transport Sociology*

E. DE BOER

Transport sociology is probably one of the most remarkable of sociological sub-disciplines not, primarily, because it covers a very complex field but because it is as much underdeveloped as it is of great potential importance, both for sociology and also for physical and transport planning. In this specialization, more than in many others, sociology comes face to face with daily life, with the fact that individuals and groups live in space and time, and not exclusively in social structures. In this way all kinds of matters which form the subjects of various sub-disciplines (education, the family, organization and industry, etc), are brought together in one framework and related to social geography. Mobility, migration and social mobility, infrastructure and social structure must be brought into association with one another.

Physical and transport planning have reached an impasse. Both sub-urbanization and the increasing use of motor vehicles are opposed, for various reasons; not, in the last analysis, because they reinforce one another, but because they seem to be unstoppable. Transport planning might very well be the most important key to urban and regional planning. Transport sociology will have to provide the insights which are needed for the employment of this key. Alas, it is not yet sufficiently developed to do so.

In Dutch the term "transport sociology" was probably first used by Groenman, not earlier than 1959. Thereafter it was not, or scarcely ever, used, although since 1972 it has been taught as a subject for transport planning students at Delft Technological University. A basically similar situation is met in English and French writings, in which aspects of the "sociology of the street" or of the "sociology of the motor car" are discussed. In the many American readers in urban sociology, the subject of traffic certainly does not appear before 1975. Examination of the German literature provides a mass of titles more extensive than those in all other languages put together. Thus Claessens in 1959 was the first to try, in *Soziologie des Strassenverkehrs* (*Sociology of Road Traffic*), to provide an outline of traffic sociology. Nevertheless, Hoettler, who carefully collated

---

Social aspects of transport: how to use social research in transport policy making, pp. 57–62. Proceedings of a conference held at West Dean 14–17 September 1980. TRRL, SR 689, Crowthorne, Berkshire; adapted for publication in the present reader.

the German literature, found it possible as late as 1975 to deny the existence of a clearly defined sociological specialization. We are at best in the initial stages of the subject: no professorial chairs, an institutional vacuum, a literature consisting overwhelmingly of occasional papers and reports, scattered among all kinds of periodicals, and publications which are only rarely specifically sociological in character.

It is obvious that no very clear picture exists of the object of transport sociology. The description that follows is thus mainly the responsibility of the present writer.

As in the case of the sociology of housing, in which both dwellings as such and the creation of accommodation are the subjects of study, transport sociology cannot restrict itself specifically to traffic (occurrences on the road) or even to transport (movements or mobility) but must at the same time consider traffic and transport policy, since otherwise too much would remain unexplained in the operation of traffic and transport and in the changes therein. The tendency towards such an extension of the field is clearly perceptible.

The elements of transport sociology are discussed below in chronological sequence, as far as possible — that is, the earliest to be developed is the first — and therefore not on the basis of any theoretical scheme.

The earliest publications dealt with traffic in a narrow sense: in particular, the behaviour of the motorist on the road and the way in which it is conditioned by the system of traffic regulations and punishments, the design of the infrastructure and the qualities of the automobile as well as its functions for the driver/owner. This complex is most systematically discussed by Schmidt-Relenberg (1968). It was with these aspects that a beginning was made, since it was in the fifties that traffic first became a problem with the rapid increase in the number of road casualties. The subject is complicated and hard to research — as Groenman noted — and it therefore needs long theoretical and empirical studies to produce any general recommendations. However, the urgency of the question demanded and demands concrete measures in the short term, with the result that the appreciation of sociology's problems is not very great. This explains the notably occasional nature of the publications and the limited accumulation of knowledge in this area. Nevertheless, a number of interesting ideas emerged. The general starting point is that deviant behaviour should be attributed to the traffic system rather than to the person in the system. Search for deviant groups, traffic education and the punishment of offenders thus have a very limited use. In traffic, general and detailed behaviour are conditioned by an intricate system of norms, of technical origin, to which we often show little insight: cyclists riding quite alone on a country road in pitch darkness are required to indicate a change of direction. Quite often complicated and unforeseen traffic situations call for an individual reaction on the part of the driver or rider and for co-operation with others. The first is impeded by the very detailed nature of the traffic regulations, the second by the absence of common objectives, other than, at best, the avoidance of an accident. It is rather a question of rivalry. Formal and informal social controls are very limited: given the closed-in nature of the private car, there is little mutual communication and one is inaccessible, and isolated. Indeed, the car is more than a rational means of transport, as is indicated by the title of Kobs essay *Werkzeug, Kongsumgut, Machtssymbol (Tool, Consumer Good, Power Symbol)* (1966). Suggestions from the sociological side point on the one hand towards a strengthening of (informal) social control (Schelsky), on the other towards the development of the traffic system: simpler norms and greater uniformity of the traffic system and of means of transport (Schmidt-Relenberg). This is, from the point of view of sociology, an interesting area of transport sociology, in that it offers good possibilities for the study of social inequality (how the categories of road-users treat each other and are treated by the judicature) and a great challenge from the theoretical point of view. A thorough consideration of this intricate system and comparison with other systems similarly over-supplied with norms, like the bureaucracy, should be of interest.

In the fifties the "traffic problem", under the influence of the increase in motor traffic, was primarily a traffic safety problem. Later, after 1960, it became also, and primarily, a question of capacity. There arose a need for reliable forecasts of transport trends, in order to make good use of limited funds for the expansion of the infrastructure. Because the behaviour of those transported was not experienced as a problem and because effort was directed solely to forecasting "trip-generation" for extensive areas, such as for motorway planning, there was no involvement of sociologists. Nor did this happen when "mode choice" became a problem, in about 1965. Pressure on the inter-city road network could be alleviated by the construction of new expressways. Bottlenecks were thus transferred to the towns, where, despite some demolition of run-down areas, there was much less possibility and willingness to make extra space for traffic. Attention was therefore focused on improving public transport, which requires less space, but without affecting "free choice of the means of travel": promoting public transport by improving its quality but without creating impediments to the use of private motor vehicles. The sparse research into choice of mode was wholly concentrated on the individual's process of choice, and on finding characteristics of modes of transport which are of importance for modal choice. This was an almost purely psychological approach with psychological theorizing at its best. Thus important traffic matters which always had the attention of the public have bypassed sociology. It is perhaps for that reason that a number of motor car related matters which are of much sociological relevance have escaped the attention of sociology.

Without too much exaggeration the motor car can be seen as a symbol of prosperity, adulthood and individual freedom in the western world and at the same time as the symbol of the consumer society with its multifarious waste. This ambiguity is related in the individual's attitude to the motor car: increasing use and favourable opinions of its superior qualities as a means of transport and, at the same time, a positive attitude to the limitation of its use. It is therefore astonishing that these phenomena have never gained the attention of sociology, any more than has the extraordinarily fascinating, extremely fierce, and international anti-motor car literature, with writings like *Les quarte rouse de la fortune* (The Four Wheels of Fortune) by the French demographer Alfred Sauvy (1970), Schneider's *Autokind versus Mankind* (1971) and *Steden, Wegen, ruimte, op weg naar de bermbeschaving* (Towns, roads, space: en route to a hard-shoulder civilization!) by H. Bakker and M. Bierman (1972).

Socio-historical studies of the penetration of the motor car in relation to its effect on society are very few in number. Only Rae's *The Road and the Car in American Life* and Moline's case-study *Mobility and the Small Town 1900–1930* (1971) deserve honourable mention. They cannot however compete with such an (admittedly exceptional) study as Kellett's *The Impact of Railways on Victorian Cities* (1969).

It was the effect of motorways in towns, in the United States in the first instance, that converted traffic problems in the second half of the sixties into social problems. The effect is of both a direct and an indirect nature: direct in the sense of the building of new routes for traffic and greater pressure on the existing street system, indirect in respect of changes in the residential pattern.

In transport planning, concepts such as "free choice of mode", "full motorization" and "family car" are common property. They give the impression that everyone can profit greatly from the motor car. Transport planning was and is mainly directed towards the smooth disentangling of current and expected transport flows and especially towards adaptations of the infrastructure to the rapid growth of motor traffic. Thus it could happen that there was a failure to take note of categories of the population, large in number, for whom cars were of little or no concern and whose contribution to the flow of traffic was slight: they caused no congestion and so no plans were made for them. The categories were the very obvious ones: children, the aged, the handicapped, housewives and the low-paid were increasingly the victims of the increase in motor traffic (De Boer, 1976; Schaeffer and Sclar, 1975). They are largely dependent for their activities on their residence and its immediate surroundings. As a result of the increased pressure of traffic, especially in older neighbourhoods, the streets can no longer be used for much else, and the freedom of movement of pedestrians, children and the aged therefore severely limited. This disrupts the process of gradual integration of the child into larger social units, and equally the ability of the aged to maintain themselves in such units. An investigation by Appleyard and Lintell (1971) made clear how powerfully traffic could affect such local social integration, including relations with neighbours.

Effects of new roads are even more radical and more easily perceptible. They are preeminently suited to provide insight into the influence of spatial changes on local society. In the United States there have therefore been intensive efforts to develop measuring instruments — complex social indicators (Wolf, 1974) — not primarily out of sympathy for the residents, but rather in order to develop objective criteria for decision-making on particular locations or plans, in view of the generally strong resistance to the construction of public works. In the case of the construction of an expressway through an inhabited locality (usually an older part of a town), a number of inhabitants and institutions are removed, internal communications become worse and the process of gradual decline (depopulation and impoverishment of facilities) characteristic of these older parts of towns is accelerated through the deterioration of the environment and of the catchment of remaining institutions. The aged and the low paid — over-represented in this context — may only with great difficulty evade the developments by means of moving or better transport. Deterioration in spatial accessibility, in the physical possibility of reaching various groupings and institutions, falls upon them exceptionally hard and one must feel concern for their social integration and mobility. Social marginality is increased by spatial marginality (Golant, 1972 and American Academy of Arts and Sciences, 1968).

The accessibility problem of the "transport-deprived" in the above-mentioned categories of the population is manifest in the construction of new roads but it is general in character, although only sporadically identified in Europe. Stimulated by road construction and the use of motor cars, various social sectors are showing an enlargement of scale, which among other things leads to a lesser density of population and institutions, as a result of which distances increase. Sub-urbanization (urban scale enlargement) goes hand-in-hand with a process of spatial specialization and segregation: concentration of certain kinds of industry in specific parts of the town and concentration of certain strata of the population in specific parts of the urban area. Specialization and segregation lead, for example to greater distances between home and work. Because these processes proceed in a spatially unco-ordinated way and independent of the existing public transport system, distances are increased even further, enhancing the use of motor cars and impairing the use of public transport (De Boer, 1976). It is a gradual process whereby — as in the United States — public transport tends finally to disappear to a large extent. Inevitably the very numerous residual categories of the transport-deprived have more and more difficulty in getting about. For sociology this poses the task, as yet hardly begun, of establishing what it means for those involved, and on the other hand what are the impacts of the efforts at forced limitation of the use of the motor car. To do this it is necessary for sociology to immerse itself deeply in daily life: to study how life proceeds in space and time and under what conditions. The methodology for the purpose is already developed: time — budget analysis, with special attention to behaviour (Szalai, 1972) and the Swedish time-space research, developed by Hägerstrand, in which the emphasis is on social and spatial circumstances (Hägerstrand, 1970). The Swedish approach in particular contributes in a quite startling manner, by a simple system of diagrams, to insight into daily life. It was adopted by leading traffic planners such as Eckhard Kutter (Matzner and Rüsch, 1976).

Transport planning itself demands the attention of sociology as much as transport. Starkie noted that ". . . the methods of analysis used by the transport planner have tended to disregard, instead of serve, the decision makers . . .: the models failed to answer the questions posed."[1] Models were not adapted to the craving for traffic restraint, for changing development in favour of public and non-motorized transport. ". . . the transport planner, perhaps preoccupied with establishing his status failed to adjust . . ."[2]. The ideas of traffic-inducement by traffic-facilities (underscoring the inadequacy of planning) and of active congestion-planning — accepting congestion as inevitable, shifting it to places where it is least harmful and even using it as an instrument of policy — used to be strongly rejected. No wonder that urban planners "found it difficult to penetrate into the closed world of transport."[3] It explains Tomazinis' remarkable conclusion from a conference on "Multidisciplinary education in transportation":

"The 2 branches of transportation — engineering and social sciences — are frequently at war with each other. Not even mutual respect for the role of each other is always apparent . . . Engineers still reveal a belief that their discipline is the essential one in the entire field of transportation. Social scientists on the other hand frequently reveal a belief that engineering studies, plans and projects are many times as wrong or detrimental to the welfare of the society as not."[4]

The new political reality of the 1970s was painful for the transport planners, who as Manheim stated ". . . can no longer hide behind a shield of supposed expertise. Rather they must be on the firing line of the political process, . . . exposing their professional judgements and value biases (implicit or explicit) to scrutiny, hostility and criticism."[5]. Reviews of methodological development testify to a radical break about 1970. Gakenheimer and Wheaton (1976) and Hoel and Meyer (1980) are unanimous in their description of four successive stages in development though these are dated somewhat differently. The first three stages are entitled: 1. conceptual development, 2. operational development, and 3. stability. The fourth one is labelled "stalemate, critical review and revisionism" and "upheaval" respectively, which needs no further explanation. It is dated "late 1960s or 1970 to present". Hoel and Meyer distinguished a fifth phase however, which they called "transition". Its characteristics may be read as signs of maturity. Those mentioned are: (a) institutional change, (b) long-range and short-range interaction, (c) incorporation of other planning concerns, and (d) (a variety of) types of projects and strategies.

It should be noted however that the changes required are so sweeping, and that planning is so long-winded, that consequently clear traces of old habits will survive for quite some time. Changes to be supported by transport sociology may be summarized after all as:

Humanization: planning for human needs and behaviour, regarding human problems like non-mobility and social impact, admitting fallability, or — citing Manheim once more: acquiring "a deep-felt humility about the professional's role and capabilities in society."[6]

Socialization: recognizing that transport is valuable only if it contributes to non-transport ends and that therefore it must be integrated with planning in other domains; stressing its function for integrating the local community; planning in interaction with its members to find for their problems solutions which they prefer.

Politicization: making subjective choice in the planning process explicit, developing alternative solutions reflecting political priorities, formulating alternative transport-policies and scenarios to confront the decision-maker with the range of choices open and with the consequences of proposed options. Webber even argues that "there can be no technically correct solutions to transport problems . . . there are no right answers: there are only the outcomes of political contest."[7] This is an overstatement however as long as there are technically incorrect solutions and as long as politics is more than pure opportunism. Transport planning is both technical and political and it should in both respects be more than haphazard, combining systematically facts and values.

Deflation and Domestication: taming traffic and its planners, shifting the emphasis from expansion of infrastructure to transport management.[8] "We may be entering an era when the transportation system is in place and the challenge may be to improve its utilization and physical condition."[9] Though normative planning theory is certainly not superfluous — Dickey's textbook is excellent in providing general guidelines — factual decision-making is receiving attention to an increasing degree, to enable the management of policy-making and implementation.[10] Gebert who reviewed the international political literature on transport for the Swiss Government in 1973 was decidedly negative about its quality: "Fallstudien wird — mit einigen wenigen Ausnahmen — die Berechtigung abgesprochen, sich unter die Politologie zu reihen" (case-studies with a few exceptions do not deserve the epithet political science).[11] Since then a number of interesting studies have however been done: Lindner (1973), Sloan (1974), Gakenheimer (1976), Pill (1978) and a series by Colcord who has been active in the field from about 1970.

Transport planners will no doubt continue to play delicate and responsible roles in decision-making. Manheim rightly devoted ample space to "the role of the professional" and "the ethics of analysis" in his textbook *Fundamentals of transportation systems analysis* (1979), knowing only too well how sophisticated analysis of the kind presented can aid the decision-maker but can deceive him as well.

Notes

1. P. 324 in D. N. M. Starkie (1974), Transport planning and the policy-modelling interface, *Transportation* **3**, pp. 323–334.
2. *ibid.*
3. Thoenig and Despicht (1975), p. 395.
4. Transportation Research Board, 1974, p. 3.
5. *op. cit.* p. 12: M. Manheim in a contribution on societal issues and transportation education (pp 10–15).
6. Manheim, *op. cit.* p. 13.
7. P. 43 in M. Webber, On the technics and politics of transport planning in Highway Research Board, 1973, pp. 43–51. His overstatement was most likely rhetorical.
8. R. Gakenheimer and M. Meyer (1979) Urban transportation planning in transition: the sources and prospects of TSM, pp 149–163 in A. Altshuler (1979).
9. Hoel and Meyer (1980), p. 17.
10. It is mentioned as important for instance by Britton Harris (p. 8) and Manheim (p. 11) in Transportation Research Board, 1974, by Hoel and Meyer (1980) (p. 19) and by Brand (pp. 15, 16) in R. M. Michaels (ed.) (1980), *Transportation planning and policy decision making, behavioral science contributions*, Praeger, New York.
11. Gebert (1973), p. 1. Richard Bolan's *Community decision behavior* (1969), reprinted in Faludi's important reader in planning theory (1973), pp. 371–394, still offers excellent schemes of the factors influencing decision making.

Literature

A. Altshuler (ed.) (1979) *Current issues in transportation policy*, Lexington Books, Lexington (Mass.).

American Academy of Arts and Sciences (1968) *Conference on Transportation and Poverty*, Springfield, Va. (National Technical Information Service).

D. Appleyard and M. Lintell (1971) Environment Quality of City Streets, the Residents' Viewpoint, in: *Highway Research Record*, **356**, pp 69–84.

H. Bakker en M. Bierman (1972) *Steden, wegen, ruimte, op weg naar de bermbeschaving*, Amsterdam (Van Gennep).

E. de Boer (1976) Mobiel en niet-mobiel, een verkenning van de sociale betekenis van ons vervoer, in: J. Overeem (ed.), *Stedelijk vervoer langs nieuwe banen?*, Den Haag (Stichting Toekomstbeeld der Techniek, Publicatie 21), pp. 47–78.

D. E. Boyce (ed.) (1985) Transportation research, the state of the art and research opportunities. *Transportation Research*, special issue, vol 19A, no 5/6 Sept/Nov 1985, pp. 349–542.

D. Claessens (1959) Zur Soziologie des Strassenverkehrs, in: *Zeitschrift für Verkehrssicherheit*, **5**, 3.

F. C. Colcord Jr., *Urban transportation decision making*. Series of monographs MIT Urban Systems Cambridge Mass. (especially no. 11 1975 with R. Lewis, Stockholm and Gothenberg: a case study).

Ch. H. Cooley (1894) *A theory of transportation*, in: Publications of the American Economic Association, **9**, pp. 223–370.

J. W. Dickey a.o. (1975) *Metropolitan transportation planning*. McGraw-Hill, New York.

R. Gakenheimer (1976) *Transportation planning as response to controversy: the Boston case*, MIT-Press, Cambridge (Mass.).

R. Gakenheimer and W. Wheaton (1976), Priorities in urban transport research, *Transportation* **5**, pp. 73–91.

A. J. Gebert (1973) *Politikwissenschaft und Verkehr*, Ubersicht der politologischen Literatur. Eidgenossische Kommission für die Schweizerische Gesamtverkehrskonzeption (GVK-CH), Bern.

S. M. Golant (1972) *The residential location and spatial behavior of the elderly*, a Canadian example, Chicago (University of Chicago, Department of Geography, research paper 193).

Sj. Groenman (1959) Het verkeer als samenlevingsvorm, in: Sj. Groenman, *Ons deel in de ruimte*, Van Gorcum, Assen, pp 74–86.

T. Hägerstrand (1970) What about people in regional science, in: *Papers of the Regional Science Association* **24**, pp. 7–21.

P. Hall (1980) *Great planning disasters*, Weidenfeld and Nicolson, London.

M. Hillman, I. Henderson and A. Whalley (1973) *Personal mobility and transport policy*, London (Political and Economic Planning, Broadsheet 542).

L. Hoel and M. D. Meyer (1980) Training and education in transportation: future directions in: Transportation Research Board, *New Directions in transportation education*, TRR 748, pp 15–21.

R. Höttler (1975) Soziologie und Verkehrsprognosemodelle, in: R. Hottler, *Soziologische Verkehrstypologie* (dissertation),Berlin, pp 1–134.

R. de Jong (1972) Herovering van de straat, sociaal-economische ontwikkeling in de 19e en 20e eeuw, in: Tj. Deelstra e.a., *De straat, vorm van samenleven*, Van Abbemuseum, Eindhoven, pp 12–23.

J. R. Kellett (1969) *The impact of railways on Victorian cities*, Routledge and Kegan Paul, London.

J. Kob (1966), Werkzeug, Konsumgut, Machtssymbol, zur Soziologie des Automobils, in: *Hamburger Jahrbuch für Wirtschafts- und Gesellschaftspolitik*, **11**, pp 184–192.

Th. Kramer-Badoni, H. Grymer and M. Rodenstein (1971) *Zur sozio-ökonomischen Bedeutung des Automobils*, Suhrkamp, Frankfurt am Main.

W. Lindner (1973) *Der Fall Massenverkehr, Verwaltungsplanung und städtische Lebensbedingungen*, Althenäum, Frankfurt am Main.

M. L. Manheim (1979) *Fundamentals of transportation systems analysis*, **11**, Basic concepts, MIT-Press, Cambridge (Mass).

E. Matzner and G. Rusch (eds.) (1976) *Transport as an instrument for allocating space and time, a social science approach*. Wien (Institut für Finanzwissenschaft und Infrastrukturpolitik der Technischen Universität, publication no. 11).

N. T. Moline (1971) *Mobility and the small town 1900–1930*. Chicago (University of Chicago, Department of Geography).

J. Pill (1978) *Planning and politics, the metro Toronto-transportation plan review*. MIT-Press, Cambridge (Mass.).

J. B. Rae (1971) *The road and the car in American life*, MIT-Press, Cambridge (Mass.).

K. H. Schaeffer and E. Sclar (1975) *Access for all*, transportation and urban growth, Penguin, Harmondsworth.

N. Schmidt-Relenberg (1968) Zur Soziologie des Individualverkehrs in Städten, in: *Zeitschrift für Verkehrssicherheit*, **14**, 4, pp 210–222.

K. R. Schneider (1971) *Autokind versus mankind, an analysis of tyranny, a proposal for rebellion, a plan for reconstruction*, Norton, New York.

A. K. Sloan (1974) *Citizen participation in transportation planning: the Boston experience*, Ballinger, Cambridge (Mass.).

D. N. M. Starkie (1976) *Transport planning, policy and analysis*. Pergamon, Oxford.

L. Szalai (ed.) (1972) *The use of time*, Mouton, The Hague.

J. C. Thoenig (1973) *L'Ere des technocrates* — les cas des ponts et chaussées, Ed. de l'Organisation, Paris.

J. C. Thoenig and N. Despicht (1975) Transport policy in: J. Hayward and M. Watson (eds.), *Planning, politics and public policy, the British, French and Italian experience*. Cambridge University Press, London.

Transportation Research Board (1974) *Multi-disciplinary education in transportation*, Special Report 150, Washington D.C.

United States Senate, Special Committee on Aging (1970) *Older Americans and transportation, a crisis in mobility*, US Government Printing Office, Washington D.C.

C. P. Wolf (1974) Social impact assessment; the state of the art, in: D. H. Carson (ed.), *Man-environment interactions*, proceedings of the 5th EDRA-conference, Milwaukee, Pt. I, bd 2, pp. 1–44, Halsted, Stroudsbury (Pa.).

F. F. Zelinka (1974) Zum Selbstverständnis der Soziologie in der Verkehrssicherheitsforschung, *Zeitschrift für Verkehrssicherheit*, **20**, 4, pp 742–760.

Part I Social Impacts of Infrastructure

Introduction

E. DE BOER

Improvements to transport systems like roads and railroads are essentially intended to improve access, and to open up residential, occupational, educational and recreational opportunities for its users. Alas, the more they seem to serve this purpose by offering high travel-speed, the less they themselves are accessible: motorways and inter-city-trains are available at relatively few places and at much higher cost than the average street and streetcar. Moreover, by enhancing regional accessibility, they often destroy local accessibility. Therefore the dominant social impact mentioned in British and French government manuals for the environmental appraisal of road projects is "effet de coupure" or "severance"[1]. Motorways for instance may cut through geographical relationships, severing residents from their neighbours, children from their playgrounds, shops from their clients. Infra-structure can however have even more incisive and pervasive social impacts. The variety, the dynamic and the interactive nature of social impacts and their implications for assessment will be treated successively.

Social Impacts

Access is an end rather than an impact of transport planning. The distribution of access (time-distance to facilities) is unequal however, both geographically and socially: people live at varying distances from facilities and differ in their ability to overcome this by means of transport. The carless and the old, for instance usually need more time and greater effort to reach the same destinations as younger people with motorized transport. Improvements of infrastructure may have redistributive effects, yielding (in the case of motorways) better access to those who had more of it already. They make other systems less attractive and cause them to deteriorate, and in the end improve access for the better-off and worsen it for the underprivileged. Mobility problems are treated in detail in Part II.

Severance. The existing distribution of access may be changed even more radically by the physical character of traffic and infrastructure. Destinations relatively near are virtually placed out of reach for pedestrians when road connections are disconnected, or when existing roads become increasingly dangerous to cross. The result may be a dramatic curtailment

19

of action space for children and of the community facilities' catchment. Relieving urban streets from through traffic and replacing village thoroughfares with bypasses may redress severance by traffic. This part of the problem seems to be of public concern in several Northwest European countries: apart from Britain certainly Sweden, the Netherlands and Germany[2]. The social function of the street itself and how it is disturbed by traffic will be treated in Part II.

Displacement. Construction or reconstruction of transport networks will as a rule require changes in land use. If its present function is for instance residential, commercial or educational it plays a very important role in the lives of (respectively) inhabitants, workers or students, defined in the Leitch Report as "occupiers". Relocation to a site nearby may be impossible, for lack of adequate housing. Marginal firms and facilities will be liquidated, older inhabitants forced into old age housing. Of course this factor also contributes to inaccess: a neighbourhood may lose its only shop or playground. Now all this may currently look a bit exaggerated now that large scale motorway building virtually has come to an end. Expansion of urban rail systems and reconstruction of existing main roads may require somewhat less additional space, but the impact is still quite impressive in urban areas where space is by definition scarce.

Migration. Changes in access and amenity (noise, pollution, vibration) may induce migration. People with higher incomes move out of an area because of loss of residential quality; in pedestrianized inner-city areas they tend to move in, ousting lower class people from the housing market[3]. Housing and local shops may even be largely superseded.

Disintegration of the local community may be the result. If people are forced to go elsewhere for a job or for shopping, if neighbours are relocated or feel obliged to leave, if strangers move in instead, social integration in the neighbourhood may decline rapidly, social contacts and other activities being less and less organized at the community level. Lower class and elderly people, especially long-term residents and "routine seekers" (striving for a stable way of living) will find it difficult to adapt[4]). But for them it may even be difficult to appreciate the process of planning and construction and to assess the meaning of the project for their life in the neighbourhood.

Project and Environment in a Process of Development

The introduction of a transport project in an urban environment doesn't suddenly cause change in a static situation. The project itself exerts a gradually changing influence on its environment in the process from conception to use by the public, which may take more than 10 years. The urban environment too is always on the move. The population of a certain neighbourhood may be ageing gradually, its land-use mix shifting towards more office-employment. The project will stimulate one trend, counteract another[5].

Stages of the Project

Planning. Location studies and political discussions will create expectations and fears of what is to come and therefore induce migration. A corridor for a road may be plotted and reserved, creating severance even if construction never takes place.

Construction. During this phase disruption as a rule is worst. Building requires more space than needed for the facility itself, existing roads may be blocked, temporary replacements primitive, if present at all. Temporary inaccess can force shopkeepers out of business, temporary construction nuisance (heavy traffic, dirt) may lead to migration of residents and therefore cause lasting impact. The *design* of the facility in horizontal alignment e.g. varying between elevating and tunneling, decides to what degree it will in the end be a barrier.

Use. The project is now deploying its full potential of redistributing access, severance and annoyance. To decide its extent it is however necessary to have a closer look at the local community.

The Floating Neighbourhood

Until now the concepts "local community" and "neighbourhood" have been used loosely. In the early days of American highway impact assessment its social component was nearly completely directed to the "community". The search for community boundaries was however — except in (small) isolated residential areas — rather hopeless[6]. Certainly the question as to what happens to a given area should be posed but the search for an answer should be guided by the notion that several overlapping communities of varying format might be found. If *individual residents* are asked to indicate on a map the neighbourhood they live in — a procedure utilized in several British studies — the result is determined at least as much by the location of their dwellings as by geographical "borders" like main roads. *Facilities* within the area sometimes serve only part of it and on other occasions a much larger area: an infant school versus a library for instance. The same is true for the action space of different *population categories* according to occupation, income or age. Toddlers for instance have only a small action space which expands gradually in the process of growing up and contracts again for the aged. The population structure indicates the degree of dependency on the direct neighbourhood. It will usually be changing, if only because of ageing of the inhabitants, with inherent repercussions for local facilities like primary schools.

Social impact of a transport project on a given area should be seen then as a changing influence on a dynamic social environment. Research into this requires posing questions like "at what stage of the project is whose community or whose facility affected?" and "how does the project affect pattern and rate of development in the area?".

Assessment and Aid

It is in no way easy to know beforehand what will be the social impact of a transport project, if only because it is not known how inhabitants of the affected area will react to planning proposals (planning impact). As Stanley and Rattray put it: "An actual project is not merely a physical facility. It is introduced by specific organizations or political institutions. It is often seen as serving the interests of specific groups in society. It may be opposed or supported by other groups. . . . These components are part of the relevant environment within which people assess the impact of a project on their lives and predict the extent of social disruption, including social severance." (p. 160).

Yet public reaction to or rather against urban motorways during the late sixties and the seventies forced the US government in particular to make systematic social impact assessments as part of the environmental impact statements (EIS) required by the National Environmental Policy Act of 1969. Therefore the US Department of Transportation issued a social impact "guidance manual" as early as 1975.

European governments reacted several years later. The British Leitch Report on trunk road assessment (1977) recommended a framework which has been officially accepted by the Department of Transport in its Departmental Standard of August 1980. It is a general framework, but strongly socio-political in character, requiring attention for six "interest groups" amongst which are "travellers" (all modes of transport), "occupiers" and "users of facilities". Severance — simply defined as "the imposition of barriers to free movement" — is for both occupiers and users one of the assessment topics. The framework was elaborated into the Department's "Manual for Environmental Appraisal" (1983). The French government's "Directive provisoire (pour) Etudes d'impact des projets routiers interurbains" stressing severance as well (coupure des cheminements et des unités fonctionelles) was introduced in 1978 (Ministère de l'Equipement etc. 1978). The Dutch Department of Transport and Public Works will add a chapter on "social aspects" to its "Guidelines for project proposals" in 1986, building in part on American and British experience (Rijkswaterstaat, 1983)[7].

Meanwhile in the US the EIS requirements created an extensive literature on social impact assessment (SIA). Important contributions were made by Finsterbusch and Wolf (Finsterbusch, 1980, Finsterbusch and

Wolf, 1981). A history of the field was provided by Wolf (1977) and a methodological review by Rohe (1982). Stanley and Rattray excellently commented upon theoretical (sociological) potentials and problems in SIA, pointing to the weaknesses in current methods and concluding that ". . . at this stage . . . in any event no formula for evaluating . . . social aspects . . . is likely to be appropriate" (p. 160/161).

Most fortunate however is the convergence in general methodological development described by Wolf in his "main pattern of steps" (*figure one*, Finsterbusch and Wolf, 1981, p. IX). Steps 3 to 6 are more or less traditional[8]. Inclusion of steps 1 and 2, problem identification and formulation of alternatives, implies that social considerations are taken into account from the very beginning of a project. There is a fair chance then that social problems in transport are solved instead of created. The "social improvement alternative" — improving social conditions while keeping traffic conditions more or less constant — might become a standard part of the procedure[9]. Inclusion of steps 7 and 8, mitigation and monitoring, may change a traditional practice of using assessments only for political decision making without, during execution of the project, caring sufficiently about and for admittedly disadvantaged interests, nor even about the correctness of the assessment. These additional steps indeed are to some extent included in Governmental guidelines and manuals, though least in the French case. However Offner's vivid analysis of before and after studies of public projects in his country is witness to a similar trend in France (Offner 1980, Introduction and Conclusions).

Social impact assessment should develop (and seems to be doing so) into an interactive process: engaging in actions of the planners and in the reactions of the planned or rather the unplanned. Since impact is only

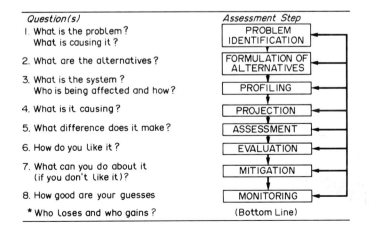

Question(s)	Assessment Step
1. What is the problem? What is causing it?	PROBLEM IDENTIFICATION
2. What are the alternatives?	FORMULATION OF ALTERNATIVES
3. What is the system? Who is being affected and how?	PROFILING
4. What is it causing?	PROJECTION
5. What difference does it make?	ASSESSMENT
6. How do you like it?	EVALUATION
7. What can you do about it (if you don't like it)?	MITIGATION
8. How good are your guesses	MONITORING
* Who loses and who gains?	(Bottom Line)

FIG. 1. Social Impact Assessment: The Main Pattern.

roughly predictable from the outside (in first round global or mini-assessments) interaction with the public is required to identify their problems, to formulate alternative acceptable solutions, to inform them about the consequences of these and to give aid in adapting to the conditions created by the solution chosen. Manheim and Suhrbier presented a roughly similar approach in "Transportation decision making, a guide to social and environmental considerations" (1975)[10].

This development could make transport planning a socially less remote affair, bringing it closer to the man in the street, the subject of Part II.

Summaries of the Selected Papers

The first article, *Fellman's Neighbourhood protest of an urban highway*, was chosen for its vivid description of life and protest in a lower income area. In Fellman's own summary:

> "Urban highways are often planned through low- and lower-middle income neighbourhoods. The social character of such neighbourhoods is probably misunderstood by many planners, who also tend to interpret minimal resistance to plans as indifference or even acceptance. The case study outlined here demonstrates the social richness and complexity of such an area. It also suggests that ignorance of effective protest techniques, disbelief in the possibility of affecting decision-makers, and a general despair over the threat of forced relocation account for low participation in a protest movement."

Fellman's argumentation underlines the need for social impact assessment of an interactive kind as suggested in the previous section. It is required for mutual understanding, positive or negative.

Cline's Urban freeways and social structure — some problems and proposals is more theoretical in character and explicitly directed towards impact assessment. After over-praising economic assessment — which is not nearly as accurate as he believes it to be — he summarizes classical sociological literature on life in urban neighbourhoods[11]. Physical environment is shown to be important and physical disruption in consequence to be socially and psychologically disruptive. Apart from disruption of "the physical framework on which the community is built", the creation of "border vacuums" (spatial marginality implying social marginality) and "separation" are mentioned as causes of social problems. The article concludes with general recommendations for research and policy.

Appleyard takes a further step in his *Evaluating the social and environmental impacts of transport investment*. His purpose was "to develop a conceptual model of the chain of social-environmental and functional interactions that take place around transport facilities". On first sight the result might seem not very insightful, the model as depicted in Figure 1 awkward, the text hardly more than a checklist. Yet the paper is in fact sound in structure and a rich source of information. A distinction is made between the impact of a transport system under relatively stable conditions — i.e. without interventions in its functioning — and under conditions of change: when the system is interfered with. It draws attention to the fact that the system as it is developing has all kinds of impacts similar to those occurring under drastic change. This implies on the one hand that impact studies might serve to redress problems around existing facilities (severance for instance) and on the other hand that studies of intervention should be comparative: confronting the ongoing process — "what might have been" — with the new circumstances. The figure not only indicates that quite a lot may change (which is hardly surprising) but also through what kind of behavioural response this might be brought about. Being a psychologist, Appleyard stresses convincingly the importance of psychic response and of adaptation, by which impact may be digested or hidden. He discerns four phases in the impact pattern of a new facility, not only the familiar planning phase (described in detail) and the familiar clearance and construction phase but an opening phase and a stabilization phase as well. This is not just the logical result of his approach, it again correctly draws attention to persistent impact and ongoing adaption. After his detailed treatment the author correctly concludes with a paragraph on strategies for assessment, suggesting criteria for content and method such as relevance to impacted populations and public comprehension. The checklist has been kept for the appendix: "an incomplete list", but quite useful for analysis.

Notes

1. G.B. Department of Transport (1982) Part B, section 4, "Community severance" and Ministère de l'Equipment etc. (1978), especially Annexe 1, chapter 1.1.2 "Effet de coupure", pp 11–26.
2. See apart from the manuals mentioned in note 1: Harder (1977), Korner (1979), Lassière (1976) and de Boer (1986).
3. The second mechanism is reported in W. Heinz a.o. (1978), *Verkehrsberuhigte Zonen in Kernbereichen*, see the literature of chapter 2.
4. The term "routine seekers" was coined by H. J. Gans (1962) to denote the behavioural style of one category of Boston West Enders in his famous book *"The urban villagers"*, Free Press, New York.
5. Offner (1980) theorized on this subject in his conclusions "l'Evaluation des investissements de transport: effets ou congruence?" (pp 90–97).
6. See the comments made by Stanley and Rattray (1978), pp 153, 154.
7. The chapter mentioned was largely based on a draft by the present writer: E. de Boer (1982), *Samenleven met infrastructuur* (Living with infrastructure), Delft University of Technology (unpublished). It was revised conjointly with a Department official F. Paes.
8. These steps are outlined for instance in the US Army Corps of Engineers guidelines for impact assessment (Finsterbusch and Wolf 1981, p. XIII).
9. As in fact according to the Dutch guidelines.
10. The report was summarized in M. L. Manheim and J. H. Suhrbier, Community values: a strategy for project planning, pp 37–47 in: Highway Research Board, HRR 380, *Citizen participation and community values*, Washington D.C., 1972, 47 pages.
11. In the Leitch Report a special appendix was dedicated to this matter. It concluded that except in cases of radical improvements of infrastructure — e.g. introducing a new transport-technique — no significant contribution to regional economic growth can be expected (pp 205–207).

26   E. de Boer

Literature

A. B. Bishop, C. H. Oglesby and G. E. Willeke (1970) *Socio-economic and community factors in planning urban freeways*, Stanford University/U.S. Department of Transportation, Washington D.C.

E. de Boer (1986) Estimating severance caused by main roads in: H. A. Becker and A. Porter (eds.), *Methods and experiences in impact assessment*, Reidel, Dordrecht (NL).

K. Finsterbusch (1980) *Understanding social impacts*, assessing the effects of public projects, Sage, Library of Social Research, **110**, Beverly Hills/London.

K. Finsterbusch and C. P. Wolf eds. (1981) *Methodology and social impact assessment*, 2nd edition, Hutchinson Ross, Stroudsburg (Pa).

G.B. Department of Transport (1983) *Draft Manual of Environmental Appraisal*, London.

U. Harder (1977) *Die methodische Erfassung und Quantifiziering der Trennwirkung von Verkehrsstraszen* (conceptualizing and quantifying severance by roads), Bundesverkehrsministerium, Gelbe Schriftenreihe 233, Bonn-Bad Godesberg.

R. J. Jain and B. L. Hutchings eds. (1978) *Environmental Impact Analysis, emerging issues in planning*, University of Illinois Press, Urbana (I11).

J. Korner (1979) *Trafikanläggningars Barriäreffekter — en litteraturstudie*, part I Problembeskrivning, begreppsanalys och teorieansats, Chalmers Technological University, Göteborg.

A. Lassière (1976) *The environmental evaluation of transport plans*, Department of the Environment, Research Report no. 8, London.

The Leitch Report (1977) *Report of the Advisory Committee on Trunk Road Assessment*, Department of Transport, H.M.S.O., London.

L. G. Llewellyn (1981) The social cost of urban transportation, pp 169–202 in: J. Altman, J. F. Wohlwill and P. B. Everett eds., *Transportation and Behaviour*, Plenum, New York/London.

L. G. Llewellyn, C. Goodman and G. Hare eds. (1981) *Social impact assessment: a sourcebook for highway planners*, U.S. Federal Highway Administration, Environmental Division, Washington D.C.

M. L. Manheim and J. H. Suhrbier a.o. (1975) *Transportation decision making, a guide to social and environmental considerations*, ACHRP, Report 156, Transportation Research Board, Washington D.C.

Ministère de l'Equipement et de l'Aménagement du Territoire, Direction des routes et de la circulation routière (1978) *Etudes d'impact des projets routiers interurbains, Directive provisoire*: directive et fiches techniques, SETRA, Bagneux (France).

J. M. Offner ed. (1980) *Etudes de suivi et processus de décision* (After studies and decision making), proceedings of the third meeting "Transport et espace", November 1980, Institut de Recherche des Transport, Arcueil (France).

J. M. Offner, A. Bieber and A. Tarrius (1982) Development of monitoring methods in some French cities, pp 167–179 in: *Social aspects of transport*: How to use social research in transport policy making, proceedings of a conference held at West Dean, Chichester, 14–17 September 1980, TRRL, Supplementary Report 689, Crowthorne, Berkshire.

Rijkswaterstaat Hoofddirectie (1983) *Handleiding projektnota's* (Guidelines for project proposals), revised edition, The Hague.

W. M. Rohe (1982) Social impact analysis and the planning process in the United States: review and critique, *Town Planning Review*, **53**, no. 4, October 1982, pp 367–382.

J. Stanley and A. Rattray (1978) Social severance, pp 140–163 in: D. W. Pearce ed., *The valuation of social cost*, Allen & Unwin, London.

U.S. Department of Transportation (1975) *Social impacts*, a guidance manual for the assessment of social impacts due to highway facility improvements, Environmental Assessment Notebooks Series, no. 2, U.S. Government Printing Office, Washington D.C.

U.S. Department of Transportation (1978) *Social impacts*, a guidance manual for the assessment of social impacts of public transportation projects. Guidelines for assessing the environmental impact of . . . Notebook 2, U.S. Government Printing Office, Washington D.C.

C. P. Wolf (1974) Social impact assessment, pp 1–45 in: D. H. Carson ed., *Man–environment interactions: evaluations and applications*, Part I, Unit 2, Halsted, Stroudsburg (Pa), Proceedings of the 5th EDRA-conference, Milwaukee 1974.

C. P. Wolf (1977) Social impact assessment: the state of the art updated, *Social impact assessment* 1977, **20**, pp 3–22.

C. P. Wolf (1979) *Social impact assessment of transportation planning*, a preliminary bibliography, Vance bibliographies P250, Monticello, Illinois.

Neighborhood Protest of an Urban Highway*

GORDON FELLMAN

Since the development of its 1948 Master Plan, the Commonwealth of Massachusetts has actively planned an eight-lane "Inner Belt" expressway for the metropolitan Boston area. The Belt would join Boston, Brookline, Cambridge, and Somerville and connect to surrounding suburbs by means of four radiating thruways. Finding that civil defense highway funds made this plan feasible, the Massachusetts Department of Public Works issued a detailed design of the Belt system in 1962. Local reaction against specific parts of the design then began.

Before 1965 the prestigious institutions of the Boston Fenway region convinced the Department of Public Works (DPW) to depress and tunnel the section of road through their area while the Brookline government pressured DPW to reduce its takings there to approximately forty homes. In Cambridge the Belt route was slated to clear over thirteen hundred working-class units in an area where little resistance was expected since low- and low-middle income people are not noted for effective political organization and protest in such matters. But by 1965 local opposition in Cambridge had also begun.

As early as 1960 residents along the proposed route — Brookline and Elm Streets in Cambridge (referred to from here on as "Brookline-Elm") — had shown their general displeasure. A DPW hearing drew 1,500 people, including angry politicians and priests, to denounce the Brookline-Elm site selections, but no organized opposition grew out of this meeting. I discovered the issue in 1963. Observing that the Cambridge weekly newspaper periodically devoted space to the Belt issue, I wondered whether the neighborhoods to be removed would respond to the highway "threat" once final plans and decisions had been announced.

The response came in autumn 1965 when several small neighborhood groups — one of them formed explicitly as a highway protest group — began discussing an areawide meeting. A petition, much like one that accompanied the 1960 DPW hearing, was circulated. Simultaneously and

*Reprinted by permission of the *Journal of American Planning Association*, **35**, 1969, pp 118–22. The accompanying map has been re-drawn.

coincidentally, a group of professional planners, architects, engineers, and sociologists met to consider pooling their skills in an effort to find a Cambridge Belt route that would do less residential damage. This group — the Cambridge Committee Against the Inner Belt — joined forces with neighborhood groups to sponsor public rallies and pressure the Cambridge City Council to favor independent restudy of the route.

While the Council adamantly opposed and continues to oppose "any and all" Belt routes through Cambridge, it did agree (not without a trace of inconsistency) to sponsor restudies and favor an alternate alignment which would take about the same number of jobs and one-tenth the number of dwellings as Brookline-Elm. (See Fig 1.) Since this alternate route crimps its growth plans, MIT has opposed it and appears to have convinced state authorities that its disadvantages out-weigh its advantages. Meanwhile, the Cambridge Committee Against the Inner Belt enlarged its scope of interest to include other counterplanning issues in the Greater Boston area and incorporated as Urban Planning Aid, Incorporated, an advocacy planning group which works on the Belt issue with the City Council and the United Effort to Save Our Cities (SOC). SOC is a protest organization stemming from the small anti-Belt groups that first met in 1965.

As a UPA member with no special qualifications for pursuing technical and political battles, I decided to abstain from activism and turn my

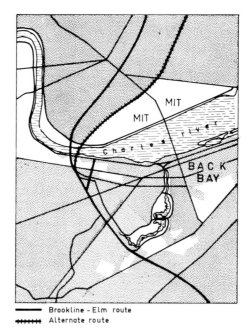

——— Brookline - Elm route
+++++ Alternate route

FIG. 1. Proposed Inner Belt Expressway Routes through Cambridge.

professional attention to understanding what was happening. Gradually, my observations and reflections crystallized in a three-part study. The first part describes the social character of the Brookline-Elm area. Reading DPW reports, I found no awareness of the nature of the Brookline-Elm population and guessed that middle class planners often implicitly and unintentionally disparage working-class housing and living patterns. I thought it would be of value to describe life along the projected pathway. Second, I wanted to learn why some people joined the protest movement and others did not — what were the political expectations and experiences of this population and how might they affect community perception of SOC activity? Finally, since I perceive SOC as largely ineffective in terms of what SOC members think they are doing, I wanted to understand why they continue to meet.

Brookline-Elm—Its Social Character

Brookline-Elm neighborhoods are similar in many significant ways to Wilmott and Young's reports on Bethnall Green and to findings from Herbert Gans and Marc Fried's studies of the Boston West End.[1] According to 1960 census figures, less than 10 percent of Brookline-Elm's homes are dilapidated. About half the homeowners have improved their properties in the past decade, although others have refrained from doing so in fear of losing their investments to highway clearance. The area is unusally well-integrated, ethnically and racially — in a sample of 120 families, 12 percent were Negro. Enclaves and scatterings of Portuguese, Puerto Rican, French Canadian, Italian, Irish, Greek, Lithuanian, and other nationalities — many of their members first and second generation — characterize the area. "Racial and ethnic harmony" appears to be a reality rather than a cliché.

Brookline-Elm provides inexpensive housing. Even though landlords can obtain higher rents from students than from working-class tenants, the nonstudent population is more than 90 percent of the whole, and median rent for all units is about sixty-five dollars a month. Sixty-seven percent of the sample feel, probably correctly, that they cannot duplicate their present rents elsewhere while only 5 percent think can; 37 percent define their present rents as low; and 20 percent consider them high.

The neighborhood's location is such that 28 percent of the sample walk to work, and 56 percent work within Cambridge. Twenty-three percent of the men and 57 percent of the working women use efficient and well-located public transportation to and from work. A major shopping district bisects the area, and 75 percent of the residents do their shopping within walking distance of their homes. Many of these also rely on local doctors and dentists.

The social structure of the area, in terms other than those of racial and ethnic composition, is typically working-class. For many people, the fundamental social unit is not the "nuclear family" of parents and dependent children in a single household but the "extended kinship" family with several generations of close — and distant — relatives living within a few blocks, on the same block, in the same building, or even in the same household. Of the 60 percent of our respondents who have relatives in Cambridge, three-quarters live within walking distance of those kin. More than three-quarters of the respondents have lived near relatives throughout their lives. Of these, 42 percent visit one or more relatives every day. Neighborhood friendships are also common — 66 percent visit friends at least weekly. Sixty percent live within walking distance of their friends' homes. These people attend churches and schools within a few blocks of home; some are their family's second generation members and students of local institutions.

This is (to borrow Gans' phrase) an "urban village" atmosphere. Few of the sample belong to organizations, use Boston or even Cambridge cultural facilities, shop in Boston or other parts of Cambridge. Shopkeepers, neighbors, and clergy are familiar from daily or almost daily contact. Obviously, such a population would be difficult to relocate without disturbing established and often comfortable living patterns. Although around a quarter of the sample would like to leave the neighborhood if leaving meant upward mobility, most residents realistically fear that relocation would mean deterioration, in terms of rents paid, physical condition of housing, and social context. Although some residents would — to their surprise — find themselves "better off" in new circumstances, most undoubtedly would not — and they know it.

Protestors and Nonprotestors

Given the fears and perceptions of Brookline-Elm residents, it is reasonable to expect massive support for Save Our Cities. It turns out that about 27 percent of the sample have engaged in SOC protest activities — attending meetings and rallies, writing letters to politicians and government officials, displaying anti-Belt posters on their houses, and joining peaceful demonstrations at MIT or on Boston Common. Twenty-seven percent is an impressive figure, considering norms for protest activities even in the middle classes, but few of that number are regular protestors by any definition. About twenty have been active in organizing and speaking out regularly in public meetings; another thirty attend fairly often but do little and say nothing; the remainder appear to have attended a meeting or written a letter out of vague hope of effect, then quickly moved back to an apathetic stance. Several of the most active SOC members do not even live in the area, but are concerned working-class citizens from neighboring parts of Cambridge.

Americans of any class are not remarkably active in local protest. Part of my study is an attempt to isolate class-specific reasons for relative inactivity in this particular protest movement. Eighty-seven percent of the sample can identify the Governor of Massachusetts, and 47 percent know both Senators' names. Thirty-one percent know the name of the Mayor of Cambridge at the time of the interviews, and 13 percent can name most of the nine City Councillors. Only 2 percent know the name of the Commissioner of the Department of Public Works, which sponsors the Inner Belt, and fewer still know the names or functions of the Bureau of Public Roads and the Department of Transportation or their officials, although they have been mentioned repeatedly in meetings and in local newspaper articles. Home-owners are more knowledgeable then renters and also noticeably more active in protest activities, suggesting that their stake in their property induces awareness. Significantly, tenants' desires to remain in the area, and their integration into it in terms of family, friends and institutions, is almost the same as that of owners.

Connection with the political system tends to take the form of knowing names of Massachusetts senators and representatives and believing, in an uncritical way, that these officials are honest and make every effort to support the interests of "little people." Disappointments and betrayals, as they are defined, are attributed to "politicians" in general but rarely in particular; to powerful local institutions, especially MIT and Harvard; and to the classic "they" who are powerful, self-seeking, hypocritical, and totally disinterested in the plight of the "little people."

Defining one's own interest and acting to protect it is a complex matter. The State Department of Public Works, in its relocation report on the Brookline-Elm neighborhoods, interprets inactivity and apathy as indifference or even support for the road plan. Do apathy and inactivity indicate resignation and acceptance, or cynical withdrawal and despair? The data of my study tend to support the latter interpretation. Part of the explanation may lie in an appalling lack of information about what is going on: fewer than half the respondents can even guess who could possibly gain by building the Inner Belt road; 29 percent claim that no one gains, leaving the reasons for constructing it a total mystery; 22 percent have no idea who might find it to his advantage; 26 percent think that politicians and construction people make something off the road; and the remainder believe that the highway would be to the advantage of drivers in general and/or suburbanites in particular. Although Governor Volpe has consistently supported plans for the road, half those interviewed do not know Volpe's stand on the road plan or believe that he opposes it. Only 21 percent of the respondents could identify the three most visible and vocal leaders of the local protest group.

Most critically, a majority of people in the Brookline-Elm area oppose the road but have no idea how to pursue that opposition. Interviewers classified 62 percent of the respondents as distraught, upset, or confused about their feelings, 11 percent as indifferent or resigned, and 26 percent as eager or pleased that the road might be built. Significantly, interviewees claim that more of their neighbors are distraught, upset, or confused than themselves. Answers to questions about voting activity suggest that respondents feel obligated to take some part in the political process but doubt their ability to affect it. It seems safe to conclude that a majority of people would prefer that the road not be built but have little faith in conventional democratic procedures for effecting change and do not know how to voice their opposition. Nonetheless, some try to be heard through rallies, public meetings, anti-Belt signs (Beat the Belt, Cambridge is a City Not a Highway), letters to public officials, picketing MIT, and participating in a bus trip to Washington for meetings with federal representatives and appointed officials.

All evidence suggests that SOC efforts alone would have had little effect without help from independent professionals. Members of Urban Planning Aid conceived of and lobbied for alternate routes. During the winter of 1967–68, the Cambridge City Council, which has supported restudy for over two years, gained substantial aid when a number of prestigious citizens, including John Kenneth Galbraith and Daniel Patrick Moynihan, agreed to serve on a special Advisory Committee to the Mayor. A technical staff, including UPA members, was set up to assist the advisory group.

Middle-class participants appear to be useful to the anti-Belt movement for two distinct reasons. First, their professional training enables them to read and to use road design specifications, both to criticize official plans and to create counter-plans. Second, the middle-class participants "speak the same language" as government officials, meeting them on their own terms as members of the same class.

Max Weber and others have illuminated the extent to which an advanced industrial society relies on "rational" criteria. Ostensibly, the public official responds rationally to criticism of his plan, re-evaluating and re-planning if he is objective, errors in his planning or if he is presented with an objectively superior counterplan. But irrational factors may also enter into the decision-making process even though an actor may believe he is evaluating rationally. When a dozen working-class housewives and a couple of husbands accompanied by a parish priest succeed in gaining a hearing with a highway planning official, the official is inclined to defend the plan his agency has made. Not only does he believe it to be reasonable, but he and his colleagues have invested much time, money, and perhaps emotion in the plan. It would be difficult for the petitioners to get him to re-evaluate it by presenting him with purely rational objections. Another nonrational basis for commitment to a plan, perhaps hardest of all to overcome, is commitment to the unstated general assumptions behind a specific project. to re-evaluate the *premises* of a plan (for instance, highways are good, this highway is important, working-class people can be relocated without too much grief) means to be forced to an uncommon level of reflection that not only threatens the specific work already done, but also induces the discomfort of having to face fundamental issues as "Is what I am doing worthwhile?"

This is where social class considerations enter. Working class people feel inadequate to criticize highway designs even though they may strongly oppose them. The world of bureaucracy, technical studies, report writing, and professional certification is beyond the comprehension of many of those in it, let alone those ouside. Therefore, on the unusual occasion when the working-class neighborhood group does gird its loins for a meeting with middle-class bureaucrats, it probably enters that meeting from a position of weakness, doubting the legitimacy of its position. At best, the petitioners suspect that they argue essentially from emotional grounds and that the official "knows more", since he argues from technical bases. To an important extent, the culture's general assumption that technical arguments are more "real" than emotional ones is implicitly shared by all parties to the discussion. The complainants have little technical expertise, and they fear that the greater knowledge of the authorities will overwhelm them and that their doubt about what they are doing will be discovered by others *and* by themselves. Therefore, it is only reasonable for them to ask from nongovernmental professionals who can aid them in evaluation, mediation, and counterplans.

The independent professional "plays the game" on the bureaucrats' terms. He doesn't talk about old ladies' love of neighborhood but about the rational observation, shared with the governmental official, that other things being equal, it is desirable to take fewer rather than more homes for a highway. However, the strength from which he argues is not only the confidence that may accompany his technical arguments, but the broader basis of sharing a common culture with the government officials. While the working-class protester gets confused when someone talks of the number of "dwelling units" to be taken by a road, rather than the number of "homes" or "families"; the professionals on both sides understand each others' language, even if they disagree on everything else. Like the officials he faces, the independent professional has attended college, shares common housing preferences, such as a low value on living near relatives; and he dresses, talks, walks, and gestures in ways more familiar and comfortable to the official than those of the working-class complainants. The official may disagree with the evaluation of the road situation made by the engineer or the systems analyst working in the interests of the working-class area, but he recognizes in him a fellow member of the middle-class community, and he respects the degree in engineering or city planning. When the middle-class advocates are luminaries such as

Galbraith or Monynihan, the likelihood that their cause will be paid some attention is all the greater.

This suggests that, like everyone else, government officials respond to plans and counterplans not only on objective terms but also on *who* proposes and supports them. The middle-class, then, by virtue of reputation, life style, *and* information, has enormous advantage over working-class residents when confronting state and federal authorities. Most of our society's formal institutions are run *by* the middle-class as well as *for* the middle-class. Contact with those institutions, unless done by force, is most easily made within the framework of middle-class culture.[2]

The Effectiveness of Protest

With this background, it is possible to try to understand the limits of effectiveness of the Brookline-Elm area protest movement. It must be recognized that the Save Our Cities meetings, rallies, letter writing campaigns, and the like are not without value — at the very least, they crystallize neighborhood discontent and provide a base from which various other activities can take off — but in the eyes of neighborhood people, the meetings are not meant as symbols but as actual means of affecting the political decision-making process. It is in regard to this function that their effectiveness may be questioned.

Brookline-Elm people engaged in SOC activities appear to have only the vaguest definitions of the political process which they wish to affect. They move between two poles: overtrust and cynicism. In the first, it is assumed that officials will respond reasonably once they get the true picture of people's feelings against the route. In this view, the problem is "getting to" the right officials at the highest level possible. If they cannot be reached, one relies on people who are well connected to make the case for the community.

The other pole is one of complete cynicism and mistrust of virtually everyone who has any power — politicians, big business, and big institutions (especially MIT in the case at hand). They are conceived as purely self-interested, with no concern for the wishes of the "little people" who live in Brookline and Elm Streets.

If the protestors doubt their capacity to make themselves heard and also sustain a fantasy that unattainable officials would help, what can they do? First, they can rely on middle-class allies, which is exactly what the Brookline-Elm people do. To this extent, they act reasonably by anyone's definition, but they also continue to meet as a protest group. What do they do in those meetings?

Primarily, the meetings serve to announce information of recent developments in discussions between the Mayor's Advisory Committee and the DPW or the Bureau of Public Roads, but the meetings are not just media for transmitting news. They also serve at least two other distinct purposes. One is laying protest plans — urging participants to write letters of protest to Congressmen, the DPW, BPR, and the Secretary of the Department of Transportation, and occasionally planning rallies, marches, and picket demonstrations. At the end of each campaign, there is some discussion on how well it went, but this Monday morning quarterbacking is almost inevitably limited to the organization and elegance of the protest event in question and rarely evaluates the effect it might have on any of the principals in decision-making positions.

This lack of evaluation suggests that the activity furnishes its own meaning. Most SOC members are bewildered by the Inner Belt decision-making process and how it can be influenced. Public agencies have no history of attempting to educate neighborhood people into enlightened participation in settling such issues, and residents lack the initiative to adequately learn the process for themselves. Meetings, rallies, demonstrations, and letter writing campaigns are ways of seeming to participate without actually having to evaluate the consequences of these activities. The impending danger of the road leads its imminent victims to want to "do something" to ward off that danger, so the protest movement becomes like a game.

In the protest game television and the press report the events with a straight face, never suggesting the futility of another petition to the Governor or pointing out that state agencies are rarely moved to change their plans by rallies. A Senator to whom a polite letter of concern is written responds with a polite answer that he will do what he can and then proceeds to sit the issue out. A representative of the university which opposes a feasible alternate route listens respectfully to petitioners while his institution takes no action. And so it goes. This is not to suggest that SOC activities will have played no role if the Brookline-Elm route is finally defeated, but it must be recognized that city officials and the prestigious Advisory Committee, not SOC, will be the main instruments of any changes. Protest activities serve at most to rally city authorities behind the residents' cause.

The other purpose protest meetings serve is more subtle. Almost every meeting is punctuated with expressions of anger at DPW and MIT, and with demands that the road be built elsewhere or not be built at all. The function of such ritualistic rhetoric is essentially cathartic. Anger, impotence, and frustration are vented verbally and harmlessly, in the company of like-minded neighbors and sympathetic outsiders. Pent-up emotions are released not through constructive work for change but in little speeches and exclamations of indignation and digust. In this sense, the protest meetings may be therapeutic for the protestors' personalities but do not help in pursuing the protest movement's aims.

Summing Up

Highway planners have made their case for the need for highways. That case is couched in the respectable, conventional language of solving traffic problems, and neither the problems nor the traditional solutions can be dismissed as irrelevant or malevolently intentioned. The study under review here attempts to examine the other side of the highway design — the nature of the people affected and their response to what they define as a threat to themselves. If the protestors are guilty of insufficient consideration of greater transportation problems generating the plan for the Brookline-Elm path of the Inner Belt expressway, planning agencies are correspondingly negligent of the nature of neighborhoods through which they would build a highway as well as the feelings and real-life situations of the people living there. This study demonstrates that the areas in question are neither decaying nor transient, and the the residents' lack of political activity indicates despondency and ignorance of political procedures rather than apathy or indifference. Protest activities may help bring discontent to the attention of public officials, but the functions of the activities seem to be at least as much to allay protestors' anxieties as to effect change.

Notes

1. Michael Young and Peter Willmott, *Family and Kindship in East London* (New York: Penguin Books, 1964); Herbert Gans, *The Urban Villagers* (Glencoe, Ill.: The Free Press, 1962), and "The Human Implications of Current Redevelopment Relocation Planning," *Journal of the American Institute of Planners*, XXV (February 1959), 15–25; Marc Fried and Peggy Gleicher, "Some Sources of Residential Satisfaction in Our Urban Slums," *Journal of the American Institute of Planners*, XXVII (November 1961), 305–15; and Marc Fried, "Grieving for a Lost Home," in Leonard J. Duhl (ed.), *The Urban Condition* (New York: Basic Books, 1963).

2. This is not to suggest that force is not sometimes valuable as a technique of persuasion. Indeed many of the gains made by black people in the last few years rely more on force than on middle-class persuasion techniques. It might be argued that force was applied precisely to the extent that it became clear to some black leaders that alliances with middle-class professionals, white and black, were getting almost nowhere. In any society, it might further be hypothesized, demonstrations of physical force, whether violent or nonviolent, emerge only as a response to the incapacity of traditional institutions to respond seriously to objections made within their framework.

Urban Freeways and Social Structure—Some Problems and Proposals*

MARVIN G. CLINE

This paper treats a newly identified force that those who build highways and other large-scale physical developments in congested urban areas have encountered. That force is society. Although a powerful force, its strength is transmitted through the political system in a more emotional way than land values or economic activity which are more commonly recognized. The force of society is expressed in anxieties and fears, frustration and loneliness, but also in loyalty and love. The intrinsically public decisions of highway building have already encountered these powerful forces in public hearings, in elections and referendums, in the press, and in legislative deliberations. They have effectively blocked some specific highway developments. Because the social sciences offer a way to understand these forces and to accommodate necessary public works to them, a beginning should now be made at a long, difficult, but inescapable study of social structure as it is influenced by large-scale physical changes, particularly urban expressways.

In the social world, as in the physical world, for each action there is a reaction. To the extent that reactions can be adequately anticipated, actions can be adequately planned. No better example of this proposition can be found than the planning and construction of highways. Consider the reactions or consequences of highway construction, and the precision with which they can be anticipated. The cost of moving great volumes of traffic from one point to another can be precisely established and related to the anticipated benefits accruing to the users of the highway. Further, the changes in the value of the regions connected by the highway can be estimated in advance, as can the changes in the value of the land through which the highway passes. All of these changes in value can be compared to the cost of moving traffic (land aquisition, construction, maintenance, etc.) so that a net worth of the highway can be stated in advance of its construction. Certain other effects (or impacts) can also be estimated in

*Highway Research Record, no. 2, pp. 12–20, Highway Research Board, National Research Council, Washington, D.C. Reprinted by permission of the Board.

advance, such as the change in accessibility of some functions and institutions (schools, churches, medical facilities, recreation areas, shopping centers, etc.) which can be used to predict changes in location of residential populations. All of these consequences have been measured after the fact[2, 7, 26, 31, 33, 38, 39] and they undoubtedly have been incorporated in the decision-making processes for most of the larger highways recently constructed.

This is an admirable accomplishment. One cannot help but be impressed by the skill with which these measures have been taken, and the accuracy of the predictions made. It is to be hoped that all aspects of planning reach this level of precision before too long.

However, one gets an impression that some consequences of considerable importance may not be included in the balance sheet, and that this formula for decision-making may be lacking some critical variables. For example, a gross variable (which may be so gross that it cannot be entered into the formula) has to do with the kind of urban structure one wishes to develop. The construction of a freeway system connecting the suburban fringes with the central city may be contributing to the destruction of the central city by enhancing the dispersion of precisely those functions which are critical to the central city. That is, it is the concentration of retail, industrial, recreational, cultural, and educational functions in the central city that makes it the vital core of the whole city. The freeway system, by enhancing the dispersion of populations, may at the same time enhance the flight of many of these activities to the new outlying population centers. This can, of course, place added burdens on the freeway system in order to make the new locations of these activities more accessible. These consequences may or may not be desirable, but they are, at least at present, inadvertent. To that extent, freedom to plan in the future is being restricted by a lack of planning in the present. At the same time, if freeway planning is not integrated with more comprehensive urban planning, the freeways may become self-defeating (the more one builds, the more dispersion, the more one has to build). Hence, they become less economic[32].

However important this variable is, it is not the only one which appears not to be included in the current methods of evaluating highway plans. Another variable involved here is becoming an increasing source of political conflict and, for the transportation planner, embarrassment. This variable has to do with the reactions to the freeway on the part of the resident through whose neighborhood the freeway is to go. It is not necessary to document the rapidly growing number of instances in which irate citizens, civic organizations, and political groups are complaining about routes, interchanges, and access streets. Every transportation official must be painfully aware of the complaints arising from this ill-considered population. To date, the primary complaint has to do with the problem of relocation, but this is by no means the only significant issue.

Those who will not be removed from the path of the freeway, who will have to live with it, may shortly discover that they too have a considerable stake in the planning of urban transportation systems. These people will be challenging a critical and implicit (rather than an explicit) assumption of highway designers—the space between the points joined by a freeway is a social wasteland, devoid of human significance. This assumption is, of course, sometimes correct as in the case of purely industrial regions, or in undeveloped suburban or rural areas. Here, the only contact human beings have with the freeway is in using it for transportation purposes.

In somewhat more developed suburban regions, the assumption is still correct in a large portion of the cases, because the freeway can be effectively isolated from the residential spaces[26]. However, referring to those very few impact studies which deemed it desirable to query residents' views of the freeways (and in each case, only suburban populations were queried), it is apparent that the freeway must be a considerable distance away from homes (200 to 300 ft) before those who consider it a nuisance are reduced to 25 percent of the population[39]. A more developed Rhode Island residential community[6] through which a freeway was driven produced a large group of residents severely disturbed by the facility. A search of the impact literature failed to turn up a single instance in which an urban population was asked its opinion about a freeway in its midst. Nevertheless, from the data just presented, an extrapolation can easily be made. Urban residents living in greatest proximity to the freeway would have the greatest objections. These residents would present the greatest challenge to the assumption that freeways through urban areas run through social wastelands. Actually, these regions may be the locale for viable, cohesive communities, to which the residents have strong attachments. Although residents may state their objections in terms of the perceived noise, smell, and danger of the freeway, it is likely that the less obvious impact of physical disruption on the social structure will likely be more damaging[13, 14].

Not all residents living in close proximity to a freeway, however, will have the same kind or same degree of objections. Physical proximity is not the meaningful variable, unless it is directly coordinated to psychological proximity. Thus, residents whose use of the physical space surrounding their homes is restricted to a pathway function (streets are important only as a means of getting to or away from the home) will not be disturbed by freeway construction beyond the inconveniences of noise, smell, and danger. This is most likely to be found in highly urban populations, living in apartment houses and oriented toward highly dispersed social spaces. These people are also likely to be high users of the freeway, and only occasional users of whatever open spaces are provided along its periphery.

Conversely, urban regions (particularly those that are most likely to be selected for freeway routes) are characterized by high concentrations of people who consider the space surrounding their homes as a living space to which they belong and in which they feel the comforts of a home. The space they are physically close to is the space to which they are psychologically attached.

A freeway traversing such a space is not traversing a social wasteland. It will be the purpose of this paper to suggest that the space and its social structure through which an urban freeway is to be constructed needs to be understood in great detail by the road designer both to avoid the harmful effects and to gain potential advantages that the freeway may have for the community.

All communities have the potential for social degeneration and blight. If the inadvertent placing of a highway helps to realize this potential, then the designer must bear the responsibility of having created more waste than a society can afford. On the other hand, if the highway can aid the community in acquiring some of the conditions of life that it values, then the designer is equally at fault if he does not discover how to produce these consequences. The time has long passed when the luxury of a hit or miss approach to social planning can be afforded.

The City as a Social System

The traditional view of the city includes a picture of the lonely, lost urban dweller, cut off from the norms and expectations of the small but stable village community, forced to lose his personal identity, and sinking in a sea of depression. This view of the nature of city life has persisted for some time, and was recently elaborated on by Louis Wirth[40]. This theorist was aware that not all urban residents were contemplating suicide. Some of them were establishing with their fellow residents very real interpersonal relations that have the character of true community behavior. But Wirth attributed this to a residual to rural living, so that right or wrong, he was again denying the city a capacity for spontaneous generating social support for its residents.

More recently social scientists have been taking a hard look at urban structure, using new and more sophisticated techniques[3, 4, 12, 22, 29]. These investigators are now arriving at a rather different view. It is apparent that urban regions produce a wide variety of social structures and populations. Even the lowest income areas can generate integral systems of living that supply their residents with a good deal of personal satisfaction, a sense of neighborhood, identification with physical region, and a great reluctance to give up residence even with the inducement of better housing. These systems of living appear to vary according to the economic status of the families, the degree of family integration, and the degree of "urbanism" of the neighborhood (an index based on measures of the fertility of the families, rates of females employed, and the number of families living in single-family housing units). For example, lower-income urban groups tend to have a great reliance on their family and extended family for their informal relation[4] and they prefer to use the local economic, service, and recreational facilities of the neighborhood[17]. Komarovsky found that urban dwellers have rather low (25 percent and lower as status decreases) rates of membership in voluntary associations[27]. At the same time, it has been noted by several investigators[3, 5, 10, 12, 15] that, as there is less formal structure in the more urbanized community, there is an increase in the rate of informal "friendship" contact between local residents. Even when the contacts are based on formal role structures such as consumer–storekeeper relations, a significantly high proportion of the urban residents (particularly the lower-income groups) prefer to transform the relationship into a personalized, informal state of affairs[37]. Lower status shoppers prefer to shop in smaller community stores where they were known by name and where informal relations with the store personnel could be established. The author does not mention the availability of credit buying in the local food store which must also be an important factor in shaping the preferences of these buyers. It can be concluded that the lower-income neighborhood can be an extended and complex social network involving geographically localized friends and relatives, many informal groups, and strong attachments to the community. Clearly, significant proportions of the urban population are on intimate terms with their immediately surrounding physical and social environment.

Also, positive feelings toward the neighborhood often develop despite inadequate housing facilities. Behind the slum lies not social chaos but a strong, satisfying community. This is an important point because it indicates the degree to which the residents of these neighborboods are willing to tolerate difficulties in order to maintain the primary social relations of the community. Apparently this is a phenomenon present in many groups living in a satisfying social system despite generally inadequate housing. An interesting example of this can be found in the classic study of Festinger, Schachter, and Back[16] of a housing project built by Massachusetts Institute of Technology for married veteran students. The development consisted of U-shaped courts of from 8 to 13 single or semi-detached houses in each. The experimenters were interested in relating the physical features of the courts (the distance between houses and the direction in which a house faced) with the kind and rate of social interactions observed. For various reasons, the residents of these courts were generally very favorably impressed with life in the project. Very few expressed any desire to leave; more than one-half were vigorous in their statements that they would not consider leaving the project at all. Friendship rates were quite high, as were the rates of informal contact. This general satisfaction existed in spite of, and seemed to compensate for, many physical inadequacies of the houses. For example, at the time of the study, many of the houses had trouble with the roof so that moderate winds could raise them and allow rain to pour down the walls. The adequate and satisfying social life was sufficient to override these inconveniences. The authors report that the typical reaction was "Oh yes, there are many things wrong with these houses, but we love it here and wouldn't want to move."

Not all physically debilitated areas have such viable social structures within them, of course, but it ought not to be necessary to argue that the knowledge of the social system through which a freeway is to go is an important datum for those who plan and decide. This is all the more true when one considers that the attachment to the physical environs is probably greater among the lower-income groups than other strata, and that these groups live in areas most likely to be earmarked for freeway construction. That is, low-income areas appear to be the preferred places to locate urban freeways. The point of the present discussion is to warn highway planners to distinguish between slum-blighted areas, and low-cost areas. Seeley[36] has suggested a critical psychosocial distinction between them: the slum is an area in which there are pathological consequences for the residents wrought by the physical and social character of the neighborhood; i.e., the true blighted area. The low-cost area may be almost indistinguishable from the slum in terms of its physical facade, but it is a place whose physical inconveniences the residents will accept in order to gain the benefits of either low rent or the social satisfactions resulting from a sense of belongingness. This is a vital distinction, and one which the highway designer must recognize if he is to avoid making serious planning errors.

Psychological Impact of Physical Disruption

There have been few studies of low-income areas disrupted by large-scale physical change. No studies have yet been done in which the source of the physical disruption is the construction of a freeway. But one important study of the effects of an urban renewal program is brilliantly suggestive of the issues that must be resolved.

This series of papers describes the residents of the West End section of Boston and their reactions to the destruction of the neighborhoods, mistakenly identified as a slum, and thus cleared. Fried[19], Fried and Gleicher[20], and Gans[21] describe the intense attachment of the residents to their neighborhood. This is the first study to establish the focus of positive loyalty to physical places (specific stores, houses, streets, etc.) as much as to the social environment of relatives and friends. The authors use the term "localism" to describe this kind of attachment to a space. It refers to a space that has the qualities of home but at the same time is public space in the sense that it is used by all residents for their various purposes. It may be thought of as an extension of home, with all the values of home. In the eyes of those to whom it is home, it is thus a space to live in rather than to pass through. It is typically composed of streets, hallways, roofs, alleys, stoops, and the fronts of stores.

Such a public space is the medium for the interaction of a great variety of people and functions. In this situation complex and intricate social systems develop. The physical aspect of the space is the framework on which the social systems are built. Although the authors limit this phenomenon to lower-income areas of high density, there is no doubt that other highly used spaces will generate social systems and the development of a strong sense of belongingness on the part of the resident of the space.

Disruption of the physical space has the potential of striking at the very foundations of the resident's sense of psychological well-being. When the residents of the West End were forced out, many of them exhibited what Fried[19] has likened to the clinical syndrome of grief. A depression similar to the experiences one has at the loss of a loved one seems to have persisted in some cases over a period of years. It should not be difficult to imagine that residents who continue to live in an area that has received such a crushing pyschological blow will develop negative feelings about the eviscerated area. And it is the feelings that the residents have for their neighborhood which are the most important determinant of the social and economic value of the area. Social disorganization almost inevitably results in physical and economic disorganization, which ordinarily can be expected to spread to adjacent areas.

Hartman[24], in describing further the West Enders, reports an interesting method of estimating resident's reactions to generally shabby and in some instances dilapidated building conditions: an index of the phsycal condition of the tenants' apartments was constructed and compared to an index of the physical condition of the building. Surprisingly, almost one-third of the apartments were in considerably better condition than the buildings. Evidence that the residents devoted a good deal of care and attention to their apartments, despite the shabbiness of the general environment, should alert even the casual observer to question whether the usual objective criteria of substandard living can be appropriately applied in this case.

Physical Disruption and Social Functioning

There is a more immediate problem than that of the pervasive impact an urban freeway may have on a viable community: the effects on the surrounding area. The impact studies have little or nothing to say to this problem outside of describing the change in economic and population characteristics of the area. The few studies in which residents were asked their opinions of the freeway are largely irrelevant to this problem because it is apparent that physical spaces occupied by the freeways in these instances were not significant psychological spaces to the residents[26, 39].

One study by the Blair Associates[6] documents a point made by Wilfred Owen[32 p. 51]. "The highway . . . can disrupt a neighborhood by thrusting itself between houses and recreational land, or between houses and schools." Blair Associates report that the highway removed four playgrounds, raised costs for police and fire protection because of the extra distances they had to travel, reduced the number of houses in the community by one-third, and increased the time it took the children to travel to school.

The implication of these points is that the highway is seen as a gap or a gash through the community and serves to separate people from each other and from the important facilities of the neighborhood. On the other hand, the gap itself has special characteristics, some of which have recently been described by two observers of the social and visual characteristics of urban space. Kevin Lynch, in an extremely insightful description of the visual qualities of the city[30] defines a sharp perceptual change in the layout of a city as an edge. This is an area that separates two regions, marking a sharp change in the characteristics of the regions on either side to the edge. There may or may not be the means to penetrate the edge from one side to the other. If such means exist, the edge becomes a seam, "a line of exchange along which two areas are sewn together." If such means do not exist, the edge is perceived as a barrier that serves to halt rather than enhance social functioning. A busy street, railroad tracks, an expressway, are all examples of barriers, whereas a park, accessible from both sides, can serve as a seam. Lynch's point is that the edge is perceptible as a barrier or a seam and will therefore serve to control behavior. Barriers will in effect repel and seams may attract.

In a similar analysis, Jane Jacobs, describes what she calls a border vacuum[25, ch. 14]. Mrs Jacobs places the emphasis on the functional rather than the visual properties of a region, and argues that when the functions that a region supports are curtailed, its utility is reduced. This in turn leads to still less use and consequently to the creation of a vacuum. A vacuum is used only by those who prefer it; i.e., those who wish to remain unseen or uncontrolled, such as criminals.

Mrs. Jacobs applies this concept to city streets that have had functions removed (e.g. streets along the edge of high-rise apartments and projects that are used only as paths), parks that offer only nonfunctional grass or asphalt walks, and stores with limited functioning (e.g. banks which close early in the afternoon). These are interesting speculations because they suggest a dimension of community space that might be causally related to the social integration of the community, and therefore related to the degree of personal satisfaction and community commitment of the residents of the area.

This analysis can be applied to the construction of large shopping centers where single-function impulse-buying shops are placed between large multifunctional "magnets." This is necessary because few people venture very far from the highly active magnets, and this number decreases as the distance from the magnet increases. Single-purpose stores at the end of a line of stores in a shopping center apparently have a tendency to fail, whereas identical stores in the midst of the flow of buyers between centers of activity apparently thrive.

This might also be applied to a typical urban area cut by a limited-access freeway; for example, an intersection of streets in such an area before construction. Retail shops are located for a number of blocks along both sides of one street which runs perpendicular to the residential streets. Such an intersection is likely to be an active and populated subregion of the neighborhood throughout the better part of both the day and night. This is the magnet of the neighborhood, the social and economic center which is so popular that the traffic flow may not serve as a barrier between the four sides of the intersection. When this microcosm is replaced with a limited-access freeway, the consequence is not merely the reduction of population, business activity, and housing. The magnets that drew people and money to the region are gone. Multifunctions have been replaced by single-function streets. Activity suddenly halts a few hundred feet from the freeway and remains dormant until one reaches a few hundred feet beyond the other side of the freeway. Even a street that turns into a bridge across the freeway is a socially empty and useless object because its only purpose is to move cars away from the area. There is no reason to go to the intersection except to travel through it, or, because it is devoid of activity, to hide. Such an area becomes, in Lynch's terms, an edge, or in Jacobs' terms, a vacuum. In any terminology, it has become a negative place, quite capable of rapid degeneration.

Conclusions and Proposals

There are three major sources of negative consequences resulting from locating a freeway in the midst of an urban area: (a) the freeway may disrupt the physical framework on which the community is built: (b) the freeway may create a border vacuum capable of rapid degeneration; and (c) the freeway may serve to separate the residents from each other and from important institutions and facilities of the neighborhood. These consequences are in respect to the residents who remain in the immediately surrounding environment and do not include the consequence of relocation of those who live and work in the path of the facility. These are both long- and short-term consequences and may not be easily identifiable by the residents themselves. However, they may be sources of serious unrest and discontent, long and costly public hearings and delay.

It would be appropriate to make some proposals at this point in order to achieve a level of constructive criticism. The psychosocial structures through which the freeways are to go need to be seriously considered in planning the facility, and such consideration will lead to improved, acceptable designs. The following are therefore proposed:

1. If some of the freeways that have been built in urban areas are examined the variety of communities through which they have been placed may be noted and the range of consequences that have been produced may be imagined. It is not necessary to be a sophisticated observer of the social scene to estimate where and what kinds of disruptions of social functions have taken place. It is possible to increase one's sensitivity to the social requirements of communities by simply looking.

2. Some social science research should be included in present plans. Sociological and social psychological methods for measuring social structure are sophisticated enough at present to allow an adequate before-and-after experimental design[1, 18, 23, 29]. Both experimental and statistical techniques are available so that the contribution of a freeway to social change can be reasonably distinguished from most other factors contributing to the change. In other words, the concept of an impact study needs to be expanded. Parallel studies are needed in the social psychological disciplines, similar to those in the economic and demographic disciplines. Until the psychosocial consequneces of actions are known, the environment cannot be fully controlled.

3. Before a freeway is built, its locale should be studied with respect to some of the following: (a) the social boundaries of the communities involved; (b) the major social needs of the residents; (c) the important social functions carried out in the neighborhood; and (d) the critical spaces within which these functions and needs operate. Above all, these should be done in cooperation with the residents.

With these data, it will be possible to minimize the disruptions at least because meaningful criteria of route location will be established. Equally important, however, is that it becomes possible, with these data, to identify the necessary disruptions in advance, and to plan for their reduction before they are created. For example, these data can suggest where and how the community must be shielded from the freeway. They can also suggest in advance which functions of the community are most in need of maintenance. Thus, if a highly used space is to be cut by the freeway, then it is apparent that the facilities for these uses should be recreated as part of the freeway structure, with easy accessibility for all residents. The roadbed might be sunken, in this case, and the functions (retail buying, recreational activities, restaurants and bars, etc.) placed on top of the freeway. This could also act as a bridge between the two sides of the road. In this manner, those critical magnets could continue to hold the neighborhood together. Without this support, such a community could easily begin to die.

Notes

1. Arensberg, C. M. (Sept. 1954) The Community-Study Method. *Amer. Jour. Social.*, **60**: 109–124.
2. *Socio-Economic Factors and the Inner Belt* (1961) Associated Industries of Mass., Economic Research Department, Boston.
3. Axelrod, M. (Feb. 1956) Urban Structure and Social Participation. *Amer. Sociol. Rev.*, **21**: 13–18.
4. Bell, W. and Boat, M. D. (Jan. 1957) Urban Neighborhood and Informal Social Relations. *Amer. Jour. Sociol.*, **62**: 391–398.
5. Bell, W. and Force, M. T. (Feb. 1956) Urban Neighborhood Types and Participation in Formal Associations. *Amer. Social. Rev.*, **21**: 25–34.
6. *The Friendly Interchange: A Planning Study of Interstate 95 and the Huntington Avenue Expressway as They Affect a Community in Cranston, Rhode Island* (1960) Blair Associates, Providence.
7. Bright, D. (Jan. 1947) *The Effect of Limited Access Expressways on Existing Street Systems: A Bibliography*. HRB Bibliography Series 1.
8. Caplow, T. and Forman R. E. (June 1950) Neighborhood Interaction in a Homogenous Community. *Amer. Sociol. Rev.*, **15**: 357–366.
9. Dansereau, H. K. (1961) Some Implications of Modern Highways for Community Ecology. G. A. Theodorson (Ed.), *Studies in Human Ecology*. Row Peterson.
10. Dean, J. P. (April 1958) The Neighborhood and Social Relations. *Forum on Neighborhoods Today and Tomorrow* 3:4, Philadelphia Housing Association.
11. Dewey, R. (Jan. 1955) A Critical Look at Freeways to Downtown Areas. *Amer. City*, **70**: 153, 155.
12. Dotson, F. (Oct. 1951) Patterns of Voluntary Association Among Urban Working-Class Families. *Amer. Sociol. Rev.*, **16**: 687–693.
13. Duhl, L. J. (1956) Mental Health and Community Planning. *Planning 1955*, American Society of Planning Officials, Chicago.
14. Duhl, L. J. (1960) Planning the Physical Environment. *HRB Bull.* **190**: 20–24.
15. Fava, S. F. (1958) Contrasts in Neighboring: New York City and a Suburban Community. W. M. Dobriner (Ed.), *The Suburban Community*. Putnam.
16. Festinger, L., Schachter, S. and Back, K. (1950) *Social Pressures in Informal Groups: A Study of Human Factors in Housing*. Harpers.
17. Foley, D. L. (1957) The Use of Local Facilities in a Metropolis. P. Hatt and A. J. Reiss (Eds.), *Cities and Society*. Free press.
18. Form, W. H. *et al.* (Aug. 1954) The Compatibility of Alternative Approaches to the Delimitation of Urban Sub-Areas. *Amer. Sociol. Rev.*, **19**: 434–440.
19. Fried, M. Grieving for a Lost Home. L. J. Duhl (Ed.), *The Environment of the Metropolis*. Basic Books (in press).
20. Fried M. and Gleicher, P. (Nov. 1961) Some Sources of Residential Satisfaction in an Urban Slum. *Jour. Amer. Inst. Planners*, **27**: 305–315.
21. Gans, H. J. (Feb. 1959) Human Implications of Current Redevelopment and Relocation Planning. *Jour. Amer. Inst. Planners*, **25**: 15–25.
22. Greer, S. (Feb. 1956). Urbanism Reconsidered: A Comparative Study of Local Areas in a Metropolis. *Amer. Sociol. Rev.*, **21**: 19–25.
23. Greer A. and Kube, E. (1959), Urbanism and Social Structure: A Los Angeles Study. M. B. Sussman (Ed.), *Community Structure and Analysis*. Crowell.
24. Hartman, C. (1962) Social Values and Housing Orientation. *Research Document 19*, Center for Community Studies, Boston.
25. Jacobs, J. (1961), *The Death and Life of Great American Cities*. Random House.
26. Kelly, J. F. (Oct. 1957) Residences and Freeways. *Appraisal Jour.* **25**: 505–520.
27. Komarovsky, M. (Dec. 1946) The Voluntary Associations of Urban Dwellers. *Amer. Social. Rev.*, **11**: 636–698.
28. Kuper, L. (March 1951) Social Science Research and the Planning of Urban Neighborhoods. *Social Forces*, **29**: 237–243.
29. Lazarsfeld, P. F. and Merton, R. K. (1954) Friendship as Social Process: A Substantive and Methodological Analysis. M. Berger *et al.* (Eds.), *Freedom and Control in Modern Society*. Van Nostrand.

30. Lynch, K. (1960) *The Image of the City*. Technology Press.
31. Nash, W. N. and Voss, J. (1960) Analyzing the Social-Economic Impact of Urban Highways. *HRB Bull.* **268**: 80–94.
32. Owen, W. (1959) *Cities in the Motor Age*. Viking.
33. Pillsbury, W. A. (1961) *The Economic and Social Effects of Highway Improvement: An Annotated Bibliography*. Virginia Council of Highway Investigation and Research.
34. Ravitz, M. J. (1957) Use of the Attitude Survey in Neighborhood Planning. *Jour. Amer. Inst. Planners*, **23**: 179–193.
35. Rubin, M., Orzack, L. H. and Thomlinson, R. (1950) Resident Responses to Planned Neighborhood Redevelopment. M. B. Sussman (Ed.), *Community Structure and Analysis*. Crowell.
36. Seeley, J. R. (Feb. 1959) The Slum: Its Nature, Use and Users. *Jour. Amer. Inst. Planners*, **25**: 7–14.
37. Stone G. P. (July 1954) City Shoppers and Urban Identification; Observations on the Social Psychology of City Life. *Amer. Jour. Sociol.*, **60**: 36–45.
38. Thiel. F. I. (April 1962) Social Effects of Modern Highway Transportation. *Public Roads*, **32**: 1–10.
39. *Traffic Impact: A Study of the Effects of Selected Roads on Residential Living in Southern Westchester* (1954) Westchester County Department of Planning, White Plains.
40. Wirth, L. (July 1938) Urbanism as a Way of Life. *Amer. Jour. Sociol.*, **44**: 1–24.

Evaluating the Social and Environmental Impacts of Transport Investment*

DONALD APPLEYARD

Introduction

This chapter deals with the conceptual issues involved in evaluating the impacts of transport systems. Like most other planning fields, the present state of impact assessment is fragmented. Techniques developed to measure the impacts of freeways concentrated on analysis of cheaply obtainable secondary data from the census, assessed values, accident statistics, crime statistics, and anything else available. In the real political world, freeways were frequently halted on the basis of community opposition defending socially or environmentally valued areas, with only a minimum of impact measurement (e.g. houses or jobs taken). As impact analysis evolved, a few direct environmental measures such as those of noise, sedimentation in the water, air pollution, visual intrusion or likelihood of flooding have been added to the checklists. In many cases these measures have been selected on the basis of professional judgement, availability of data or ease of measurement.

More recently research has moved towards measuring the psychological and behavioural responses of surrounding residents to transport systems or changes. Among these have been studies of the impacts of the BART rapid-transit system, of freeways, of traffic and of airports.

There are now therefore three parallel measurement trends in impact analysis, the first searching for economic indices such as land value, rents or other indicators of migration behaviour, the second focusing on environmental measures, and the third on attitudinal responses. My concern is to develop a conceptual model of the chain of social-environmental and functional interactions that take place around transport facilities, in order to relate these current measurement points in the impact process, and to show how inadequate present measures are in gaining a true picture of the impact process. No doubt this model is also incomplete

*From David A. Hensher and Peter Stopher, eds, *Behavioural Travel Modelling*, Croom Helm Ltd, 1979, pp 797–814. Reprinted by permission of the publisher.

and will benefit from extensive discussion. Others may see it as unnecessarily detailed, and beyond the budget of any current impact study. If, however, we can lay out all the impact relationships we may see more clearly at which points measurement is more effective. Strategies of measurement selection are discussed at the end of the chapter.

A Conceptual Model of Environmental Impacts

Consider the impacts of a hypothetical transport system first under relatively stable conditions, then under conditions of change.

The Stable Impact Model

The model diagrammed in Fig. 1 describes transport-environment relationships at two points in time. The left-hand column describes relationships under relatively stable conditions; the second, later in time, describes them under conditions of change which may have been initiated in several ways. Each column graphs the *seven* main components of

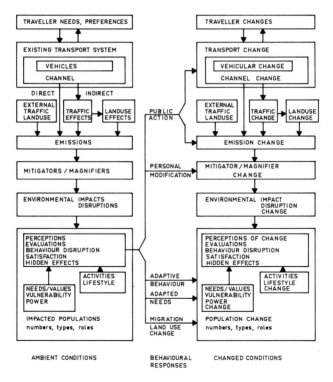

FIG. 1. The Socio-environmental Impacts of Transport Change.

environmental impact; the *traveller needs and preferences* that create the transport system in the first place, the *transport system* under study, the *transport and land use generated* by the studies system and that derived from other *external causes*, the *emissions* created directly and indirectly by the system, the environmental factors which *mitigate or magnify* the impacts, the *environmental impacts themselves, and the impacted populations*. These entities interact back and forth in a feedback system in which the results of traveller needs and preferences impact surrounding populations, and those populations endeavour to minimize the negative impacts. The model is, of course, complicated by the fact that travellers and impacted populations are sometimes the same people, torn by internal conflict.

Traveller needs and preferences. The desire for mobility is what creates transport facilities, whether it be a neighbour walking past one's front door, or an airport which impacts a sizeable area of landscape. Impacts can therefore be affected as much by changes in traveller demand as by a facility itself and the impact of most systems is directly related to the number of travellers they have to carry.

The transport route. The transport system itself contains a number of environment-affecting elements. *People and vehicles* (e.g. cars, buses, trains, airplanes, bicycles, pedestrians) are the primary and mobile elements of the system; *channels and change-points* (e.g. streets, freeways, track tunnels, airports, off-ramps, bus stops, stations, ports) make up the support and enclosure facilities. These combine into *systems*, whose impact we treat only briefly in this chapter.

It should be noted that while the people and vehicles on the transport system can change gradually over time, growing, diminishing or changing composition, facilities are lumpy investments, have lumpy impacts when constructed, and have therefore been the focus of most controversies. Traffic creeps up on communities slowly and imperceptibly.

Generated and extraneous systems. Transport often generates transport, especially at change points. Bus routes generate pedestrians at bus stops, transit stations can generate cars, buses, bicycles and pedestrians. As with transit systems, the secondary transport impacts may be more negative than the direct impacts of the facility. An underground BART line may have no impact on the above residential neighbourhood, but the station may have powerful effects.

Transport also provides a market. It generates land uses, again usually at change points. Shopping centres have clustered at freeway intersections, commercial uses have gathered around transit stations, industry around airports. However, it is extremely difficult to separate out the causal effects of land-use generation, since land uses locate for combinations of reasons, and since most urban areas are served by mixed transport systems. Transport systems extraneous to the one studied may generate their own transport and land uses. All of these may impact on a social and physical environment. In complex urban situations such as downtown San Francisco, the effects of BART on such land uses as office construction remains a matter of opinion[20]. In simpler suburban situations these impacts may be possible to sort out.

Emissions. While the more commonly identified emissions are those of noise, vibration and air pollution, emissions such as danger, visual images, glare, darkness and the presence of travellers with prying eyes are of similar character. Emissions, at the source point of the transport system, may or may not impact directly the surrounding population, and therefore may not necessarily require measurement unless identification is required for their direct control, as in the case of controls over vehicle emissions of various kinds.

Mitigators and magnifiers. Between the transport route and the impacted populations the emissions can be dampened or accentuated. Channels and change points can in many ways mitigate the impact of transport vehicles. Streets by their width, channel design, parking, barriers or landscaping can modify the impact of traffic. Distance from the facility itself modifies impact. On the other hand, glare-creating sound-reflecting channel walls can accentuate discomforts. Facilities that are designed to be compatible with the neighbourhood are likely to be more acceptable than those which affront its character. Identification of these elements can be crucial in situations where emissions cannot be controlled and compromise is necessary.

Environmental impacts and disruptions. The point of impact or disruption is the point where it is likely to hurt. There is an environmental interpretation of this point and a social interpretation. Both are necessary to understand complete impacts. The environmental interpretation tends to measure the spatial distribution of impact over an impact zone. A typical measure is that of noise level. Noise contours are now commonly measured around transport facilities. Similarly, it is possible to measure air-pollution levels, erosion, water pollution and a chain of ecological effects. The disruption of exisiting environmental connections and systems, such as the blockage of watercourses, the disruption and siphoning of wind patterns, the interruption of views, and neighbourhood character can also be recorded. These impacts can be measured at any point in the environment surrounding the transport facility. Impact analyses of transport facilities travelling through natural landscapes have commonly employed a series of contour maps, sometimes computer-generated, which have recorded existing environmental qualities and in some cases predicted environmental impact[19].

A social interpretation of environmental impact concentrates more on where people are or are likely to be in the surrounding environment, and takes measures at these points. Instead of treating the environment as the equi-important space, the places where people live, meet or carry on other activities are the primary points of environmental measurement. Hence, in the BART impact study we planned to carry out measures at individual houses, on street blocks, at community facilities, and on local access paths[1], and in Lassiere's work on evaluating transport plans, impacts are measured at each home site[13]. Similarly, in a study of the impacts of high-rise buildings in San Francisco, Dornbusch calculated the number of pedestrian exposures to high noise levels from the extra traffic generated by predicted high-rise buildings. Such measures assume that the environmental impacts on facilities or activities will be a cause of disturbance, and in many cases assumed perceptions are extrapolated from other research studies.

Impacted populations. The most critical impacts are on people, the environments they value, the resources that they command and their sense of power or powerlessness. In the final calculus the question is who has gained and who has lost, in what ways, by how much, for how long?

Population characteristics. The social and psychological impacts of transport systems ultimately depend on which populations are being impacted, how, and in what degree. Neither are people all alike. Some are more susceptible to impact than others.

The most important strategy is to search for those most *intensely impacted*, that is, those who experience the most intense negative environmental impacts and social disruption for the longer duration, and to search for those most *vulnerable* to impacts. Vulnerability, a term coined in the Buchanan Report, refers to those most sensitive and least able to cope with negative environments, for instance, families with small children who are especially vulnerable to traffic accidents, to the old and infirm who may be most sensitive to local access, to low-income groups least able to move away when conditions worsen. Who belongs to the most vulnerable groups is still an empirical question. It is therefore necessary to look at a number of personal characteristics of the impacted population, particularly income, age and family composition but also length of residence, time spent in the home, travel modes and patterns, home ownership, health problems and infirmities, ethnic and sex differences.

Any one person will be playing a number of *roles*. Assessments must therefore be careful to avoid double-counting. In a politicized context, populations may form interest or neighbourhood or block groups, with coherent viewpoints about the impacts on their constituency. Perceptions of the impacts on activists will have to be taken into account, though there is no substitute for assessing the impacts on the silent majority. The actual and perceived *power* of impacted populations may also affect their response to a transport facility. Around San Francisco airport more complaints are received from affluent residents who live in the hills at a distance from the airport, than from the poorer groups who live under the flight patterns. Power may depend on income and education, or on group cohesion. Those who have a sense of power or real power are more likely to articulate any negative impacts.

An accounting of the numbers of different groups impacted by a transport facility will begin to clarify its distributional effects. But the question remains how much and in what ways are people impacted. Moderate income groups, for instance, may feel more vulnerable to impacts that affect rent, local access and neighbourhood facilities, while affluent groups may be more concerned about impacts on the natural landscape. There is no single index of impact.

Activities and travel. The activities in which people engage or desire to engage may affect their vulnerability to negative environmental impact. People are interrupted by traffic more when trying to sleep, when talking or watching television, than when eating[2]. Ball-playing in the street is more vulnerable to traffic impact than gardening or chatting. Residential land use in general is more susceptible to negative impacts than are commercial or industrial uses. Similarly, walking trips are more likely to be disrupted than car trips.

Indoor activities are defended from impacts by protecting facilities such as homes, gardens, or any building which provides shelter. The numbers of people engaged in different activities and the degree of activity disturbance or disruption can thus become another measure of social impact. The British, for instance, have concentrated on "severance" as an index of the disruption of neighbourhood access and interaction. It has been measured by changes in length of pedestrian trips[3] across a freeway alignment, based on origin-destination surveys. More recently they have concentrated on changes in perceived distance[14]. The activities people engage in can be assessed through behavioural observations and land-use surveys.

Perceptions, evaluations and behavioural disruption. Perceptions and evaluations arise from the interaction of environmental impacts and the population's characteristics, usual activities and travel patterns. Important also is each individual's background experience, especially recent experience, his past and present expectations and value dispositions. For instance, more-educated groups have higher expectations and are thus more likely to evaluate environments critically. Educated groups are also likely to be more aware of negative impacts, hidden effects and better alternatives than are the less educated. Even so, some environmental impacts will probably go unperceived, due to behavioural adaptations or their invisible nature.

The range of perceived environmental impacts and behavioural disruptions is impressive. Appendix A identifies a number of those that have been mentioned in resident surveys. These impacts are described in *negative* terms as increasing with the presence of a transport system. This is only one side of impact, however. Impacts can also be positive. They can decrease hazards, improve micro-climate, orientation and reduce noise levels. The critical measure is the *change* from previous levels.

The list could be more finely divided or more compactly grouped. These are matters of judgement. Under stable conditions the losses, destruction and disruptions will probably be forgotten and therefore be seen as unimportant, whereas in conditions of change such impacts will come to the fore. These impacts and disruptions are usually listed as separate, yet there are several causal relationships between them. Environmental conditions, for instance, affect social linkages, privacy and sense of turf. It is beyond the capacity of this chapter, however, to outline such relationships.

The most important information concerning these impacts is how *significant* the impacted populations consider the impacts to be, which impacts are of most concern, i.e. to which ones are they most *vulnerable*, and which impacts do they consider to be the most *intensive*.

In appearance, responses and behaviour are a much softer area of impact assessment than environmental measurement. Subjective judgements are more likely to vary between groups, there will probably be no consensus, and yet they may well change over time. It seems like quicksand. Yet the chance of keeping in close contact with what the impacted population feels is politically less hazardous than the pursuit of professional measurements that may have no popular relevance. Besides, there are scaling techniques, sampling and survey-research methods that provide a level of reliability in assessing responses even to some of the more intangible kinds of impacts.

Satisfaction, disturbance and acceptance. In impact measurement there is frequently a quest for the single index of evaluation. Are people generally satisfied, how much are they disturbed, how much are they willing to accept? People can respond to such questions but their responses vary, for instance depending on how subjective or objective the question is. If they are asked their personal feelings about an environment, responses are more likely to be affected by *personal dispositions*. If they are asked to evaluate the environment, they respond more to *environmental conditions*[6]. If asked to compare their situations with others, their responses will differ from their direct response to one situation.

Even if we can obtain some reliable estimate of satisfaction, for instance, by creating an index from a number of questions, there is the still more fundamental question of how serious do we consider dissatisfaction to be, and how many have to be dissatisfied before we consider the impact to be unacceptable? In impact studies by agencies, who wish to construct facilities, it is tempting to minimize dissatisfaction by trying to determine levels of acceptability. Opponents, on the other hand, are after higher levels of environmental quality than mere satisficing. The establishment of standards of acceptability will necessarily be a matter of debate. Proposals for standards of traffic capacity for residential streets presently range from 2,000 vehicles per day to 14,000 per day[2].

Power. Perhaps the most significant effects of transport investments are their differential impacts on the economic and political power of various groups. The effects of environmental impacts on the economic resources of different groups, on their employment, markets and land values, and the effects on their political power, community or group solidarity, must be recognized. These are seen as beyond the scope of this chapter, but must not be ignored for those reasons.

Hidden effects. Some impacts may only be discerned by scientists or by professionals who measure impact. Health hazards are the most obvious of these. The effects of air pollution, prolonged exposure to high noise levels, perceptual overload or lack of exercise may all have serious effects on health, effects which have yet to be discovered. No list of perceived and measured impacts can therefore be taken as final and definitive.

Behavioural responses. While we have now described the possible impacts of a transport facility, we have so far not dealt with people's responses to these conditions. These modes of response must be taken into account, for they may be instrumental in dampening or accentuating levels of dissatisfaction.

Adaptation. People may simply adapt their perceptions and behaviour to an intrusion. They may psychologically screen out noises, either by not mentioning them, or by habituating themselves so well to them that they pass unnoticed. They may engage in adaptive behaviour, by moving to the back of the house, discontinuing use of the garden, prohibiting their children from playing on the street, accompanying them to school. Finally, they may adapt their value systems to the situations, modifying their demands for a better environment, resigning themselves to poor conditions.

Adaptation-level theory may help explain this latter phenomenon. It argues that people adapt to certain levels of environmental stimulus, depending on their previous "pooled experience". They tend to become indifferent to these conditions, reacting more strongly as situations deviate from the adaptation level. Under long exposure to changed stimuli, adaption level will change[11]. This theory suggests that an assessment of adaptation levels, and adaptability, be a matter of attention in environmental impact research.

One kind of adaptation is to be found frequently in interviewing, when residents act defensively in front of a strange interviewer. Admission that chosen residential conditions are less than acceptable would be an admission of poor judgement, or lack of resources. Some of this behaviour can be examined with the theory of cognitive dissonance[10]. When people have made a decision, they tend to reduce or screen out any dissonant or negative factors in that choice in order to maintain a consistent view of their condition. This is somewhat similar to the "halo" effect, wherein the beneficial factors in a situation so colour overall attitudes that negative factors are discounted. These attitudes are probably much more common among less-educated groups who engage in what anthropologist Rosalie Cohen calls "relational thinking" as contrasted to "analytical thinking"[5].

Adaptation is not always painless. Some of the more severe environmental impacts, especially those which cause loss of the home, or valued neighbourhood characteristics, can cause grief. It will be important to look behind the facades and into histories of adaptation if the true impacts are to be measured[15]. For as Rene Dubos[9] reminded us, man adapts too easily to adverse environmental conditions at unknown cost. Karl Marx used the term "false consciousness" to describe working-class acceptance of such conditions. It takes a long time to cast off such adaptations. On one London street reported in Britain's *Community Action Journal*, four children were killed by passing traffic before the residents finally protested.

Modification. Personal modifications to the environment to minimize or mitigate impacts are a common occurrence. Closing windows (35 per cent of our San Francisco respondents kept their windows closed because of traffic), drawing blinds, locking doors, erecting fences, planting vegetation or installing outdoor lighting are just some of the modifications people make. Some of these are to their own houses, some to the surrounding property.

Public action. In the case of severe impacts, people may become more active. Some engage in environmental behaviour such as erecting barricades, milling-in on the street, sitting in front of the bulldozers, or chaining themselves to trees. Others protest through social channels, signing petitions, attending meetings, voting for politicians, organizing neighbourhood groups. The intent of these actions is to bring about more powerful modifications to the environmental impact of the transport facility, such as reducing vehicle volumes, diverting trucks, the construction or elimination of a new facility or some other change such as emission controls.

Migration and land-use change. If conditions deteriorate beyond a certain point and protests are ineffective, residents and others may move out, although environmental conditions are not the only reasons for moving. In some cases they are forced to do so by the transport agency. But when people move out, others move in. Such changes in population and land use are a common consequence of a transport facility. Studies of BART have shown that incomes rise with distance from the tracks, although this may be due more to the influence of the existing railroad rights of way and arterial streets than to BART itself. Similarly lower-income groups tend to live around airports. On the other hand, in Britain no correlation was found between traffic volumes and the income of residents on those streets[10]. There is, however, a clear tendency for commercial land uses to locate and be zoned for more heavily-trafficked streets.

These four kinds of adaptive behaviour seek to work out satisfactory solutions to an environmental conflict. While three of them are personal adjustments to the system, public action attempts to modify the system by prevention or amelioration of its negative effects. The crucial point for impact analysis is that this kind of adaptive behaviour reduces dissatisfaction and makes the impact of the transport facility appear to be less negative than it actually is. Those who remain may be screening out the impacts at some psychological or financial costs, others who would not tolerate it have been forced to leave. It will be tempting for transport agencies to ignore these hidden impacts, but it is essential that such behaviour be monitored if true measures of impact are to be obtained.

A stable situation is one in which these adaptive adjustments have been made as far as possible within the constraints in which people operate. Since people are not entirely free, we will always find some who have been unable to adapt. The "deprived" who lack the wish to or cannot move, frequently are among those forced to remain living by transport facilities. We have found old people on heavily-trafficked streets unable to sleep at night for the traffic, yet unable to move.

Impacts of a Transport Change

We have discussed a relatively stable situation that evolves around transport facilities when they themselves stabilize their volumes of traffic. When a new transport facility, or a dramatic change in vehicle characteristics or volume is planned, the impacts must be seen against such ambient conditions.

The conditions of a transport facility will change and to some extent accumulate over time, as the facility itself changes. There appear to be four main phases in the impact pattern of a new facility: the *planning phase*, when planning is under way before physical changes have yet occurred; the *construction phase*, which, in the case of large investments, may take many years; the *opening phase*, when construction is complete and vehicles begin to run or fly; and finally the new *stabilization phase*, when major changes cease to take place.

The planning phase. During this phase when plans are under way, no primary environmental impacts occur beyond those that are in the minds of the impacted populations, although these may lead to various kinds of satisfaction, and adaptive and anticipatory behaviour resulting in secondary impacts. During this phase, the important factors are the simulations made of the proposed investments, the degree of diffusion throughout the impacted population, and the population's previous experience with similar investments.

The *simulations* include verbal reports, such as environmental impact reports as well as visual presentations, graphs, diagrams, plans, perspectives or models. Many of these are subject to distortion. The proponents of transport investments seek to minimize any suggestion of negative impacts. Robert Caro in his book on Robert Moses[4] for instance, described in detail how the presentation perspective of his Lower Manhattan bridge was shown from a bird's eye view which portrayed the bridge as a thin matchstick-like structure touching down on the Battery Park, whereas in fact, the piers were to be six-storey massive concrete piers, blocking the view of all the office property along the park front. An opponent's presentation, on the other hand, took a viewpoint from below ground level using equivalent exaggeration to depict the worst aspects of the project.

The institutionalization of environmental-impact reports has increased substantially the amount of information on projected impacts of transport projects, even though they have been criticized for irrelevancy, inaccuracy and deliberate distortion[8]. Such impact reports unfortunately rely on the shaky base of the few empirical studies of impacts that have been carried out. Their predictions are inevitably open to question since each situation is unique. Whereas physical impacts such as shadowing visual intrusion and description of access are predictable, behaviour, its emissions and response, may depend on unpredictable events such as accidents or crimes, political elections, economic recession or other changes in the historical or local climate of values.

The *diffusion* of information about the project is another issue. For many years, if projects were quietly developed behind the scenes, they could often be announced at the last moment, with little participation from any impacted populations. This might lead to shock and last-minute protests. More commonly today, information and participation diffuse information about investments early in the planning stages. Even so, it is not uncommon for opponents or losers to be left out of the participatory process. In either case the efforts are to stress the positive aspects of preferred schemes. In the anticipatory stage, then, impacts are subject to distortion, rumour and exaggeration. Controversy may bring out different opinions on impacts and increase the quality of impact prediction. However, this will depend on the degree of expertise available on each side of the controversy.

Analogies from previous transport planning experience and the credibility of the proponent agency will do much to create or allay suspicion among the impacted populations. Prior to the opening of BART, Bay Area attitudes towards the system were very positive, yet few in our interviews had ever travelled on a transit system except for Disneyland's monorail. Such lack of experience meant that BART publicity was virtually the sole source of information about the system, a highly unpredictable situation.

An example of anticipatory impacts was the spate of office building that took place in San Francisco before and during the construction of BART. Anticipatory attitudes were to be found around other BART stations, where substantial numbers feared that future development would impact their neighbourhoods in a negative manner. Expectation and fears are therefore the primary psychological impacts in this phase and can cause migration, change of land use, protests or other forms of response.

The clearance and construction phase. This is frequently the most negative phase of a transport project. In larger schemes, sites have to be cleared, people may be moved from their homes, work places eliminated, whole neighbourhoods with shopping centres and other valued facilities may be demolished and replaced. This first part of the phase is predominantly destructive with few compensating features, unless the area being destroyed is universally disliked or viewed with neutral feelings.

Clearance and destruction also generate trucks and other heavy vehicles which create dirt, dust, noise, vibration and other unpleasant environmental impacts that lower the social image of an area. In the construction phase the new facility emerges from the noise, mud and dust. Although this phase is usually minimized in transport planning and forgotten once the new system is open, it is frequently so painful that impacted populations migrate or simply go out of business. The construction of a major subway or freeway system can change the patterns of traffic, and therefore, business for numbers of years — lengths of time during which some businesses are unable to survive. During this time the appearance of the surrounding areas can be blighted, crime may increase and permanent damage can be done.

During this phase opposition may peak as opponents try to prevent construction taking place. While some have sat in front of bulldozers to stop freeways, others have attacked workmen installing street barriers to protect neighbourhoods from through traffic. Attitudinal surveys taken during this phase may find little praise for the facility except that which looks forward to its ultimate completion. Towards the end of construction, on larger projects like fixed-rail transit systems, there is sometimes a hiatus while the finishings are complete and before the system is opened.

The opening phase. When vehicles begin to run, the purpose of the investment is fulfilled, the feared or hoped-for impacts are actually felt. This too can be a highly charged period. It could be a "honeymoon", or a disaster. There may be surprise or disappointment. If the investment is large it will capture the attention of the media, and if controversial, may stay in the public eye for several months or years. This will be a time when people are most aware of and articulate about environmental impacts, since change has just occurred. Traffic, noise, nuisance levels, strangers, parking problems and visual description can suddenly materialize. Later on people may adapt to these changes, habituate themselves to new routines and screen out the negative impacts, but meanwhile it can be an important time to interview people for they are especially articulate about the impacts at this time. Transport agencies, however, are usually unhappy about this prospect, frequently arguing that attitudes in the opening phase are "unfair" to the projects since the bugs will not have been worked out. Yet, the environmental impacts of this opening phase may balance negative with positive. While the negative intrusions may be seen at their most acute, the newness and cleanliness of the facility usually cast it in a positive light.

The stabilization phase. This phase may be the most difficult to identify, since stabilization may never quite take place. It may be characterized by a stabilization of attitudes, of behavioural adaptations, of physical modifications or populations and use change. All these phenomena, including patronage of the facility and surrounding vegetation may continue to change without ever stabilizing. The only way to assess this will be repeated surveys over time.

The Comparative Nature of Impact Assessment

Clearly transport impacts are relative in nature. They change over time and are obfuscated by extraneous influences. All this makes accurate assessment of environmental impacts an almost impossible and very costly task.

The Impact Profile

There is rarely any clearly definable *before* situation to compare with what may never be a stabilized *after* situation. Since impacts may peak at certain points in the process, particularly after construction begins, and at the time of the opening, continuous or at least intermittent impact measures may be the only way to catch the longitudinal profile of impact.

Secular Effects

Unfortunately the transport-impact process is not isolated from the rest of the world. Several other transportation, land-use, population and environmental events may be taking place in the impact zone of the facility during the period of measurement. For example, in the case of BART, if automobile traffic increases in the Bay Area generally, with its attendant congestion, noise, air pollution, BART-area residents may benefit — relative to others — if use of BART maintains automobile traffic at its present level in their neighbourhoods, or even if the increase in their local traffic is less extreme than it is in areas distant from BART. In order to gain an accurate assessment of transport impacts, it is necessary therefore to evaluate environmental and social changes in areas identical to the impacted zone, in places where no equivalent transport facility has been placed. In the BART study, residential neighourhoods equivalent to two of the impacted neighbourhoods were selected as control sites to assess these secular changes.

What Would Have Been?

Finally, comparisons should be made between what actually happens and "what would have been" had there been no transport facility — the No-build Alternative[7] — or had alternative investments been made. In the BART impact programme there was extensive debate over the characteristics of what was called the NO-BART alternative. A decision was finally made, for instance, to assume that a fourth Bay Bridge crossing would not have been built. As can be imagined, this decision will have profound effects on assessments of BART's relative impact.

Strategies for Impact Assessment

This rather complex picture of the environmental and social impact process creates formidable measurement problems. If all cannot be measured, how do we select samples? Selection will vary depending on whether the assessment is to be an empirical study of an existing system, or a prediction of future impacts.

Criteria for Selection of Impact Measures

In order to arrive at priority measures some criteria are necessary. The following appear to be the most critical:

Relevance to impacted populations. The most important criterion from a social and environmental viewpoint is relevance to the population impacted, whether they are aware or not. The question then is relevance to whom? This criterion is more often forgotten than one would imagine. In too many impact studies, lists of professionally-selected environmental measures are taken without any reference to populations. In several known cases these measures have been taken only to find out later that the impacted populations have different concerns.

Comprehensiveness. Measures should not omit impacts that are or may be significant to some group.

Reliability. Measures should have some reliability, and their gathering should be the object of careful objective and explicit sampling and measurement.

Public comprehension. In most studies public comprehension of the results is extremely important, especially if policy is to be affected. Measures which are meaningful to the public are therefore more powerful than those which are obscure, technical or otherwise incomprehensible.

Cost. The criterion that ultimately and, in most cases, primarily determines the selected impact measures and the sampling procedures is cost. Unfortunately, this often results in taking the easiest measures rather than the most relevant.

Priority Measures

Intuitively weighing the above criteria, especially relevance, the following might be the order of measurement priority. Note that these are points of measurement on the impact model presented in Fig 1. The methods of measurement are shown in the parentheses.

Population groups. Identify the principal interest groups among the population who are likely to be most intensely impacted and most vulnerable to impacts and their relative resources.

Population values. Following the criterion of relevance, the first measures should estimate what the impacted population holds to be of most environmental and social value, which environmental qualities they judge to be most important (interviews, meetings with cross-sectional sample).

Derived impact measures. From the above desired qualities, environmental quality measures could be derived. This was the strategy of the BART Residential Impact Study[1]. The principal impact measures can be taken, preferably at points of population vulnerability, such as homes, activity centres, access routes (field surveys, aerial photo, map analysis).

Distributive effects. The distribution of the population in the zones of various impacts can provide some crude measures of the numbers being impacted. The numbers of residents subject to different traffic volumes is, for instance, a useful measure, even though the correlation of traffic volume with environmental impacts is complicated[2] (map analysis, census, traffic flows).

Perceived impacts. Directly asking the population to evaluate impacts will provide the most relevant and publicly comprehensible information, even though it is more costly. It will also act as a check on the environmental measures (interviews, meetings).

Behavioural impacts. Changes in population composition and land use will be useful but subject to time lag and census collection. Micro-behavioural impacts, like accidents, also take time before patterns emerge. Interference with activities such as street play are more difficult to obtain (census, observation, interview).

Impact sources, mitigators and magnifiers. The identification of impact sources and the separation of impacts from different facilities begins to be very complicated. Carefully sampling different situations becomes necessary probably using quasi-experimental research designs. Environmental impact depends here on land-use impact methods.

Hidden effects. Health effects require extremely careful epidemiological or laboratory studies.

Conclusion

Where budgets are constrained it may only be possible to obtain measures of the first four categories. Even so this would entail meetings and interviews with selected members of the impacted population. This is still an unusual procedure in most environmental-impact assessments, which rely primarily on Derived-impact Measures. The goals of basic research in the field should be to endeavour to validate and correlate the various measures in order to identify the most relevant and reliable. This would involve taking samples of the whole array of measurements and correlating them with each other. An attempt was made on the BART Residential Impact Study to carry out such a wide array of measures.

Appendix A: The Negative Impacts of Transport Systems; An Incomplete List

Hazards	impacts which *increase* the chance of earthquake, flood, fire, unfenced heights, deep water, etc.
Traffic hazards	danger due to vehicles, live rails, etc.
Crime	danger due to criminal activity, street assault, burglary, car theft, etc.
Health	threats to health through air pollution, lack of sunlight, water pollution, garbage and trash.
Exercise	constraints on physical exercise through lack of athletic facilities, walking difficulties, etc.
Overcrowding	lack of space to carry out desired activities, loss of parking facilities, etc.
Loss	loss of homes, work places, community or other facilities.
Noise, vibration	noise and vibration levels which interfere with desired activities and are unpleasant.
Air pollution	fumes, smells, smoke, dust and smog which are unpleasant to breathe, a nuisance to clean and which obscure desirable views.
Darkness, glare	blockage of light into buildings, shadowing of public and private spaces, glare of headlights into windows, bright reflective surfaces.
Micro-climate	unacceptable increase in wind levels, exposure to rain, snow.
Disruption of access	local vehicular access to various parts of the community, cycle and pedestrian access, public access to valued environments and facilities such as shorelines, beaches, lakes, rivers, viewpoints and other amenities.
Disorientation	invisibility and poor signing of significant and desirable destinations.
Destruction of valued places	destruction of, intrusion upon, erosion and deterioration of valued natural, historic and community environments.
Territorial invasion	invasion of territory which individuals, streets, neighbourhoods and communities feel "belong" to them, for which they care and feel responsible even if they are not owned.
Privacy intrusion	from prying eyes, the presence of strangers, distracting events.
Disruption of neighbourhood	reduction of contacts on the street, through noise, presence of strangers, unpleasant conditions.
Oppressiveness	environments which through their vast scale and authoritarian nature diminish human identity.

Reduction of choice	loss of activities, uses and places that lent diversity and life to a community.
Ugliness	environments which are unpleasant to the senses of sight, sound, smell or touch, or are littered with trash, dilapidated.
Visual disruption, intrusion	environments that disrupt the character of an existing landscape, neighbourhood or city, that block desired views.
Regional image	reduction in the quality of the regional image.
Natural loss	loss of wildlife habitats, ecological riches and other valued natural features.
Artificiality	environments which lack natural materials, outdoor views, open windows, vegetation.

Notes

1. Appleyard, D. and Carp, F. (1974) The BART residential impact study: a longitudinal study of environmental impacts, in *Improving Environmental Impact Assessment: Guidelines and Commentary*. T. Dickens and K. Domeny (eds), University of California Press, pp 121–6.
2. Appleyard, D. with Gerson, M. S. and Lintell, M. (1976) *Liveable Urban Streets: Managing Auto Traffic in Residential Neighbourhoods*. US Department of Transportation, Government Printing Office, Washington, D.C.
3. Bor, W. and Roberts, J. (1972) Urban motorway impact. *Town Planning Review*, **LXIII**, 4, pp 299–321.
4. Caro, R. A. (1974) *The Power Broker: Robert Moses and the Fall of New York*. Vintage Books, New York.
5. Cohen, R. A. (1969) Conceptual styles, culture conflict and non-verbal tests of intelligence. *American Anthropologists*, **71**, 5.
6. Cralk, K. H. and Zube, H. E. (eds) (1976) *Perceiving Environmental Quality: Research and Applications*. Plenum Press, New York.
7. Crane, D. A. and Partners (1975) *The No-Build Alternative: Social Economic and Environmental Consequences of Not Constructing Transportation Facilities*. National Co-operative Highway Research Program, Washington, D.C.
8. Dickert, T. (January–May 1975) Approaches to environmental impact assessment *DMG-DRS Journal Design Research and Methods*, G.1, pp. 10–15.
9. Dubos, R. (1965) *Man Adapting*. Yale University Press, New Haven.
10. Festinger, L. (1957) *A Theory of Cognitive Dissonance*. Row, Peterson, Evanston, Illinois.
11. Hedges, B. (1973) *Road Traffic and Environment: Preliminary Report*. Social and Community Planning Research, London.
12. Helson, H. (1964) *Adaption Level Theory*. Holt, Rinehart and Winston, New York.
13. Lassiere, A. (1974) *The Evaluation of Transport Plans at the Strategy Level*. UK Department of the Environment, London.
14. Lee, T. and Tags, S. (1976) The social severance effects of major urban roads in *Transportation Planning for a Better Environment*. P. Stringer and H. Wenzel (eds), Plenum Press, New York.
15. Marris, P. (1974) *Loss and Change*, Institute of Community Studies. Routledge and Kegan Paul, London.
16. McHarg, I. L. (1971) *Design with Nature*. Doubleday, New York.
17. Perloff, H. (ed.) (1969) *The Quality of the Urban Environment*. Johns Hopkins Press, Baltimore.
18. San Francisco Planning and Urban Renewal Association (1975) *History of Intensive High Rise Development in San Francisco*. Final Report.
19. Steinitz, C., Murray, T., Sinton, D. and Way, D. (1969) *A Comparative Study of Resource Analysis Methods*. Department of Landscape Architectural Research Office, Graduate School of Design, Harvard University.
20. Webber, M. M. The BART experience — what have we learned?, *Institute of Urban and Regional Development, Monograph No. 26*. University of California, Berkeley (1976).

Part II   The Street

Introduction

E. DE BOER

The street is a commonplace, or at least used to be so: rejected as vulgar by the middle-class, as trivial by social research. Social life in the street was marginal, deviant. Only this aspect has been studied in some detail, in William Foot Whyte's classic *Streetcorner society* (1955) for instance.

Because of neglect and disdain the street could easily lose its function as a common area and be handed over to motorized traffic. A pre-war American design-reaction to resulting unsafety was the Radburn principle creating segregated road-structures for pedestrian and vehicular traffic[1]. The neighbourhood unit formula (Perry, 1929) implying isolation from through-traffic was developed in order to isolate neighbourhoods from the big bad town, to make a better town, one which consisted of rural communitites[2]. The environmental area as introduced by Buchanan (1963) had the opposite purpose: to enhance or restore environmental quality to urban neighbourhoods by diverting traffic[3]. Since the measures taken were however often only the simplest ones — the erection of barriers in streets — the effect on amenity was equally poor. At about the same time there were strong segregational tendencies in traffic planning. New towns like Stevenage, Cumbernauld and Lelystad (NL) were built with independent road-systems for motorized and non-motorized traffic. Town centres were pedestrianized on a growing scale in the interests of shopping and tourism. However, segregation may safeguard walking and cycling, but it confirms disintegration of the street and its social functions.

A growing concern about liveability and a revaluation of urban life stimulated the pursuit of reintegrating the street, of bringing life and people back on the street. The writings of, for instance, Jane Jacobs and Hans-Paul Bahrdt were influential in changing the urban planners' mind, in English and German speaking countries respectively. Jane Jacobs stressed the presence of a flourishing community life and street use in older neighbourhoods. Bahrdt moreover supported the value of impersonal and detached urban life with his theory of socio-cultural urbanization[4]. According to him, urbanity is characterized by polarization of activities into a public sphere ("Oeffentlich", open, anonymous) and a private sphere (closed, individual). Both spheres should be protected by the architect and town planner, lest the outstanding qualities of urban life — freedom, tolerance, cultural progress — be threatened. The backbone of the public sphere is — as might be expected — public space: the street, the square, the market. There are therefore two social motives for recapturing the street from the automobile, one to protect liveability in residential streets and one to foster urbanity. The first one is vigorously at work in the Netherlands and in Germany[5]. The purpose of the Dutch "woonerf"-concept — literally "living yard" — is not to expel the car from residential streets but to create room for other activities, and to equalize pedestrian and vehicular uses. For this the street must be restructured, pavements eliminated and traffic made quieter. The Germans use the term "Verkehrsberuhigung" (traffic-quietening) for the entire process. There is a tendency towards more comprehensive measures, "Verkehrsberuhigte Zonen" or — in Dutch — "Verblijfsgebieden" (literally: staying areas), both in town-centres and in residential quarters[6]. Delft, the best Dutch example of modern traffic policy has several of those areas[7]. Demonstration "Verblijfsgebieden" financed by central Government have been established in Rijswijk and Eindhoven[8]. With growth in scale however the accommodation of traffic, and the redistribution of impact and public participation may cause increasing difficulties in planning. Particularly when large scale change is brought about all at once, as with demonstration projects, trouble can be expected, since environmental impact and consequent public reaction can be rather unpredictable. This is why such projects, intended as design show-cases, can hardly serve as examples for planning. A piecemeal approach is more to be recommended: starting at a number of places where support is certain and then gradually expanding traffic integration, pace and direction according to the degree of success. The end-state need not be defined clearly but at any step in the process motorized traffic — which to some degree will simply vanish — should be carefully redistributed. Main streets which at the end bear a considerably heavier traffic load must somehow receive compensation for this. Appleyard (1976) who compared traffic control policies in different countries put forward in his last chapter (pp 259–310) some useful suggestions, for planning. Before however embarking in a "streets for people" operation, questions of purpose, of street functions afterwards and of the bounds of possibility should be answered.

The purpose of restructuring residential streets is twofold: giving priority to its primary use and to those most dependent on it. The primary use of the residential street is implied in its name. It is of passing importance only for drivers, but of lasting importance for the people living and staying in the street. Research in Amsterdam, moreover, has shown that at no point in time during the day were more than 50 per cent of the population outside their residential precinct[9]. So changing priorities is simply a matter of redistributive justice. This is even more true for the second purpose: giving an equal right to use the street to those most in need of it: children, handicapped and elderly people. For them it is an essential first or last link with the outside world. If they cannot use it, their development or social integration is seriously threatened.

The street ought to become richer in environment, functions and activities, but what may seriously be expected? How much life can be brought back on to our present streets? To what degree are different functions compatible? What makes the street a socially interesting place, especially in the city is its indefiniteness or perhaps the tension between different contrasting functions. The street is a *public place*, open for everyone and for all kinds of activities, yet in a sense it is private too, as an extension of the adjacent buildings: shopping streets, residential yards. The street is both a *canal* of all kinds of transport (traffic, water, electricity etc.) and a *bridge* to the outside world, giving access. The street provides confrontation (meeting and exchange) and severance, anonymity and privacy, for passers-by and residents[10].

Creating and recreating a living street is finding the balance appropriate for the circumstances. These are rather different from the conditions for street life in past centuries, which nostalgia sometimes longs for. De Jonge unravels them in his "Recapture of the Street?", amply considering street-activities as well.

Summaries

De Jong's Recapture of the Street? surprisingly opens by treating the political function of the street. His argument is however convincing. The political meaning of the street is indeed of first importance. It shows how essential common things may be. The street is a "peaceful" meeting place for people, for the community. Democracy was born on the street and it is renewed and oppressed there as well. The street has however declined considerably. Various expressions of social life have vanished, or still are visibly vanishing from it. The causes are partly techno-infrastructural (rails, sewers, cars), partly economic in character: the concentration of production in large firms for instance. Interest in social reform left the street and was directed more to organizing trade unions and the like. A more modern mentality, emphasizing achievement, speed and lack of time, was an additional factor in causing decline.

There was little protest at the demolition of the street. Indeed, it had serious drawbacks: stench, noise, and frequently chaotic conditions. At present the specialized street is dominant: the residential street, the shopping-street, the motorway, the class-street.

Maybe the tide will turn: there are now pedestrian precincts in inner cities, tourism makes the street more lively, culture is back on it, and counter-culture is predominantly street-culture.

The next paper, *The environmental quality of city streets, the residents' viewpoint* by *D. Appleyard and M. Lintell* demonstrates that even a residential street need not be devoid of social meaning, providing it is not overrun by motorized traffic. This has been selected because it is suggestively illustrated by a study of charming simplicity and amazing effectiveness. Dutch research on "woonerven" is not nearly as pervasive.

Citing the author's summary:

"Field interviews and observations were carried out on three similar San Francisco streets with differing traffic levels to determine how traffic conditions affected the liveability and quality of the street environment. All aspects of perceived liveability — absence of noise, stress and pollution; levels of social interaction, territorial extent and environmental awareness; and safety — were found to correlate inversely with traffic intensity. Traffic increases were also accompanied by the departure of families with children from these streets. Responses were nevertheless muted for a number of probable reasons, including environmental self-selection, adaptation and lack of a target for resentment". The results of this study are suggestive but unrepresentative since only three cases were investigated. It was replicated in 1974 by interviewing 400 people in twenty-one streets throughout the city. The results of this second study pointed in the same direction. The position of the medium street was however less clear-cut. These streets were often in the process of transition from light to heavy traffic and problems were therefore felt more sharply. (Appleyard, 1976).

Studies like these, financed respectively by the city and by US-DOT, are an expression of growing concern about traffic conditions. Their results support efforts to polarize infrastructure in what might be called "away and stay types".

Schmidt-Relenberg in fact advocates such a polarization in his paper *"On the sociology of car traffic in towns"*. His perspective is a different and more restricted one though: traffic safety. The author argues that role-behaviour in traffic should be as rational and habitual as possible since uniformity and predictability are beneficial to co-operation between traffic participants. The objective determinants of role-behaviour which are distinguished include the vehicle, the system of norms concerning behaviour (traffic rules) and the structure of traffic facilities. Alas, the car has for the individual a number of functions other than that of a means of transport. It is a consumer commodity and, what is worse, a medium and symbol of freedom, status, prestige and power. A good deal of irrational behaviour may thus be expected. This should be counteracted by other determinants of behaviour. Yet the system of traffic rules imposes a "disproporiate burden of superfluous regulations and information upon the driver, which prevents or retards habituation". Non-observance of these norms is consequently perceived as quite normal. Transgressions may even be enforced by the objective traffic situation. Because moreover deviant behaviour is hardly ever sanctioned, the whole norm-system is ramshackle.

Neither can infrastructure meet with Schmidt-Relenberg's approval. There is too much variety in traffic situations to enforce habit. Yet the most important point of application for improvement is found here[11].Two different types of infrastructure, in practice only rarely found in a pure state, the network system and the circular system, should be applied exclusively in transport planning. The network system is egalitarian, admitting users of all kinds, regulated predominantly by social control. The circular system is hierarchical, with limited access (for e.g. cars only) controlled formally and guiding its users maximally by the physical characteristics of the facility itself.

In the end it is clear that the author has directed his analysis too exclusively towards safe car-driving. The egalitarian system is not applied to residential areas, which in fact is what we are currently striving for.

In 1968 however there was not yet much awareness of the social drawbacks of motorized transport in Europe. The fortunes, or rather misfortunes, of the carless were not discovered until a few years later. This is the theme of Part II.

Notes

1. The Radburn-principle was developed by Clarence Stein and Henry Wright at Radburn, New Jersey in 1928.
2. C. A. Perry (1929) The neighbourhood unit, in: *Regional Survey of New York and its environs*, New York.
3. C. Buchanan (1963) *Traffic in towns*, London, Her Majesty's Stationery Office.
4. H. P. Bahrdt (1961) *Die moderne Gross-stadt*, Rowohlt, Reinbek bei Hamburg. J. Jacobs (1961) *The death and life of great American cities*, Random House, New York.
5. The Dutch and German governments moreover made considerable propaganda for it. The report of the Interdepartementale Werkgroep (1974) was distributed free. So was a 64 page leaflet, full of planning suggestions by the Bundesregierung (M. Eichenauer a.o. 1979, *Wohnstrassen der Zukunft*, Bonn, Bundesministerium für Raumordnung etc.).
6. R. Monheim, a German champion of non-motorized traffic, states in his introduction to Heinz a.o. (1978) that more and more towns are beginning "mit der Planung von Fussgängerzonen gesamtstädtische Dimensionen anzupeilen", i.e. are moving towards comprehensive pedestrian planning.
7. The town was a pioneer in creating woonerven, it has a sector-plan preventing through-traffic in the inner city and a number of recently constructed bicycle-routes. In the German leaflet of Eichenauer (see note 5) there are quite a few photographs of situations in Delft. After recommending Delft as an outstanding object for design-excursions it warns ". . . please remember: the city-government is continuously overburdened with guided tours. These can be done without. . ." (p. 59).
8. The Department of Civil Engineering of Delft Technological University has with great success given post-university courses on the subject from 1978 on (Hakkesteegt, 1982). The courses are multi-disciplinary in character, treating theory, research, planning and design from several perspectives. I myself am making the sociological contribution.
9. V. Vidakovic (1980) *Mens, tijd en ruimte*, uit de dagboeken van 1400 Amsterdammers (Man, time and space; from the diaries of 1400 Amsterdammers), Dienst Ruimtelijke Ordening, City of Amsterdam, pp 31–41.
10. Other lists of functions can be found in e.g. Appleyard (1976) and Heinz (1978)
11. Suggestions for improvements in the other spheres were not quite so spectacular and partly outdated. Therefore these were left out.

76   E. de Boer

Literature

D. Appleyard a.o. (1981) *Liveable streets*. University of California Press, Berkeley.

S. Anderson (1978) *On streets*, M.I.T. Press, Cambridge (Mass.).

B. Bach (ed.) (1981) *Van woonerf tot woonwijk* (From woonerf to residential quarter), proceedings of a series of meetings of the Dutch Royal Institute of Engineers (KIvI), The Hague.

Tj. Deelstra a.o. (red.) (1972) *De straat vorm van samenleven*, a collection of articles to the exhibition from 2–6 till 6–8–1972, Van Abbemuseum Eindhoven.

D. Garbrecht (1981) *Gehen, ein Plädoyer für das Leben in der Stadt* (Walking, a plea for life in the city), Beltz, Weinheim and Basel.

J. Gehl (1971) *Livet mellem husene* (Living between homes), Architektens Forlag, Kopenhagen. (In Dutch 1978, *Leven tussen huizen*, Walburg Pers, Zutphen.)

J. Gehl (1980) The residential street environment, *Built Environment*, **6** no. 1, pp 51–61.

D. H. ten Grotenhuis (1979) *The woonerf in city- and traffic-planning*, Municipality in Delft (NL).

P. Hakkesteegt (ed.) (1984) *Cursus 'Inrichting van Verblijfsgebieden'*, Stichting Postakademiale Vorming Verkeerskunde, Delft.

W. Heinz a.o. (1978) (Studiengruppe Wohnungs und Stadtplanung, Frankfurt). *Verkehrsberuhigte Zonen in Kernbereichen* (traffic-restrained zones in town centres). Schriftenreihe Städtebauliche Forschung des Bundesministers für Raumordnung, Bauwesen und Städtebau, 03065 Bad Godesberg.

Interdepartmentale Werkgroep Verkeersveiligheid in woongebieden (1974), *Interim-rapport, Verkeersleefbaarheid in steden en dorpen*, Ministerie van Verkeer en Waterstaat, The Hague.

S. Peters (ed.) (1977) *Fuszgängerstadt*, Callwey München.

The Recapture of the Street?*

RUDOLF DE JONG

Socio-economic Development in the Nineteenth and Twentieth Centuries

In the sixties, the street[1] was rediscovered and re-conquered as a field for political and cultural action: sit-downs, "events", provocations. Immediately the opponents of the Bomb, the provos and other demonstrators were rebuked: "You are dragging politics into the streets; that's just what the Fascists did!" This reproach reveals blatant misconceptions of the street, of fascism, and of democracy. What the Fascists brought to the street was not politics, but violence that swept politics and democracy from the streets. Where dictatorship reigns, the street is silent, people in buses and trains will not talk about politics, notices appear on the periphery of street life — in the cafés, at the hairdresser's — NO POLITICAL DISCUSSION ON THE PREMISES. In the heyday of Stalin's terror, so it is told, you only had to look hard at someone in the underground to reduce him to a state of panic, and in the street people hardly dared look into each others' faces: here the street is dead, robbed of its social function as the peaceful meeting-place of people.

Power is in the Streets

Nazism went to extremes to isolate human beings completely from the street, with the Star of David Jewish people were obliged to wear on their clothes. A German Jew whom a mixed marriage exempted from deportation, has written about this star, "Today I ask myself once more as I have asked myself and all sorts of people, hundreds of times before, 'which day in those 12 years of hell was the worst for the Jews?' Neither I nor anyone else has ever given a different answer than: the 19th September 1941. From that date the Star of David had to be worn (. . .). Of course, I had been cut off from common life since 1933, and the whole of Germany had been cut off since that date; however, as soon as I had left my home and the street where I was known behind me, I was able to submerge in the great general flow. And it was a submerging, despite the fear of being

*Reprinted by permission of Van Abbemuseum, Eindhoven, The Netherlands.

recognized and molested at any moment by some malevolent passer-by. But now I was identifiable by anyone at any time and this mark isolated and outlawed me. . ."[2].

Authoritarian governments have always had a deep-seated fear of the street and its lack of order. In Europe, absolute monarchy is symbolized by the increasing distance between its palaces and the street — the fortified castles in the cities, such as the "Steen" in Ghent and Antwerp, or the Tower of London, the walled Kremlin, the Bastille in Paris. How Florentine absolutism developed is to be seen in the different situations in relation to the street of the Palazzo Vecchio and the Palazzo Medici on the one hand and the Pitti Palace with its special escape route, completely detached from the street on the other hand. The Escorial and the palace at Versailles of the Sun King Louis XIV lie far removed from the bustle of the street. Today, fear of the street still manifests itself at the first real threat to authority. Martial law means that the street is "prohibited". There is a curfew: processions, demonstrations and gatherings are forbidden.

Yet democracy itself was born on the streets. In the market place, to be exact. Quite literally. This market — over 2,500 years old is still to be seen. It is the Agora in Athens. Everywhere where people have some civil rights we can find some kind of free street, from the Roman Forum to Speakers' Corner in Hyde Park. The gardens of the Palais Royal in Paris, open to the road so that anyone could enter, although it was the private property of the oppositional Duke of Orleans, were an island of liberty in Absolutist-reigned France on which the French Revolution had its first "voice". The street retained a vital role in the entire course of the French revolution. The great movers of the revolution were not in the clubs of the ideologists, the Girondists and Jacobins, they were in the street. The street, — the market women, — fetched the King from Versailles to the capital; the street toppled the Bastille. The democratic moment and aspects of revolution do not stem from the Estates General, the National Assembly or the Convention, but from institutions much closer to the street, the communes, and even more directly from the self-administering districts and sections of Paris. Here, socialist and social concepts were realized for the first time direct from the street itself: the right to work, to receive public assistance, price ceilings, the delivery of bread and other foodstuffs, etc. During the Paris Commune of 1871, this kind of social decision was taken by the city quarters and their sections. The democratic and socialist mass movements of Europe and the United States would be unthinkable without the street . . . propaganda passed on by word of mouth, demonstrations and meetings, posters. Often the conquest or the violation of these rights were the direct issue of the struggle. In the streets the social contradictions of society, its misery and luxury were exposed. In the memoirs of socialists and in anniversary editions of old socialist newspapers you will read how a first encounter with the Socialist movement would often take place on the street, through hawking of socialist papers, demonstrations, police appearance, sometimes through the street ballad.

In the nineteen sixties, too, political action took to the street in order to achieve further democratization. It started in the United States in Montgomery, with the famous bus boycott — the public transport system is itself an extension of the street — aimed at getting equal rights for the black population. In Amsterdam, the Provos sought the restitution of all manner of democratic rights of which the streets had been robbed in the thirties, a period of declining democracy: demonstration, propagation . . . sitting. The Berkeley Campus Uprising began as a protest against an attack on the freedom of the campus as an open concourse.

In an "old-fashioned" way, the street plays an important role in the Third World. Take the Casbah of Algiers during the Algerian War of Independence: by taking to the streets the Algerian people prevented a subsequent civil war between Ferhat Abbas and Ben Bella. In the same way the Egyptians revoked Nasser's decision to resign after the Six Day War. The street resisted Russian Imperialism in Budapest in 1956 and in 1968, with altogether different methods, in Prague; it resisted American Imperialism in the Dominican Republic upon the entry of the US Marines and in Hue during the Tet offensive.

A temporary highpoint in Europe was the Paris student revolt of 1968 when posters as a political weapon, expression of art and source of information reappeared on the streets, together with street discussion, street threatre, action committees and the street's classical defence construction, the barricade. "Le pouvoir est dans la rue", "Power is in the streets!", was a Parisian battle cry.

The Street went Downhill

All power to the streets! Remarkable as it is, the slogan was coined at the very moment when the street appeared to be dying. This brings me to my actual theme, the development of the street in the nineteenth and twentieth centuries. In brief, this is its progress: with the increasing differentiation of economic and social functions, our street-world became at first particularly lively, perhaps more exciting than ever before. On the street one encountered a variety of economic and social phenomena. Then things went downhill. The continued differentiation of economic life was no longer visible on the street; on the contrary, it was impoverished because all kinds of functions disappeared and the street itself was subjected to a process of differentiation.

Different kinds of road were developed for the various needs of transport, shopping, living and working. But the very thing that gave the street its particular character was the coming together of all kinds of expressions of social life; people working, children at play, passers-by with a purpose, or just strolling (that word has a very old-fashioned ring now), all manner of street furniture and means of traffic and transport. And all this on a basis that I shall call "unorder." I borrow the term from Kropotkin to denote something that is neither chaos nor a strictly controlled order, but a commingling, not without collisions, which seeks and creates its own order from case to case, based on a few generally accepted concordances. The relationship between people consists half of anonymity (but without alienation) and half of familiarity.

It would be interesting to study the image and significance of the street in literature and art. The lively street of the first stages of industrialization, with its great social differentiations, is vividly described in the novels of Dickens, Victor Hugo, Dostoyevsky and Zola. Street scenes and street-scapes always play a very important and at times a very independent role here. In later literature the street does not seem nearly as important; only when boys play a major role do we encounter the street.

For the painter Breitner, the Amsterdam of 1900 was still a very positive source of inspiration. With the Frans Masereel the street becomes a symbol of loneliness. The empty street as an established theme emerges with the surrealist Willink. Emanating from this deserted, dead street which also appears in the dream sequence at the beginning of Bergman's film, *Wild Strawberries*, is a feeling of total desolation and totalitarian threat.[3] Pictures from the days of the occupation, with armed soldiers and tanks in empty streets, represent the oppression of tyranny more poignantly than pictures of street fighting or even razzias. The street also appears prominently as a danger, as a threat, in books about the war period, for example in Marga Minco's *Bitter Herbs*.

Things Vanished

Let me try to trace its breakdown, beginning with the things that have now nearly or totally vanished.

(1) *Animals and nature*. A hundred years ago chickens scratched for grain on the spot now known as the Rembrandtsplein in the centre of Amsterdam. In the outskirts the milkman still did his rounds with his cow. Now even the dogs and horses have disappeared. Only the birds have been able to survive. With the growth of the cities the distance to the urban periphery and nature beyond grew wider and wider.

(2) *Street-trades*. The hawker, the butcher's boy, the general repairs man, the street-peddler, beggars, and pavement artists, the local police-man, they were at the same time also street "characters": the cabby, the butcher's lad, the peddlar, they were the stuff of street life. Other trades have remained; the market is still a feature of some isolated quarters. Taxi-driving appeared as a new profession, but the speed and detachment of the motor car isolates the profession from the street.

(3) *Professions* at the edge of the street, which determine its facade; such as the workshops of small industries, — the smithy, the shoemaker's. Their signboards suffered the same fate. The buildings, housing, offices and banks that took their place turned the street front into a dead wall. Only the shop survived. Shop windows became even more exciting and spectacular.

(4) *Celebrations and recreation.* Street ballads and street music, the fair.

(5) *All kinds of aspects of life* formerly seen in the streets. Drunkeness; offenders being taken to the police-station; various curiosities; illness and death (straw used to be laid before the houses of the seriously ill).

(6) *Official and military displays*, processions and parades.

(7) *Children* and children's games.

(8) The street as a *school of life*.

The last point may seem questionable. If we divert our attention from the systematic list for a moment and turn to the actual appearance of the street with all its means of traffic and transport, tools and trade accessories visible along its facade, the diversity of clothing (according to class and status) and uniforms, of games, then we shall see that the street was a school, especially for the young working-class boy. It confronted him with a thousand objects and situations, all with a name, a word of their own not available in his home. The linguistic poverty which is at present so conspicuous, with the handicap it bestows on the working-class child even before it starts school, may be connected with the impoverishment of the street. The street urchin of the past rarely seemed to suffer from a lack of words! Not so, however, the factory child. The mental atrophy of factory children can be explained by their long working-days and the monotonous and soul-destroying work; the lack of contact on the street may have been an additional factor. Even if the street may not have offered "anything worth learning," quite a lot *could* be learned. The literature of memoirs confirms this. In the boyhood memories of working-class children the street regularly plays a very important role much more so than for the sons of the bourgeoisie, who tend to speak more of house and family. The effects of moving out beyond the city limits into the country are frequently described in reminiscences. The often described "nozems", "halb-starken", "half-baked bullies", led by boredom into acts of provocation, are perhaps the progeny of the dead street.[4] A fine suppression of women was implicit in the ban on free movement in the street for teenage girls. Woman's conquest of the freedom of the street is one of the most important positive developments in the last hundred years.

Transport Differentiating and Killing the Street

The disintegration of the street parallel to the disappearance of all manner of expressions of life in it came about by a progressive differentiation until finally "the street" was replaced by many kinds of street.

1. The construction of pavements. In a city like Amsterdam this was only done about a hundred years ago. The pedestrian was simultaneously protected, but banned to the edge of the street. How long he resisted is evident from photographs of street scenes in New York and London taken around the turn of the century; in these metropolises pedestrians still used the whole road. Now that pavements have disappeared again from many old city centres, where the whole road has become a pavement and traffic is forbidden, it is becoming clear how much the harmonious balance of the street has been distorted by the pavement.

2. The construction of wide streets and the filling in of canals for the sake of the traffic. It is astounding how soon "traffic" was used as an argument to defend the destruction of houses and filling-in of canals eulogising the miracles that the new roads were to perform. Behind much of the mania for clearing and filling-in there lurks a fetish for technical progress, not to mention the economic interests of the building contractor. The canals of Amsterdam (of which nineteen disappeared either partly or completely in the second half of the nineteenth century) clearly served as streets: commerce on the water (the flower market on the Singel is all that remains), all kinds of transport; removals; playgrounds. Beside savings in the costs of maintenance, hygiene was named as a reason for filling in the canals — a fallacy. Their function of open drainage was now taken over by those remaining, while plans for a modern sewerage system were neglected.

3. Rails. When the first rails were laid for the tramway, a fixed track for one means of transport, protest arose against it because while the other users of the road had to give way to the tram, the tram did not have to give way to them. Railways and the underground break the unity of the street. They leave the common arena and create one of their own, exclusively for one purpose. The underground is virtually the model of today's channels of traffic: an unobstructed road, crossings at different levels, and most important, a traffic flow steered by means of signs, passages and subways connecting platforms and exits. The public transport vehicle has detached itself from the street, but at the same time it remains a piece of street which one shares with other people.

4. Public utilities, along with the underground, received their own systems: gas, water, drainage, electricity, telephone. The street became three dimensional and lost a succession of functions and trades.

5. Lastly, the private car has hardly any contact with the street. In itself this is no catastrophe, travellers in coaches and cabs were just as isolated from it and were even raised above its turmoil. But what modern high speed travel has achieved, in a fatal manner and in the shortest time possible, is the destruction of the road's equilibrium. One single purpose has attained predominance, has aquired the monopoly for which every-

thing is sacrificed; the others have been driven out, either totally or into special roads. Today we are familiar with motorways and traffic routes, commercial streets, industrial streets and residential streets. In high-rise buildings specialization has been taken even further: gallery and lift: more roads which offer next to no experience.

What streets still have in common is their boredom, their monotony and their lifelessness. Differentiation even extends to age groups — streets full of children, streets grown old. The colour of the street with its anonymous but bright and multifarious throngs has practically vanished. Only the large cities have genuine, if crippled, streets. But Constant Nieuwenhuys's complaint applies here just as much, if not more so:

> "So much public space is forbidden ground to the pedestrian that he is forced to seek his social contacts either in private areas (houses) or in commercially exploited ones (cafés or rented halls), where he is more or less imprisoned. In this way the city is losing its most important function, that of a meetingplace."[5]

Hardly anywhere has the city-centre grown, despite the tremendous growth of cities and streets. Once the whole town would more or less fulfil this function. Traffic and the differentiation of the streets led to more and more space being claimed by the road. One-third of the Los Angeles area and two-thirds of the centre consist of space eaters, traffic routes, roads, parking lots, garages, service stations and so on. In this city with its millions of inhabitants public transport no longer exists although the motor car gets in its own way, hinders the flow of traffic and is a major cause of the notorious Los Angeles smog. A chance meeting in Los Angeles is out of the question. The city is virtually a huge suburb. There is no city-centre.

Yet the small suburb has the most acceptable street. Here traffic does not yet dominate, there is still nature and fresh air and children can play. This shows the dire state of the urban street. For the suburbs are an escape from the city (a very old one indeed: the phenomenon was discovered in Ur; Rome had its villas outside the city, Amsterdam had its country houses on the river Vecht in the seventeenth century). The escape corresponds to the desire, as Mumford says, to withdraw like a monk and live like a lord;[6] two of the very kinds of people to keep away from the street! Living on the outskirts was the privilege of the urban élite until modern traffic brought fundamental changes. These, however, meant the decline of the advantages of suburbia. Los Angeles itself is the great example here. Mumford calls it a "mass suburbia" which has become an anti-city.[7]

Mass-production, Mass Consumption and Mass-movement Against the Street

Traffic is not the only culprit of course. We have already mentioned various other technical and economic developments which helped to destroy the street, such as banks and offices on the street front and especially the disappearance of all manner of street trades. The factory with its mass production and mass consumption destroyed the street's economy. The street-population was also changed: the "mass" on the street used to be a heterogenous group, the "people" — a fairly vague concept met more often in older socialist literature than in more recent writing. Gradually the term "masses" came to signify the proletariat of the factory, a much more homogeneous group, much further from the street, locked in (fourteen hours a day and more in the beginning) in factories far from the town centre and frequently far from the residential streets.

The "people" were on the streets; the streets were the birthplace of the battle for civil and social rights, revolution and uprising meant street battles and barricades. The songs of the revolution like "La Carmagnole" referred to the street.

In Delacroix's picture of the revolution of 1830, *La Liberté guidant le Peuple*, we see not only a worker, but also the radical intellectual and the street urchin joining the symbolic female figure on the barricades. The street boy probably played quite a large part in all "barricade revolutions". In *Les Miserables* of Victor Hugo one of the characters is Gavroche, the street-arab, mocker and idealist at the same time who meets his end on the barricades. Daumier depicted the ragamuffin who was the first to occupy the throne left by King Louis-Philippe in 1848, taking his seat with the exclamation, "My, that's soft!"

The factory drove Gavroche behind its walls (one of the justifications for child labour was that it kept children off the streets!) and separated the proletariat from the radical journalist. The factories often lay at the periphery or around the city. The proletariat did appear in the streets now and again, but their presence was neither constant nor taken as a matter of course. When it demonstrated on the streets it could not do this without organizing a "demonstration". One could not simply assume the territory to be one's own any more. One had to show one's (quantitative) power. Socialist thinking shifted too. The vehicle for the socialist advance would no longer be the street, but the organization, the party, the union. This shift can be observed in Marxists and anarchists alike. For the latter, anarcho-syndicalism aiming at action within the factories became paramount. In Spain where anarcho-syndicalism was accompanied by a more direct street anarchism, tensions arose at times between the two currents. On the outbreak of the civil war in 1936, victory over Fascism in the streets enabled a successful social revolution to take place in the factories.

It was also the sheer mentality of modern capitalism that did harm to the street, the emphasis on ever increasing efficiency, speed and a constant state of transit. The street is not a place to be in, but to move over, an effect exacerbated by the tremendous distances to be covered and the growth of both roads and towns.

The socialists and communists had essentially the same mentality as their capitalist opponents: admiration of technology and great expectations of its social results. "Catch up and overtake" (capitalist America), was Stalin's motto for Soviet Russia. Greater productivity, better products and fairer distribution was the reformers' promise. The "Palaces of Culture" in Eastern Europe and the "Bastions of the Working Class" as the huge buildings of the labour organizations were called by their members, were anti-street. Today the workers in our welfare states have been able to afford their own cars, and the unions and traditional parties of the left will not risk a serious attack on this great murderer of streets and people. Protest against hig-speed traffic and its moral consequences was much more violent at the time of the car's triumphal entry than in our days. We have accepted that every year millions of adults and children fall victim to the traffic. Dailies, magazines and jokes before 1940 make much more of these evil consequences of automobile traffic than they do now.

Cleaning the Street Socially and Physically

Has there never been a protest, then, against the destruction of the street as a common property? It does appear as if the street's existence is only just being discovered, now that it is disappearing, just as the beauty of nature was only discovered after man had become a city-dweller. The first complaints arose not because of the social aspect of the street, but because of the mutilation wrought on beautiful townscapes by demolishing buildings and filling-in of canals — at any rate; these protests were the first to be registered.

The tearing-up of the street began with the tearing down of old popular quarters whose poor inhabitants were powerless to assert themselves. Added to this was apathy and even admiration for the new "architectural glories", the palaces which gradually occupied the space of whole quarters.

Real popular resistance arose only when popular festivals were outlawed. In The Netherlands the "Eel Uprising" of Amsterdam (when eel pricking was forbidden) made history in 1887, It was the most violent of a series of outbreaks provoked by the outlawing of fairs. Resistance in the economic sphere occurred when street trading was restricted by new regulations. This resistance however was more a matter for those directly concerned than for the whole quarter.

Progressives have always been against the street. They identified the street with its poverty and they turned their attention to better housing and dwelling conditions. In our century they built better houses, situated in often (but not always!) monotonous streets. Socialists paid little or no attention to the social functions of streets and town quarters. "Back to nature", was the solution propagated by the youth movements, and the garden cities, propagated at the end of the nineteenth century. The folk-dancing around the Easter fire in the camps of the youth movements between the two world wars, was far removed from the violent dance of the Carmagnole of the revolutionary Paris in the last century.

To the social democrats, the anarchizing "unorder" of the street was completely alien, as it was to the architects and city-planners of the interbellum who saw everything in a functional light.

In 1924, Le Corbusier wrote in his books, *Urbanism* —

> "The street is a machine for movement: a factory where the equipment must guarantee that one can move. The modern street is a new organ. We must invent new kinds of streets, equipped like factories."

The open strips which the "new architecture" put in place of closed blocks did improve housing but not in every aspect the street facade. In 1927, "Opbouw", the organization of the Dutch "New Architecture" formulated the following five points about town-planning:

1. The constantly expanding volume of traffic caused by an ever expanding economic competition makes the organization of traffic the basis for urban planning.

2. Concepts in the sphere of urban planning have to be rid of the aesthetic habits still adhering to us from earlier generations.

3. The closed townscape must be seen from these angles, and has to give way to the open townscape.

4. The closed townscape is an aesthetic idea of architecture which will prove to be useless with our growing traffic, for it is irreconcilable with the unobstructed view that lively traffic needs.

5. Aesthetically valuable buildings must not be allowed to remain on their original sites if this is detrimental to major public interests.[8]

Before we, in 1972, express our horror and indignation at these statements of the "*avant garde*" of 1927 we should perhaps cast light from an opposite angle on the image we have given of the street of the past. All the foregoing might suggest that the street of the past was ideal. The fact that drainage was one function of which the street was relieved changes our perspective already. The entire history of town and street is a history of a relentless battle against pollution, stench and noise![9]

Mumford's books highlight the two sides, positive and negative, of all kinds of urban developments and changes throughout the ages. An example is the wide squares and boulevards in Paris, originating partly from the times of the French Revolution and partly from Haussmann's well-known projects. His boulevards have a clear authoritarian structure and purpose, which is not surprising since they were intended as a deterrent against the building of barricades in times of turmoil. At the same time, the boulevards mean light, air and trees, a greater scope for contact; and they had their own beauty. This was also true of the railway and the tram. They widened the scope for communication and provided the people with contact with the outside world.[10] The rules of the road applied to everyone and had a democratizing effect.[11] The old urban working quarters may have had a very well established community-life, but this was very closed and traditional. Old people who had always lived there commanded great authority. Frequently they were proud of never having ventured beyond a tiny section of the town. At the end of the eighteenth century, when the city was no larger than today's centre, Amsterdam had nineteen different dialects, some of them spoken over only a few hundred square metres. One of these is even difficult to pinpoint on a map — the language of the fish market. This market was situated roughly on a site where today a quite unique, albeit highly international, language is spoken: the steps of the National Memorial.

Radio, telephone and television have taken over some functions of the street. The disappearance of many street trades is a loss for the strolling pedestrian, but no one will mourn those desperately hard and unprofitable professions which were replaced or made easier by modern technology.

The Class Street

We have been referring all along to "the street", but in fact we see a social hierarchy of streets. At the side of the belt of canals, Amsterdam of the golden seventeenth century, planned its working quarters (of the "Jordaan") with much narrower streets. Even so the street remained fairly democratic. Everyone had access to the canals and the "common" streets were often the most pleasant.

With the industrial capitalism, however, came a street which was no longer deserving the name of "street": the slum in the quarters of the destitute. It is true that the pre-capitalist city knew destitution too, but the industrial slums were something new. The destruction of the traditional means of production and the exodus from rural areas drove people into factories and slums.

In the chapter on original accumulation in *Das Kapital*, Karl Marx related the now classical story of the Duchess of Sutherland. Between 1814 and 1820, the Duchess had fifteen thousand people driven off "her" land and their houses and villages devastated because sheep breeding, employing a few shepherds, brought in more income than all her tenants' rents. What became of the fifteen thousand? Some of them were able to eke out an "amphibious" existence on fishing for a while, until they were driven out once more. That is where their story ends, and that of the slums, doubtlessly their one remaining refuge, begins.

In a slum, the street which is no longer a street but a gutter is as degraded as the holes that serve as houses. The social functions of a street in the deprived but not decayed traditional working districts are largely lacking here.

The street in the destitute districts of the developing countries and that of the slums of the ragged industrial proletariat of the nineteenth century, have a great deal in common. Social contact there is much weaker than in the old working districts which retained some of the character of an autonomous village, shaped by highly personal relationships. The slum dweller has no pride in his area. He "came down" and "ended up" there and even if he is born there, his great aim is to get out. The advantages of economic development, such as plumbing, drainage, electricity and paved roads passed these streets by. In the nineteenth century it needed the sickness and death of cholera to bring about any communication between the slums and the better-off areas and get clearing-schemes under way. The nature of the connection between the slums of Europe then and the deprived town quarters in the Third World now becomes quite apparent in the "accommodation" of the foreign labourers[12] in Western Europe and the negro ghettos in the United States (inhabited by recent immigrants from the southern states).

In practice the distinction made here between an urban working district and a slum is not always so clear. Slums and distress dwellings often arose and still do in old working-class districts.[13] The expression "the district's degenerating" is a very pregnant and topical one from this angle. But generalizations should be handled very carefully. Slums can be subdivided into innumerable kinds, slums of hope, and slums of despair in which most of the inhabitants have given up any hope that things might get better; slums housing people who have jobs and the completely pauperized slums of the permanently unemployed.[14]

The "class-street" is naturally also very undemocratic. It is a street hostile to strangers, which severely restricts its most important function of being a space open for all. The black American "devalues the white street". In the black street, the white feels insecure.

On being confronted with slum quarters and streets, earlier progressive generations thought first of all of better accommodation. But the improved accommodation was beyond the financial reach of the asocial and the poorest of the proletariat. The socialist movements consequently did not involve the poorest of the poor. The idea that the quarter itself might redeem and restore both street and district by the self-organization of its inhabitants is comparatively recent. The spark for the arduous growth of awareness is frequently the fight for improvements or against deterioration in public services — public transport, electricity, water — which are usual in normal streets. One of the greatest incidents of unrest in New York was provoked in a poor negro quarter by the rationing of the water supply during a heatwave. A successful action in a New York slum consisted of the dumping of rubbish in better streets in order to force the community to provide this social service for the poor of the quarter as well. In the famous diary of Maria de Jesus a slum-dweller in Brazil, water supply is a central theme; "I got up to fetch some water." Something like a community feeling, not yet a campaign, but a common grumble, occurs when public transport and electricity prices rise.[15]

A New Future

Is the street approaching a new future? On one side we see inconceivable destruction wrought by the car and the erection of gigantic buildings: skyscrapers, factories, banks and offices which have become just as alien to the street as the palaces of Absolutist princes. On the other side there is not only the resistance of the inhabitants against the destruction of their quarters and the political campaigns we mentioned already, but there are also solid economic forces at work, to the street's advantage.

The Lijnbaan, created out of the ruins of Rotterdam's old city centre, returned the street to the pedestrian and gave space not only to plants, but even to art. Cities which had been bombarded in World War II frequently led the field here: Cologne, Bremen, Düsseldorf, Coventry. Increasing tourism has had a good influence on the street in many ways. It has given old historic towns and the canals of Amsterdam a new economic value; it enlivened the street and its facade with boutiques, cafés, restaurants.

Still more important are the increase in daily leisure and the higher standard of living. The number of people with time to spare, students and other young people who populate the street, has grown. Among the provos, particularly the non-intellectuals among them, one could encounter Gavroche's descendants who had at last left the factories. The "masses" to some extent have become the people in the street again. The city and the street enjoy a higher esteem among today's young people than in previous young generations.[16]

Late-night opening has returned. Snack bars, pizzerias, small cafés, self-service shops and boutiques open up, making the street front more open and varied again. There are sometimes desperate efforts to bring art and culture closer to the street; open museums with free entry, for example. When the European football cup was won, the spontaneous fiesta even conquered the streets of Rotterdam and Amsterdam. The off the peg dress of the white-collar proletariat no longer calls the tune in the streets. A motley crew, hailing from all four corners of the earth make a closer look at the public in the street rewarding again. The counter culture born of prosperity and leisure needs the street and is itself of great value to it. For counter culture the street has become a meeting place and an information centre and an arena for economic activities: the sale of jewellery, door-to-door trading with publications, musicians, etc.

The Amsterdam of 1973 shows the dual history of the street very clearly. There is dilapidation and decay, pollution and stench, the fruits of the coalition between the car consumer and capitalist economic interests. It is supported by an urban council, dominated by socialists and communists, which pass all responsibility on — according to the best liberal-capitalist tradition — to the central government with the pretext of insufficient funds. The counter-forces are those which make the panorama and life of the street freer, more vital and democratic. Both these forces, sometimes stronger, sometimes weaker, are active in every town.

If the (childless) streets of the town centres are regaining some of their street character now, other kinds of streets are fighting back too. The accent in the word "reanimate" in the phrase "reanimate the street", is on "animate", not "re-". To reconstitute the street of the past would be unthinkable. Mankind's greater mobility has altered its significance and its role. We use and know many streets, and move house often. This means that we are less bound to one street, we have a more impartial approach to it. Consequently we are more open to change.

The traffic-free pedestrian concourse is not a reconstitution either: here the pedestrian has a monopoly. In their book, *Communitas*, Paul and Percival Goodman see the essence of a city as the existence of a place which serves as a strolling and meeting ground for those at leisure. Only a square and perhaps a few mainstreets could have this function. However streets given exclusively to pedestrians might be boring and could even bring disadvantages. Was the essential characteristic of a street not the dynamic and flexible equilibrium of the most diverse functions? It is the "unorder" that challenges the imagination. The Paris street revolution of 1968 coined the motto "le pouvoir est dans la rue" but also the much more important slogan, "Let imagination rule". Will the street be recreated according to this ideal and contribute to this aim? Perhaps it is good to remind the reader that the streets can be categorized into dead ends and streets with open exits.

Notes

1. Very little literature exists to my knowledge on the street as such. The subject is of course encountered in all kinds of books on the city, and these books fill whole libraries. I was thus able to make fruitful use of the following studies: Lewis Mumford's *The Culture of Cities* (1938) and *The City in History* (1961) (The latter has appeared recently in Penguins but with a drastically reduced bibliography); *The Historian and the City*, eds Oscar Handlin and John Burchard, M.I.T. 1963; *Traffic in Towns, a study of the long term problems of traffic in urban areas*, the so-called Buchanan Report, London 1963; Paul and Percival Goodman's *Communitas — means of livelihood and ways of life*, 2nd ed., New York 1960; W. Seidensticker: Die City im Umbau, Essen 1967; Kevin Lynch: *The Image of the City*, Cambridge 1960, and of the literature given in the footnotes below!
2. Victor Klemperer *LTI, Notizbuch eines Philologen*, Leipzig, Reclam 1968, pp. 204, 206.
3. The atmosphere in the film *The Third Man* by Orson Welles is evoked chiefly by the dead streets and sewers of the post-war city. In various films of the age of motorized traffic the motorway plays an important role, connected with loneliness, terror and downfall — *La Strada, Le Weekend, Easy Rider*.
4. Dr W. Buikhuizen, *Achtergronden van nozemgedrag*. (Background to the behaviour of bullies), Assen 1966. The author does not include the character of the delinquent street

itself in his survey. The statement of a bully, "I feel awful on Sunday (. . .) that's such a boring day (. . .) all you can do is stroll around town," (p. 209) reveal the character of the street.

5. Constant Nieuwenhuys: "New urbanism", in: *Delta, a review of arts, life and thought in the Netherlands*, autumn 1967, p. 57.
6. Lewis Mumford, *The city in history*, p. 553.
7. Kenneth E. Boulding calls this city "an agglomeration created by and poisoned by the automobile. Under no circumstances could Los Angeles be called a city in the classical sense of the word . . ." See *The historian and the city*, p. 143. Denis W. Brogan refers to "an area . . . strangled in its freeways," *ibid.*, p. 164.
8. *Opbouw* 10 no. 1, 1927, p. 81, cited by Arthur Lehning, *De internationale avant-garde tussen de twee vereldoorlogen*, p. 51.
9. In a serial on environmental pollution in *Intermediair* of 10th December, 1971, A. C. Nielsen wrote an interesting article called "Money does not stink" about these evil-smelling aspects of the city in the course of the centuries. Even the Romans had special streets for their water supply and drainage. And dogs were forbidden by the law. In the oldest collection of by-laws of Amsterdam (dating from 1413), we see environmental regulations including a decree outlawing the dumping of slaughter waste in the canals (Mr M. F. H. Oldervelt in *Zeven eeuwen Amsterdam*, publ. A. E. d'Ailly, part 5, Amsterdam, p. 233).
10. In Salford — Friedrich Engels once called it the classical slum — the change from the horse-drawn tram to the very cheap electric tram in 1903 was of great cultural significance for the poor when for the first time it became possible to get out into the parks. See Robert Roberts, *The classic slum, Salford life in the first quarter of the century*, 1971, pp 115–116. Roberts himself grew up in that "classical" slum.
11. Even the private car has its place in the history of street revolts. In 1958 the dictator of Venezuela, Jimenez, was toppled; the revolution began with the protest of hooting cars.
12. The presence of foreign workers greatly influence the west European street and its facade. Traditional colonialism had affected the street indirectly; in the wider context of technological economic growth. Before the War, Holland had its Chinese street merchants (peanut vendors) and its Indonesian-Chinese restaurants.
13. Amsterdam's renowned Jordaan is called the Kingdom of slums in L. M. Herman's little book *Krotten en Sloppen* (deprived quarters and alleys), 1901. It is interesting that the problems of today are just the same.
   For the most run-down houses, the relatively highest and often absolute highest rents were taken. The occupant of these hovels could still not afford the rents of houses in the new buildings, because although cheaper compared with the gain, the rents were too high. The worst houses had the worst public utilities (water, toilet). The difference lies in the level of destitution; hovels then were worse and more numerous than today. On the problems of constructing social accommodation in a capitalist system, see the catalogue of the exhibition *Bouwen 20–40*, the Dutch contribution to *Het Nieuwe Bouwen*, Van Abbemuseum, Eindhoven 1971, particularly the article by J. Nycolaas. (published in German as well)
14. For a typology of the slum and its tenant see Marshall B. Clinard, *Slums and community development. Experiments in self-help*, New York 1966.
15. Here, too, we should be wary of easy generalizations. Latin America has fairly well organized *barriadas*; sometimes they owe their existence to an organization, For a barriada is often a taking possession of the soil, where one settles, organizes oneself to attain rights on this soil, later to obtain water, electricity and similar amenities. See Jose Matos Mar, *Die Barriadas von Lima*, Zürich 1966, and Talton F. Ray, *The politics of the barrios of Venezuela*, Berkeley, 1969.
16. In an article *Bewogen jeugd contra bedreigde stad* (moved youth against a threatened city) by J. S. van Hessen, *Akademiedagen* 15th–16th April, 1971, Koninklijke nederlandse akademie van wetenschappen, part 22, Amsterdam 1972, there is reference to a Bohemian-style urban proletariat of the last century as a stylistic model for today. Despite the contradiction of Bohemian and proletariat, this definition reflects the change well. In recent years the concept of proletariat has begun to shift markedly in that it is being extended to include students, the underground culture, in short, the street.

The Environmental Quality of City Streets: The Residents' Viewpoint*

DONALD APPLEYARD and MARK LINTELL

Protests and research about the environmental and social impact of transportation systems have paid most attention to the problems created by new freeways through urban areas. But while these are the more dramatic instances of traffic impacts, the rapid growth of vehicular traffic has swamped residential streets in cities across the United States and in other countries. Traffic on city streets may affect as many, if not more, people than traffic on freeways. In San Francisco, approximately 60 percent of the city's major streets (those with a daily traffic volume of over 10,000 vehicles) are lined with residences.[1]

Studies of urban streets (such as the current TOPICS program of the Federal Highway Administration) have concentrated almost exclusively on increasing their traffic capacity, through devices such as street widening, signalization, and one-way streets, with no parallel accounting of the environmental and social costs of these alternatives. Wilfred Owen (1969) recently directed attention to the role that city streets play in the environmental quality of cities as "the main corridors and front parlors" of the city, but even he did not point out that people also have to live along city streets. To our knowledge, the only empirical studies of life on city streets, apart from some studies of traffic noise and a Michigan study of the economic and environmental effects of one-way streets (Michigan, 1969), have been those carried out in Britain since the Buchanan Report (Her Majesty's Stationery Office, 1963 and Chu, 1971).[2]

The investigation reported here is a small-scale attempt to identify the environmental concerns of those who live on city streets in San Francisco. It is a pilot study using observation and open response interview techniques, and does not pretend to have statistical significance. The results however are suggestive. The project grew out of the San Francisco City Planning Department's concern over increasing traffic on the city's

*Reprinted by permission of the Journal of the American Planning Association, 35, 1969, pp. 84–101.

streets and the side effects of widenings and other proposed changes in the street system. It was one of a series of studies of environmental conditions made in San Francisco during 1969 and 1970 (San Francisco City Planning Department, 1969–70).

Study Streets

Of the street blocks selected for a general study of street living three streets are reported upon here to serve as a model of the research approach and because they contrast the effects of traffic on similar types of streets. The street blocks chosen were adjacent north-south residential streets in the northern part of the city.

Traffic

The major environmental differences between the streets were their traffic levels. The first street, which we shall call HEAVY STREET, was a one-way street with synchronized stop lights and a peak hour traffic volume (at the evening rush hour) of 900 vehicles per hour (average 15,750 vehicles over twenty-four hours). The second street, MODERATE STREET, was a two-way street with a peak traffic flow of 550 vehicles per hour (average 8,700 vehicles over twenty-four hours); the third street, LIGHT STREET, had a volume of only 200 vehicles at peak hour (average 2,000 vehicles over twenty-four hours).[3]

Speeds on all streets could rise to forty-five miles an hour or more but only on HEAVY STREET was the speed controlled by the synchronized lights. Traffic volumes had increased on HEAVY and MODERATE STREETS ten years earlier when they were connected to a freeway at their southern terminal. Through traffic was dominant on MODERATE and HEAVY STREETS, and traffic composition included more trucks and buses on HEAVY STREET than on the others.

Population

The three study blocks were part of a residual Italian neighborhood that also included other white residents and a small but growing Oriental minority. By social class, education, and income the streets were relatively homogeneous. Contrasts, however, occurred in age, family composition, ownership, and length of residence.

LIGHT STREET was predominantly a family street with many children. Grownup children were even returning to bring up their own children there. One-half of the people interviewed were homeowners, and the average length of residence was 16.3 years. HEAVY STREET, at the other extreme, had almost no children on its block. It was inhabited mostly by single persons of all ages from 20 years upward, with many old people, especially single elderly women. The average length of residence on HEAVY STREET was 8.0 years, and people were nearly all renters. Rents were also somewhat higher on HEAVY STREET, averaging $140 a month among our respondents, whereas those on LIGHT STREET averaged $103. MODERATE STREET stood in between. Average length of residence here was 9.2 years and the average rent was $120. (See Table 1.)

Environment

The three streets were typical San Francisco streets, with terrace houses or apartments built up to the building-line, very few frontyards and very

TABLE 1. *Street Profiles*

Street Characteristics	HEAVY STREET	MODERATE STREET	LIGHT STREET
Peak hour traffic flow (vehicles/hour)	900	550	200
Average daily traffic flow (vehicles)	15,750	8,700	2,000
Traffic flow direction	one-way	two-way	two-way
Vehicle speed range (mph)	30–50	10–45	10–35
Noise levels (percentage of time above 65 decibels at the sidewalk)	45%	25%	5%
Accidents (per annum over a 4 block length)	17	12	. . .
Land uses	Residential (apartment blocks, apartments)	Residential (apartment blocks, apartments, single family homes), corner store	Residential (apartments, single family homes), corner store, small business
Street width (feet)	69	69	69
Pavement width (feet)	52	41	39
Sidewalk width (feet)	8.5	14	15
Average building height (no. of storeys)	3.5	3.0	2.5
Interview sample:	HEAVY STREET	MODERATE STREET	LIGHT STREET
Mean household size (no. of people)	1.5	2.6	2.7
Percentage renters	92%	67%	50%
Mean household income ($1,000's)	6.6	8.1	10.0
Mean income/member of household	4.4	3.1	3.7
Mean number of school years completed	14	13	15
Mean length of residence (years)	8.0	9.2	16.3
Mean rents ($ per month)	140.00	120.00	103.00

Source: Traffic statistics and accident counts were obtained from the San Francisco Department of Public Works, Traffic Engineering Section. All other information came from interviews, summer 1969

few gaps between the houses. The architectural style ranged from Victorian to modern. The buildings were finished in either wood, stucco, or brick and were of white or light colors. They were pleasant-looking blocks. The streets were each fairly level, with a slight gradient to the south. They were close to various shopping and community facilities.

Study Design

Two sources of information were used in the study. Detailed interviews lasting about an hour were held with twelve residents on each block, composed of three equal age categories, the young (under twenty-five) the middle-aged (twenty-five to fifty-five), and the elderly (over fifty-five). This was not a very large sample but since they represented about 30 percent of the households on each block, their attitudes were probably representative of those on the three blocks. Second, systematic observations and, where possible, objective measurements of pedestrian and traffic activity on the streets were carried out.

The study design stemmed from earlier papers by Appleyard and others (Appleyard and Lynch, 1967; Appleyard and Okamoto, 1968) which proposed environmental criteria to be used in transportation system design. The criteria identified in the earlier studies were hypothetical in nature and for this investigation were slightly modified to cover the probable concerns of those living on urban streets. Five major criteria categories were employed to describe the character and day-to-day use of the street and the concerns and satisfactions of the residents. The interview was introduced as a survey of what the resident thought of his street, inviting suggestions for its improvement. The residents were not told that we were primarily interested in the effects of traffic.

The criteria categories were:

Traffic hazard: concerns for safety in the street associated with traffic activity.
Stress, noise, and pollution: dissatisfaction with noise, vibration, fumes, dust and feelings of anxiety concerning traffic.
Social interaction: the degree to which residents had friends and acquaintances on the block, and the degree to which the street was a community.
Privacy and home territory: the residents' responses to intrusion from outside their homes, and the extent of their sensed personal territory or turf.
Environmental awareness: the degree to which the respondents were aware of their physical surroundings and were concerned for the external appearance of the buildings and the street.

Each question in the interview was related to one of the above categories, though some answers had relevance to more than one. The answers were independently rated on a five-point scale as "environmental quality" ratings by the interviewer and another member of the study team according to a general description of each criterion. Disparate judgments were discussed and a consensus rating was eventually recorded. No attempt was made to weight the responses in terms of their overall importance to the residents although this report emphasizes the main points of concern for the residents as expressed in the interviews. To make these findings more understandable we have graphed the responses in cartoon form.

So far, a public report on the study has met with considerable response in San Francisco. The general concerns of the study, and many of the individual conclusions, have been featured in the local press and on television. Furthermore the officially adopted San Francisco "Urban Design Plan" (San Francisco, City Planning Department, 1971) incorporates many of the recommendations for limiting through traffic on residential streets and creating "protected residential areas."

Traffic Hazard

Accident counts were equally high on HEAVY and MODERATE STREETS (means of seventeen and twelve accidents per year over a four-block length).

The danger of traffic was of concern to inhabitants on all three streets, but especially so on HEAVY STREET (ratings 3.7, 3.8). (See Table 2.) These findings are not surprising, since the need for "safe intersections" was the most repeated concern in a concurrent citywide survey of city residents (Kaplan et al., 1969).

HEAVY STREET is a one-way street with synchronized stoplights which enable bunches of vehicles, already with momentum from traveling downhill, to travel through at speeds of up to fifty miles an hour. The fast speeds were frequently mentioned in the responses. The very heavy traffic volumes on HEAVY STREET made it unsafe for children, and even for people washing their cars. For residents trying to manoeuver out of their garages, a one-way street has advantages over a two-way street, since the driver only has to look one way, but getting a car into a garage can be more difficult since the driver either has to swing across the traffic flow or pull to one side and wait for a lull. Excessive speed was the cause of most of the perceived traffic safety problems, especially on HEAVY STREET. Residents, seeing a large number of cars speeding down the hill, would wait for someone to make a false move or would listen for the screeching of brakes. Several residents wanted the speed limit on HEAVY STREET reduced.

LIGHT STREET, with only a small amount of through traffic, had problems of a different nature. It tended to attract the occasional hotrodder who was, in some instances, a greater menace than the steady stream of traffic on HEAVY STREET. He appeared without warning, often jumping the stop signs at intersections, and was extremely dangerous for children playing in the street. Another problem on LIGHT STREET was the temptation to park where it was immediately convenient. Delivery trucks often parked on the corner when making deliveries to the grocery and blocked the view down the cross street for motorists approaching the intersection.

Residents of MODERATE STREET perceived less safety problems arising from traffic than did the residents of HEAVY STREET. However, they were concerned about traffic dangers. As one respondent put it, "There have been some accidents and I am taking precautions."

Apart from the direct effects of traffic on the feelings of safety, there were some indirect effects. The continuous presence of strangers on HEAVY STREET, even though they were in automobiles, evinced some feelings of fear. One young housewife had frequently been "hassled" from passing cars, and some of the older ladies on HEAVY STREET were "afraid to stop and chat."

As can be seen from the aggregated ratings, there was a consistent trend through all age groups to consider LIGHT STREET as being safe, MODERATE STREET as being neither safe nor unsafe, and HEAVY STREET as being unsafe.

Stress, Noise, and Pollution

Measurements of noise levels were made on all three streets. The sound levels were determined through the use of Sound Survey Meters, utilized at four periods during a weekday; early morning (6:30 to 8:30 a.m.), late morning (11:00 a.m. to 12:30 p.m.), late afternoon (5:00 to 6:00 p.m.), and early evening (7:00 to 8:00 p.m.). In each measurement period, fifty consecutive measurements were made at fifteen second intervals at corner and midblock locations on each street. To translate these measurements into a useful measure of average conditions, the percentages of time that the noise exceeded certain A-weighted decibel levels [dB(A)] were calculated. From these we computed a traffic noise index,[4] a recognized measure of noise problems, which can be used to predict probable dissatisfaction due to noise. (Griffiths and Langdon, 1968.)

On HEAVY STREET, noise levels were above sixty-five decibels 45 percent of the time and did not fall below fifty-five decibels more than 10 percent of the time except in the early morning. These noise levels were so high that the traffic noise index read right off the scale. The two-minute sample sound level recording in Fig. 2 illustrates the uneven character of noise due to the waves of cars that flowed down the street, and to the occasional noisy vehicle which exceeded seventy decibels.

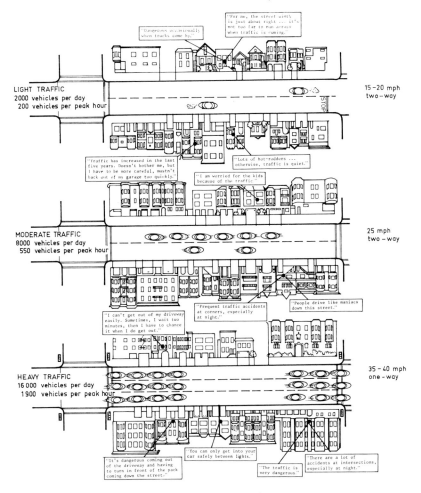

FIG. 1. Traffic hazard.

On MODERATE STREET, sound levels were above sixty-five decibels 25 percent of the time. By the traffic noise index, the noise level (6.5) would be rated as "definitely unsatisfactory." On LIGHT STREET, the quietest of the three, sound levels rose above sixty-five decibels only 5 percent of the time, meaning that one-half of the residents would consider the noise level "unsatisfactory" and one-half "satisfactory."

The two-minute sample sound level recordings on MODERATE STREET show that the noise levels tended to be more variable than on HEAVY STREET but in the same range, whereas the sound level chart on LIGHT STREET shows an ambient noise level much lower than the other two streets.

TABLE 2. *Mean Ratings of Traffic Hazard. (Low traffic hazard ratings were given to responses indicating feelings of safety and security from traffic and other related incidents. Rating: 1 = very safe, 5 = very unsafe.)*

Question	HEAVY STREET	MODERATE STREET	LIGHT STREET
What is traffic like on this street, how would you describe it? Does it bother you at all?	3.7	3.2	2.2
Is it ever dangerous on your street and around your home? (traffic accidents; incidents, etc.)	3.8	3.0	2.5

The traffic is very dangerous. — Traffic accidents are frequent at both intersections, especially at rush hours. — Traffic is fast, the signals are set fast. — It's dangerous for children because of traffic. You can't wash your car on the street for fear of being knocked down and if water is sprayed on passing cars, they get very angry. — I think it is a highly accident-prone area, I often hear screeching brakes. — This street is murder; I like European streets better. (HEAVY STREET)

It's a busy street, I don't trust the children on the sidewalk. — Hear brakes screeching at corners at night. — It's difficult backing out of the garage because of traffic. — Accidents and near-accidents frequently at (intersection). — Sometimes dangerous with commuter traffic between 5:00–6:00, especially round grocery on corner. — There's something deadly about the street. (MODERATE STREET)

Sidewalks are fine; kids can play, buggies or strollers get round cars very comfortably. — Children have to be taught care in crossing the street. — Traffic is getting worse. (LIGHT STREET)

After the danger of traffic itself, traffic noise, vibrations, fumes, soot, and trash were considered to be the most stressful aspects of the environment on these three streets. (See Table 3.) On HEAVY STREET, the noise was so severe that one elderly couple was forced to try to catch up on sleep in the daytime. Many, especially the older people, were unable to be objective about the other characteristics of their street because these stresses totally colored their perceptions of their environment. Adjectives such as "unbearable," or "too much" or "vulnerable" were typical of the responses.

As with traffic hazard, the large mass of vehicles was not always the major problem. It was often the lone individual or the unusual vehicle that disturbed the situation. This was certainly true of HEAVY STREET where the large majority of cars were reasonably quiet and passed by at a smooth even flow. The real offenders were sports cars, buses, and trucks. The steady drone of traffic was certainly bad, but the random deep-throated roar of a bus or large truck, with the accompanying shudder that rattled every window, unnerved the most hardened resident, especially when it continued day and night. The screeching of brakes at the inter-sections added to the distress.

TABLE 3. *Mean Ratings of Stress, Noise, and Pollution. (Low stress, noise, and pollution ratings were given to responses indicating lack of nuisance, adequacy and suitability of street lighting, local services, road and sidewalk width, and good street maintenance. Rating: 1 = low stress, 5 = high stress.)*

Question	HEAVY STREET	MODERATE STREET	LIGHT STREET
Is there anything that bothers you or causes you nuisance on and around this street?	4.5	3.3	2.6
Are you ever troubled by noise and/or vibration?	3.7	2.5	2.4
Are you bothered at all by dirt, pollution, smells, glare? Does it to your knowledge cause any ill health?	3.4	2.9	2.0
Is there adequate street lighting?	1.4	2.0	2.4
Is the street too wide or too narrow?	2.1	1.9	1.7
Are the sidewalks too wide or too narrow?	2.5	1.8	1.3
Do you have adequate local services: garbage collection, street cleaning?	2.2	2.1	2.1
Is your street well maintained, are front-yards, planting, sidewalks, etc., well kept up?	1.5	1.8	1.9

Traffic noise bothers me, during the day, but it's heavy at night also. — I am bothered by the exhaust from traffic and noise. Lately the trucks have been returning to this street, even though they are banned. — Troubled by traffic noise, mostly trucks and motorbikes. The street acts like an echo chamber, especially for sirens. It continues day and night. — Bothered by noise and vibration. I have to straighten pictures frequently. — Noise is terrible from traffic. I can feel vibration even up on the fourth floor, especially from buses. — Have to take a nap during the day as don't get enough sleep at night because of the traffic. — The street is well maintained by old ladies washing down front steps once a week. — Other than traffic, it has a very nice appearance. — It's absolutely disgusting the amount of litter there is. — It's terribly dirty and we often have traffic fumes. I sometimes leave only the rear window open. (HEAVY STREET)

The car gets dirty because it is parked on the street. — Smells from big trucks, not very often. — Bothered by vibration from trucks sometimes, and by noise of hotrodders revving up. — Feel helpless as far as traffic is concerned, I can never finish cleaning. — It's a dirty street, I have to be a janitor and sweep the street. People in cars dump cigar ash and beer cans in the gutter. — It's getting worse because of traffic; getting dirtier. The rot has set in. (MODERATE STREET)

Sometimes bothered by noise of the occasional big truck which will wake the baby. — Motorbikes occasionally make a noise. At night sounds of hotrodders frequently. — Street well maintained. Usually someone sweeping, my mother or people next door. — A very relaxed happy family neighborhood, perfect. It makes me very happy. — There are parking conflicts, parking is a pain because outside people put their cars in the driveways. (LIGHT STREET)

Residents on HEAVY STREET had petitioned for a sign prohibiting trucks and buses. The sign was installed, but it did not mention buses. It was small, the same color as the background, and was seldom seen. In any case, the law was not enforced, so truck drivers had learned to continue on their way with impunity. Noise problems were not so acute on MODERATE STREET, where people were more bothered by the fumes, dust, and soot which penetrated into their living rooms and bedrooms. LIGHT STREET had a few complaints of occasional noise.

Other forms of pollution. The condition and cleanliness of the buildings of the three streets were generally high. Maintenance and clean appearance were clearly important to all the inhabitants. HEAVY STREET was constantly on show to outsiders who were traveling through it, and the owners of the buildings were careful to maintain a high standard of cleanliness despite the "digusting amount of litter." The *appearance* of a quality environment was therefore maintained — and paid for through higher rents — but because the street did not encourage people to be outgoing, tenants were reluctant to accept responsibility for the street itself. Therefore, they avoided picking up trash and were slow to defend the street against vandalism and abuse.

On MODERATE STREET, concerns for trash, dust, and soot, where specifically referred to, were more pronounced than on HEAVY STREET. This street was going through a difficult stage. Traffic and traffic problems were increasing, and there was no clear demarcation between public territory, which was the responsibility of the city, and local territory, which might have been the responsibility of the residents. People in parked cars had been observed dumping the contents of ash trays and beer cans into the gutter. Even so, it was still seen as a "good respectable place to live" and sidewalk maintenance by the local inhabitants helped to keep up the appearance of the street.

LIGHT STREET was very seldom seen by outsiders and so the issue of maintenance was a local matter. This street was also seen to be changing and residents had noticed signs of deterioration. As one resident put it, "The quality of [LIGHT STREET] is getting better in that people take great care of their properties, but worse in that there is more traffic and more cars on the street." Indeed, the responses showed that many inhabitants took an interest in looking after the cleanliness of the street, and some had planted their own trees.

The only other inconvenience mentioned was the crowded parking conditions. Many suburban commuters and users of the nearby shopping center were parking on all three streets and taking up parking spaces of the residents. In response to questions concerning the adequacy of street lighting, garbage collection, and street cleaning, respondents considered the three streets to be without serious problems.

In reaction to all these issues, each age group found HEAVY STREET

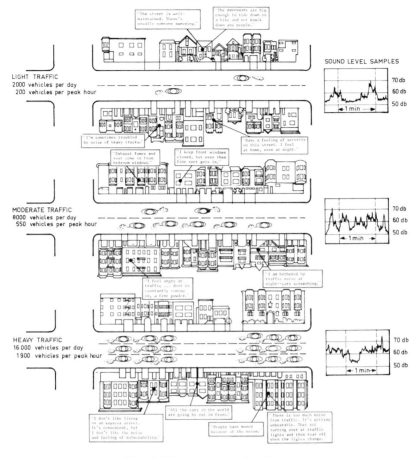

FIG. 2. Noise, stress, and pollution.

more severe, and the old- and middle-aged groups found MODERATE STREET worse than LIGHT STREET. The only exceptions were residents under twenty-five, who were more critical of LIGHT STREET. People on LIGHT STREET tended in many cases to be more aware and more critical of their street, while those on MODERATE STREET were more apathetic.

Social Interaction

Residents were asked a series of questions about the friendliness of the street, the numbers of friends and acquaintances they possessed, and the places where people met. Each respondent was shown a photograph of the buildings on the street and asked to point out where any friends, relatives, or acquaintances lived.

On LIGHT STREET, inhabitants were found to have three times as many friends and twice as many acquaintances on the street itself (9.3 friends and acquaintances per person) as those on HEAVY STREET (4 per person). The diagrammatic network of social contacts in Fig. 3 shows clearly that contact *across* the street was much less frequent on HEAVY STREET than on LIGHT STREET. The friendliness on LIGHT STREET was no doubt related to the small amount of traffic, but also to the larger number of children on the street and the longer length of residence of the inhabitants. The statements of the inhabitants corroborate this.

On HEAVY STREET, there was very little social interaction. With few if any friends (0.9 per respondent) the residents did not consider it a friendly street. Although it might be argued that this was primarily a

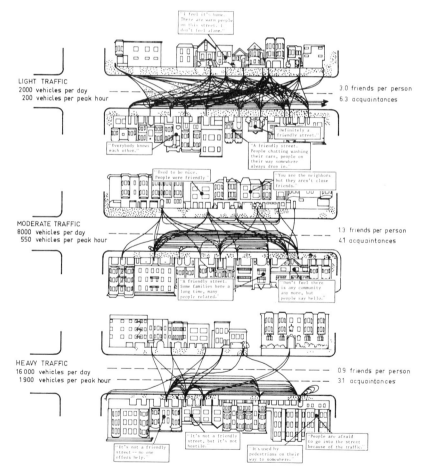

FIG. 3. Social interaction. Lines show where people said they had friends or acquaintances. Dots show where people are said to gather.

consequence of the life style of those living on HEAVY STREET (Keller, 1969), the sense of loneliness came out very clearly, especially in the responses of the elderly. As for MODERATE STREET, residents felt that the old community was on the point of extinction. "It used to be friendly; what was outside has now withdrawn into the buildings. People are preoccupied with their own lives." Some of the families had been there a long time, but the number of longtime residents was diminishing. As other respondents put it, "It is half-way from here to there," "An in-between street with no real sense of community." There was still a core of original Italian residents lamenting that "There are no longer any friends and acquaintances around here." The average number of friends and acquaintances per respondent was only a little higher (total 5.4 per person) than on HEAVY STREET.

There were sharp differences between age groups. The middle-aged residents on the three streets possessed a similar number of friends, although those on LIGHT STREET had more acquaintances. This age group was probably more mobile and better equipped to make friends than the other groups. The young and old, on the other hand, who had many less social contacts on HEAVY STREET than on LIGHT STREET, appeared to be more affected by the amount of traffic, especially in establishing casual acquaintanceship with neighbors in the street.

From the notations of street activities drawn by the subjects on the map of the streets (see Fig. 3), it can be seen that LIGHT STREET had the heaviest use, mostly by teenagers and children. MODERATE STREET had lighter use, more by adults than by children, and HEAVY STREET had little or no use, even by adults. The few reported activities on HEAVY STREET consisted of middle-aged and elderly people walking on the sidewalks but seldom stopping to pass the time of day with a neighbor or friend. Reports on MODERATE STREET indicated that the sidewalks were more heavily used by adults, especially by a group of old men who frequently gathered outside the corner store. Children and some teenagers played on the sidewalks, mostly on the eastern side of the street (probably because most of their homes were on the eastern side and they didn't like to cross the road except at the crossings). On LIGHT STREET, people used the sidewalks more than any other part of the street, but children and teenagers often played games in the middle of the street. Children also used the sidewalks extensively because of their gentle gradient and their width. Again, a corner store acted as a magnet for middle-aged and elderly people, and a tennis store across the road attracted a small group of young adults. Front porches and steps on LIGHT STREET, and to a certain extent on MODERATE STREET, were used for sitting, chatting with friends, and, by children, for play. The residents of HEAVY STREET regretted their lack of porches.

In conclusion, there was a marked difference in the way these three streets were seen and used, especially by the young and elderly. On the one hand, LIGHT STREET was a lively close-knit community whose residents made full use of their street. The street had been divided into different zones by the residents. Front steps were used for sitting and chatting, sidewalks by children for playing, and by adults for standing and passing the time of day (especially round the corner store), and the roadway by children and teenagers for playing more active games like football. However, the street was seen as a whole and no part was out of bounds. This full use of the street was paralleled by an acute awareness of the physical environment (as will be described in the section on environmental awareness).

HEAVY STREET, on the other hand, had little or no sidewalk activity and was used solely as a corridor between the sanctuary of individual homes and the outside world. Residents kept very much to themselves so that there was no feeling of community at all, and they failed to notice and remember the detailed physical environment around them. MODERATE STREET again seemed to fall somewhere between the two extremes. It was still quite an active social street, although there was no strong feeling of community. Most activity was confined to the sidewalks, where a finely sensed boundary separated pedestrians from traffic. The ratings in Table 4 reflect these differences between the three streets, particularly the perceived lack of meeting places for old people and play places for children on HEAVY STREET, where mean response ratings usually exceeded 4.0.

Privacy and Home Territory

A number of questions were asked to gauge whether inhabitants felt they had sufficient privacy, and whether they had any feelings of stewardship over their streets.

In their responses, residents of LIGHT and MODERATE STREETS, especially middle-aged residents, evidenced great pride in their homes and streets. (See Table 5.) On HEAVY STREET there was little peace and seclusion, even within the home, and residents struggled to retain some feeling of personal identity in their surroundings.

Perception of individual privacy was high throughout this area, perhaps because of the feeling of "privacy and seclusion that exists in any middle class area", as one respondent put it. Inevitably, in a tightknit community like the one that existed on LIGHT STREET, life on the street tended to intrude more into a person's home than it would on a less friendly street, but the residents had achieved a good balance wherein they maintained their own household privacy and yet contributed to the sense of community. As one woman enthusiastically put it, "Only happiness enters in". Children and young people often preferred the lack of seclusion because they liked to be part of things. On LIGHT STREET a satisfactory

TABLE 4. *Mean Ratings of Social Interaction. (Ratings of high social interaction were given to responses indicating friendliness and community feeling, a wide variety of friends, relatives and acquaintances, and intensive use of the street space. Rating: 1 = high, 5 = low.)*

Question	HEAVY STREET	MODERATE STREET	LIGHT STREET
Do you think this is a friendly street? Do you think there is a feeling of community on this street?	3.2	2.0	2.0
Where do people congregate on the street if at all?	4.4	3.2	1.4
Where do children play if at all?	4.5	3.0	1.7
Where do teenagers gather if at all?	4.7	4.1	3.0
Where do adults casually meet and chat outside if at all?	4.1	2.5	2.7
Do you have any friends and relatives who live on this street?	4.2	3.2	2.8
Which people on this street do you know by sight?	3.5	2.8	1.8

. It's getting worse. There are very few children, even less than before. — The only people I have noticed on the street are an older couple in this building who stand outside every night, otherwise there are only people walking on their way somewhere. — Everybody on (HEAVY STREET) is going somewhere else, not in this neighborhood. — Friendly neighbors, we talk over garden fences. — It's not a friendly street as people are afraid to go into the street because of the traffic. (HEAVY STREET)

Friendly street, many people related. — Friendly street, several families have lived here a long time. — There are no longer any of my friends around here any more. Dislike most about street? I don't know neighbors any more. I feel helpless not knowing anyone in case of emergency. — Doesn't feel that there is any community any more. However, many say hello. — There's nobody around. (MODERATE STREET)

Friendly street, people chatting washing cars, people on their way somewhere always drop in. — The corner grocery is the social center. I get a kick to go up there and spend an hour talking. — All family people, very friendly. — Kids used to play in the street all the time, but now with a car every two minutes, they have to go to the park. — Everybody knows each other. (LIGHT STREET)

balance had been achieved between a feeling of privacy and contact with the outside world. Even on HEAVY STREET residents occasionally enjoyed the street activity. ("I feel it's alive, busy, and invigorating.") However, for the majority, the constant noise and vibration were a persistent intrusion into the home and ruined any feeling of peace and solitude.

Figure 4 shows the residents' conceptions of personal territory. Even though legally a householder's responsibilities extend to the maintenance of the sidewalk immediately outside his building, residents on MODER-

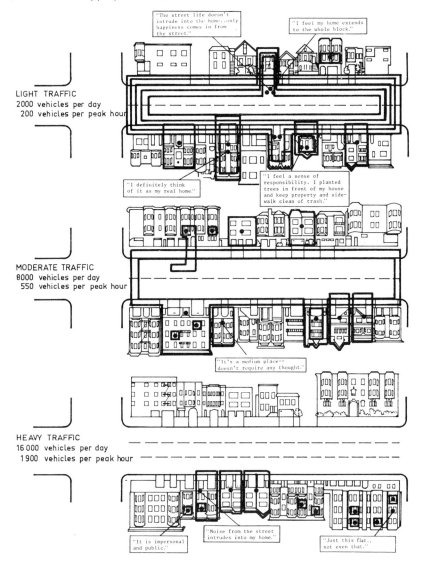

FIG. 4. Home territory. Lines show areas people indicated as their "home territory."

ATE and LIGHT STREETS considered part or all of the street as their territory. However, the HEAVY STREET resident's sense of personal territory did not extend into the street, and for some, mostly renters in the large apartment blocks, it was confined to their own apartment and no further. This pattern of territorial space corresponds to the pattern of social use of each street. The contrast between the territorial restrictions of those living on HEAVY STREET and the territorial expansiveness of

TABLE 5. *Mean Ratings of Privacy and Home Territory. (High ratings of privacy and home territory were given to responses indicating seclusion, lack of intrusion or invasion, extended personal territories, and a sense of belonging and responsibility. Rating: 1 = high, 5 = low.)*

Question	HEAVY STREET	MODERATE STREET	LIGHT STREET
Do you think that your street is relatively secluded?	3.4	2.1	2.4
Do you feel that your street is overcrowded or cramped?	3.3	1.6	2.0
Do you find that street life intrudes into your home life at all?	2.9	1.2	1.8
Do you feel that your privacy is invaded by neighbors or from the street in any way while you are in and around your home?	2.5	1.6	2.2
Where do you feel that your "home" extends to; in other words, what do you see as your personal territory or turf?	3.0	2.3	1.2
Do you think of this street as your real home, where you really belong?	2.9	1.9	2.1
Do you feel any sense of responsibility for the way the street looks and for what happens on it?	2.6	2.8	1.3
If an outsider criticized your street would you defend it?	3.0	2.2	1.6

Do you think of this street as your real home where you belong? — Definitely not. It's hard to say where we feel our home is. — Where do you feel your home extends to? — Just this apartment, not even that. — There is a raging war between the residents and those terrible commuters from Marin. The residents want to dynamite patches of the road to slow traffic. — My outdoor space is the roof or the fire escape where I may have plants. (HEAVY STREET)

I am out there with a broom from one end of the block to the other. I am known as the "woman with the broom." (MODERATE STREET)

I tend the sidewalk trees outside the house and the rose bushes in the front. — I like our little street, even though I am not a home owner. — I keep it clean of debris, pick up broken bottles, notify people of anything wrong. — I feel my home extends to the whole block [very emphatic]. — I always clean the street, take in dirt off the street, pick up nails, broken glass and paper. At least ten people take care of the street. (LIGHT STREET)

those on LIGHT STREET is one of the more salient findings of the study. The residents on LIGHT STREET are quite similar in this respect to those West End Italians in Boston who considered the boundaries between house and street space to be quite permeable (Fried and Gleicher, 1961). In sum, HEAVY STREET was seen as considerably less private than the other two streets, especially for those most confined to the street, the young and the old.

Environmental Awareness

Street dwellers were each asked to recall all important features of their street, to judge whether their street was in any way different from surrounding streets, and to draw a map of their street.

Figure 5 is a composite of all the maps that each person drew for his own street. The responses to the questions were much richer in content — and more critical in character — on LIGHT STREET than on the other two streets. This can be partly explained by the greater differentiation of frontyards and smaller houses; but it clearly stemmed from an increased awareness of the street environment by the residents themselves.

Interest in the street as evidenced by the maps drawn varied by age group. LIGHT STREET had tremendous appeal for children, who recalled individual buildings, frontyards, steps, particular parked cars, manhole covers, telegraph poles, and even the brickwork setting around the base of a tree. Many of these detailed elements were obviously encountered during their play on the street. On MODERATE STREET, where there was less street activity, the maps of children and young people were accordingly less rich.

Middle-aged people on the other hand seemed to have a more complete impression of their street. Their recollections included combinations of buildings, sidewalks, the roadway, and the traffic itself. For them, LIGHT STREET was seen as a collection of individual buildings with differences in frontyards and porches. MODERATE STREET was much more straight-walled. Residents had accurate memories of driveways, pedestrian crossings, and road markings (possibly because it was seen as a traffic route with finely defined boundaries).

HEAVY STREET was seen overwhelmingly as a continuous traffic corridor, straight-sided without a break for cross streets, and packed with cars. The traffic itself was an easily identified characteristic of the busier street.

As for the responsiveness of the street environment to the needs of the street dwellers, LIGHT STREET once more showed up well. (See Table 6.) Two trees had been planted in the sidewalk, other plants were thriving in the occasional frontyard, and flower boxes were prevalent. On HEAVY STREET, the sidewalks were too narrow to allow anything to grow except the very small bushes that flanked the doors of one or two apartment buildings.

Study Conclusions

1. The intensive traffic conditions on HEAVY STREET led to both stress and withdrawal. Those people who found the traffic conditions intolerable, especially those with children, had moved elsewhere, and the

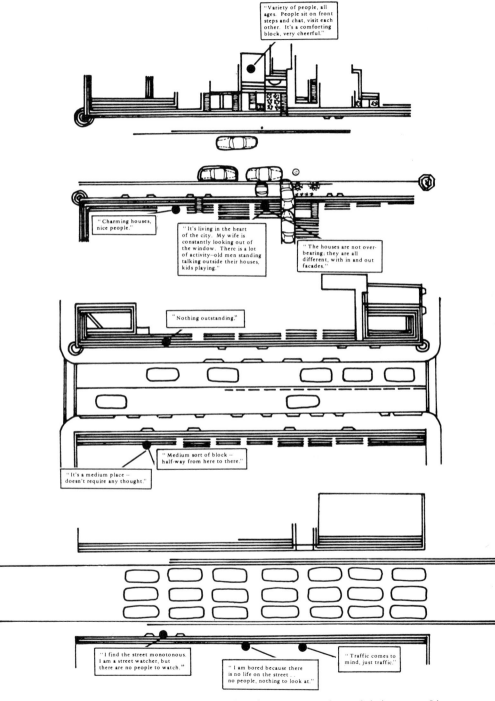

FIG. 5. Environmental awareness. Composite of maps people drew of their streets. Lines indicate number of times feature was drawn by residents.

TABLE 6. *Mean Ratings of Environmental Awareness. (Ratings of high environmental awareness were given to responses that described the street as having a distinct sense of being a particular place and different from other streets, and that were full of rich, varied, and affectionate detail. Rating: 1 = high, 5 = low.)*

Question	HEAVY STREET	MODERATE STREET	LIGHT STREET
Do you find your street and the life that goes on there interesting? Do you get bored by life on this street, do you find it monotonous?	3.3	2.9	2.3
What parts of the street do you like most? What parts do you find least attractive?	3.1	2.6	2.1
What first comes to mind when you think of your street?	2.3	3.1	2.5
Could you please try to draw a map of what you think of as this street showing all the features of the street and the buildings that stick in your mind no matter how trivial they seem to be.	2.7	2.5	2.1
Do you think this street is different from surrounding streets, is it special or unique in any way?	2.2	3.6	2.1
Do you think there are many different kinds of people on this street? Can you describe them?	3.4	2.1	1.8

I dislike the sterility of the surroundings. — I don't like the fact that there is no greenery. — The first thing that comes to mind are apartment buildings, small apartments, five to six units. This wasn't so until ten years ago when they made the street one-way, before that there was a feeling of neighborhood. — Physically it feels as if you are looking over a void, the street is nonexistent. — The street facade is extremely unmemorable, dull brick or bland plaster. The surfaces are flat and static. — First thing that comes to mind, fast traffic. — It's absolutely dead, not even any night life, nothing. (HEAVY STREET)

Different from other streets in that it has a yellow line down the middle, others don't. — It's all dull, which is what I seek. — First thing that comes to mind, cars especially. (MODERATE STREET)

The houses are not overbearing, they are all different with varigated in-and-out facade. — It's like living in the heart of the city, my wife is constantly looking out of the window. There is a lot of activity — men standing talking outside their houses, the kids playing, etc. — Variety of people, all ages. People sit on front steps and chat, visit other people. It's a comforting block, very cheerful. — I like the set backs, they give individuality. (LIGHT STREET) people who lived there at the time of the survey had either withdrawn from the street or had never become engaged in it. They only used it when they had to, they had few local friends and acquaintances, and they had become oblivious to the street as a living environment. If they could, they lived at the backs of their houses. For those who treated HEAVY STREET as a transient residence, this condition was tolerable. Those who had to treat it as a permanent residence because they were too old or too poor to leave suffered.

In contrast, those who lived on LIGHT STREET were very much engaged with their street. They saw it as their own territory. Their children played on the sidewalk and in the street. They had many friends and acquaintances (over twice as many on the average as those on HEAVY STREET), they noted many more features of the street when they were asked to make a drawing of it, and they were generally much more aware of their street. Despite all this, the rents on HEAVY STREET were higher. Perhaps the apartments on that street, because of their higher exposure and turnover, were more available to a transient population.

The living conditions of those who lived on MODERATE STREET lay somewhere in between the other two, but the residents' levels of satisfaction were lower than their middle position might suggest.

From our results we can state some hypotheses about the apparent effects of traffic on the environmental and social quality of these streets (see Fig. 6). These hypotheses should be tested in later studies.

a. Heavy traffic activity is associated with more apartment renters and less owner-occupants and families with children. The income levels of the residents are in a similar range.

b. Heavy traffic is associated with much less social interaction and street activity. Conversely, a street with little traffic, and many families, promotes a rich social climate and a strong sense of community.

c. Heavy traffic is associated with a withdrawal from the physical environment. Conversely, residents of the street with low traffic show an acute, critical, and appreciative awareness of and care for physical environment.

2. There are some exceptions to the above conclusions. Many respondents on MODERATE STREET had chosen that street for its livable environment. MODERATE STREET, however, was changing from a quiet residential street into a major traffic corridor. Therefore, the residents there were often more dissatisfied than those on HEAVY STREET. Their original expectations for the environment were higher and their disappointment was therefore greater.

On LIGHT STREET some respondents perceived the occasional hot-rodder as worse than the traffic on HEAVY STREET for similar reasons. When people expect traffic to be heavy, their behavior adapts to the situation and traffic is tolerated. When they expect it to be light, a

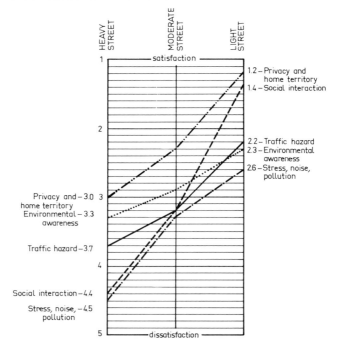

Fig. 6. Environmental quality. Note: The following interview questions were chosen to represent the "environmental quality" criteria illustrated in this figure. Traffic hazard: What is traffic like on this street, how would you describe it? Does it bother you at all? Stress, noise, and pollution: Is there anything that bothers you or causes you nuisance on and around this street? Social interaction: Where do people congregate on the street, if at all? Privacy and home territory: Where do you feel that your "home" extends to; in other words what do you see as your personal territory or turf? Environmental awareness: Do you find your street and the life that goes on there interesting? Do you get bored by life on this street, do you find it monotonous?

hot-rodder is especially intrusive. In conclusion, people were dissatisfied with the streets with lighter traffic when their environmental expectations were not realized either through an environmental decline from a previously higher quality or from deviant traffic behavior.

3. The appearance of environmental quality was found to be quite different from environmental quality as revealed by the comments of the residents. HEAVY STREET was well maintained and appeared to be of high quality to the outsider (for example, to the city urban design staff in earlier field surveys of the area). The residents were aware of its high status, yet the presence of heavy traffic lowered its quality below that of more modest-looking streets.

4. The pattern of interview responses suggested that the issues of safety, stress, condition, pollution, privacy, and territoriality, followed closely by neighborliness, were of primary concern to the inhabitants of all the

streets. Issues such as sense of identity, environmental interest, appropriateness, and individual self-expression were not considered important if the other issues were seen as problems.

5. The general trend was toward increased traffic on each of the three streets, with the prospect that the environment of each street would decline further.

Discussion of Conclusions

Objective observations of environmental quality, through traffic flow and noise counts, showed that environmental conditions on HEAVY STREET were particularly severe. Though complaints were numerous, however, they were not so strong as one might reasonably expect. There had been very little public complaint or protest by any group. Why was this?

One major reason appears to be that the erosion of environmental quality had been subtle and slow, taking place over a period of ten years or more. During this time the workings of *environmental selection*, and *environmental adaptation* had been allowed to operate. These are important phenomena to consider in measurements of response to environmental quality.

1. The workings of *environmental selection* may be stated as follows: an environment tends to be selected by those groups who find it most amenable, and to be rejected by those who find it least amenable. Hence when traffic increased on HEAVY STREET, families with children moved away, and single people and couples whose local environmental needs were less but who valued accessibility tended to replace them. The principle does not work perfectly, however. Those who are unable to select their preferred environment through lack of financial, informational, or psychological resources become "locked in" to certain environments, and are therefore likely to suffer the most from changing environmental quality. On HEAVY STREET the older people, finding it too costly and too much effort to move, experienced severe discomforts, and the families who had to remain on MODERATE STREET experienced the loss of friends. Similar predicaments face lower income populations.

People may select a less than ideal environment for reasons other than lack of resources. Many make a *compromise*, sacrificing amenity for the benefits of, for example, an easily available apartment or accessibility to other parts of the city. The apartments on LIGHT STREET had less turnover so they were seldom on the market. Others make *errors of judgment*. Visually HEAVY STREET is a well-maintained high quality street. Therefore an apartment hunter might be deceived. Another kind of error is the *inability to predict future deterioration*. When many of the present inhabitants moved in to HEAVY and MODERATE STREETS conditions were good. Since then they have worsened.

2. By *environmental adaptation* we mean that those who remain in one environment for a length of time will become adapted (or resigned) to it whether or not it is or has been pleasant, especially if they see no future change in sight. Evidence for this phenomenon can be found in this study, especially in some of the more indifferent responses on HEAVY STREET. (Such evidence can also be found in the research literature in this field [Sonnenfeld, 1966; Wohlwill, 1968].) Those with low expectations or aspirations may be content with any environment.

Besides private adaptation, there appears to be a more publicly oriented defensive kind of adaptation. Most people are stuck with the choices they have made. When an interviewer arrives at the door and asks if there is anything they dislike about their environment, people may not wish to complain even though they may privately acknowledge that their environment is unsatisfactory. They may refuse to complain in order to keep up their social image and the sales value of their property, or through reluctance to admit that they have limited resources or have made an error of judgment.

Individual and family adjustments to a deteriorating environment were further muted because there was no clear public target for resentment, only the individual automobiles and trucks. No particular agency was threatening the environment or initiating changes. This worked both ways; residents' hopes were not raised that anything would be done about their problem, but neither were their frustrations focused sufficiently for them to band together in protest.

Despite the private nature of the adjustments and the slowness of the deterioration, a majority of the inhabitants were still well aware of their plight, as their comments tell.

One final and more positive finding of this study was what it told us of life on a "good" residential street, namely LIGHT STREET. Since we cannot hope to improve urban environments without some positive goals to work toward, LIGHT STREET performs a critical function.

Environmental Proposals

1. Policy usually has to be made without the benefit of adequate research, and this study is no exception. The strongest proposal resulting from the study was the designation in the adopted Urban Design Plan (San Francisco City Planning Department, 1971) of "protected residential areas" throughout San Francisco. These are areas which will be protected from through traffic by policies such as the improvement of public transit; the concentration of traffic on the city's main arteries by increasing their capacity through separated grades, selective widening, parking controls,

and so on; and the blocking of through traffic by devices such as rough pavement surfaces, "necking down" entrances, bending alignments, landscaping, lighting and sidewalk treatment, all of which would slow traffic down to a residential pace (and incidentally provide more street recreation space).

2. On streets where traffic flows and speeds could not be reduced, ways of ameliorating conditions were proposed. These included sidewalk protection by means of trees, low walls, hedges, and so on; the provision of alternative play spaces to divert children's activities away from the dangerous street; the protection of residences from glaring street lights, car lamps, and the view of passing vehicles through the planting of trees; the clear definition of parking spaces; and the encouragement of inhabitants to exercise some interest in their own frontyards and sidewalks through provisions and subsidies for private planting, benches, and the like.

Environmental Studies

Environmental conditions on residential streets will not be improved unless means of determining acceptable and unacceptable conditions are available. Present planning thought is running against the formulation of standards, as planners have come to realize the variability of population needs and situations and the difficulties of scaling environmental conditions. Yet without standards or specific guidelines, planning controls will remain amorphous and ineffectual. There is an urgent need at the very least to articulate unacceptable environmental conditions for particular groups. These conditions might be couched in the form of environmental performance standards.

The field of noise abatement, which has progressed quite far in trying to set environmental standards related to behavioral response, has encountered some difficulties. Simple decibel ratings (for example, forty-five decibels as a tolerable level inside residences) have to be modified by the "duration, frequency, substantive content of the sound and individual differences" (U.S., Department of Housing and Urban Development, 1969). The Traffic Noise Index (Griffiths and Langdon, 1968), developed in Britain, attempts to take a few of these factors into account. The Buchanan Report (Her Majesty's Stationery Office, 1964) identified "vulnerable" populations. But what about standards which will allow people to feel comfortable on sidewalks, or to cross the street, which encourage neighborliness, allow privacy and an ample sense of personal territory, or which promote care and interest for the physical environment of the street? These are even more difficult measures to scale. The effort to measure pedestrian crossing delay times as an indicator of residential quality, which was used in the *Kensington Environmental Management Study* (Greater London Council, 1966), was an interesting attempt in this direction. The work report here is not substantial enough to develop such indicators, but this is the direction of our research.[5]

Research Implications

The results of this study are suggestive but obviously unrepresentative. Our a priori groupings of issues under criteria headings proved a useful way of organizing the interviews and observations. More studies examining larger numbers of street conditions and types of population are clearly required. Such studies should use more structured questionnaires that would allow subjects to make their own ratings and selections from adjective and other check lists (Craik, 1967; Shaffer, 1967). They should also use a more comprehensive set of observable environmental indicators (such as pedestrian delay times, counts of street activity, closed windows, drawn blinds, parked cars, trash, flower boxes, and other signs of personal care) and a finer assessment of traffic variables (including flows at different times of day and night, speed levels, traffic composition, traffic control signals, and so on).

Multivariate analyses of interviews, traffic composition, and environmental indicators would then allow us to understand the ways in which factors tend to cluster, and to develop predictive models from regression analyses of response to various conditions. With such models, indices (similar to the traffic noise index) could be established to predict subjective responses to environmental phenomena such as levels of privacy; neighborliness, street identity, stress, and sense of safety for residential streets. The ability to predict the flow and speed of traffic from environmental conditions, given the desire lines operating in an area, would allow the control of speeds and flows at environmentally acceptable levels. We know that signs do not control speed. What are the effects of rough surfaces, trees, "necking down" streets, and street bends on these traffic variables?

Finally, more extensive surveys to assess the numbers of people who actually live under the deteriorated environmental conditions of streets with heavy traffic are needed. In a recent book, J. M. Thompson (1970) calculated that one million people in London would be living within 200 yards of the proposed motorway system. The implication was that one million people would be suffering from a deteriorated environment. Such accounts of conditions in a U.S. metropolitan area might have a significant impact on the allocation of investment to environmental improvements.

Authors' Note: *We are indebted to the San Francisco Department of City Planning (Director, Allan Jacobs) for supporting this project through an urban planning grant from the U.S. Department of Housing and Urban Development, under the provisions of Sec. 701 of the Housing Act of 1954, as part of their Urban Design Study, and for permission to use the drawings. Elizabeth Seltzer assisted with the drawings and Hugo Blasdell carried out the noise surveys and analysis.*

Notes

1. Estimated from Report no. 4, San Francisco Planning Department (1969–70).
2. For example, the Barnsbury Environmental Study (Great Britain, Ministry of Housing and Local Government, 1968) and the Pimlico Precinct Study (City of Westminster, 1968).
3. All traffic statistics were obtained from the San Francisco Department of Public Works, Traffic Engineering Section.
4. The traffic noise index is a function of the 50 per cent noise level and the difference between the 10 per cent and 90 per cent levels.

$$TNI = L_{50} + 4 \ (L_{10} - L_{90}) - 30$$

   This figure has been shown to correlate with expressions of annoyance. Our budget did not allow us to take the customary hourly samplings over the full twenty-four-hour period.
5. A study of a larger residential area in Oakland, California, is now under way supported by small grants from the U.S. Department of Transportation and the National Institute of Mental Health.

Literature

D. Appleyard and K. Lynch (1967) "Sensuous Criteria for Highway Design." In J. L. Shofer and E. N. Thomas, "Strategies for the Evaluation of Alternative Transportation Plans" (Research Report, the Transportation Center, Northwestern University, Evanston, Illinois).

D. Appleyard and R. Okamoto (1968) "Environmental Criteria for Ideal Transportation Systems," in Barton Aschman Associates (ed.), *Guidelines for New Transportation Systems* (U.S. Department of Housing and Urban Development, Washington, D.C.).

C. Chu (1971) *Urban Road Traffic/Environmental Research and Studies: A Selective Annotated Bibliography* (Centre for Environmental Studies, London).

City of Westminster (1968) *The Pimlico Precinct Study* (London).

K. H. Craik (1968) "The Comprehension of the Everyday Physical Environment," *Journal of the American Institute of Planners*, 34 (January): 29–37.

M. Fried and P. Gleicher (1961) "Some Residential Satisfactions in an Urban Slum," *Journal of the American Institute of Planners*, 27 (November): 305–315.

Great Britain, Ministry of Housing and Local Government (1968) *The Barnsbury Environmental Study* (Islington, London).

Great Britain, Ministry of Housing and Local Government (1969) *Great Improvement Areas*.

Greater London Council (1969) *Kensington Environmental Management Study*, publication 39 (London).

I. D. Griffiths and F. J. Langdon (1968) "Subjective Response to Road Traffic Noise," *Journal of Sound and Vibration*, 8 (1): 16–32.

Her Majesty's Stationery Office (1963) *Traffic in Towns* (The Buchanan Report) (London).

M. Kaplan, S. Gans and K. Kahn (1969) "Social Reconnaissance Survey, Part 2," San Francisco Urban Design Study, San Francisco City Planning Department.

Michigan, Department of State Highways (1969) "The Economic and Environmental Effects of One-way Streets in Residential Areas."

W. Owen, "Transport: Key to the Future of Cities." In H. Perloff (ed.), *The Quality of the Urban Environment* (Baltimore: Johns Hopkins Press).

San Francisco City Planning Department (1969–70) "Preliminary Reports," nos. 1 to 8, San Francisco Urban Design Study.

San Francisco City Planning Department (1971) "The Urban Design Plan for the Comprehensive Plan of San Francisco."

M. T. Shaffer (1967) "Attitudes, Community Values, and Highway Planning," *Highway Research Record*, 187.

J. Sonnenfeld (1966) "Variable Values in Space Landscape," *Journal of Social Issues*, 22 (January): 71–82.

J. M. Thompson (1970) *Motorways in London* (London: Andworth and Co., Ltd.).

United States, Department of Housing and Urban Development (1969) "Noise Abatement and Control: Departmental Policy, Implementation Responsibilities, and Standards," unpublished circular (September).

J. F. Wohlwill (1966) "The Psychology of Stimulation." In R. Kates and J. F. Wohlwill (ed.), *Journal of Social Issues* 22 (January): 127–136.

On the Sociology of Car Traffic in Towns

NORBERT SCHMIDT-RELENBERG*

Until now there have been few forays into the sociology of traffic and next to no results from empirical research. This is astonishing, for traffic has become one of the great unmastered problems of industrially developed societies and this alone should be enough to spur analytical science into action. Traffic is of particular interest to sociology, for it is a process which is extensively determined by society and operates in its own kind of social contexts. To this extent an analysis of traffic can enrich sociological theory. Finally the conclusions of research might be converted into model suggestions or at least serve as a basis for applied techno-political measures.

In the following exposition I shall consider motorized traffic only in its urban manifestations, especially in discussing the concrete problems of political and technical planning. This does, however, require some introductory theoretical considerations which have a wider context themselves and so apply at least in part to traffic in general.

Traffic as a Social System

At the most general level, *traffic serves as a connection between two places*: we leave one place and try to reach another. To that extent *traffic is in principle not at end in itself* but the means to an end, namely the connecting of place to place; so it demands rational behaviour or at least makes rational behaviour seem advisable. In this sense, traffic resembles other rationally-orientated activities such as work in goods production, the purposes of which lie beyond the actual activity and turn it into the mere execution of the means. In the case of traffic, there is the additional non-rational, sportive variant of conduct: driving at random and for the fun of it. From the individual's point of view, participating in traffic becomes an end in itself. But compared with the proportion of traffic as the purpose-orientated connection of place to place, recreational motoring can be ignored as a peripheral phenomenon.

*Zeitschrift für Verkehrssicherheit, 1968, pp. 210–222, TUV-Rheinland Köln.

Considered sociologically, traffic is a *social system* with largely technical determinants and therefore has a comparatively strong coercive nature. It is a social system typified by *utterly standardized behaviour and minimal integration of the participants*. Traffic participation is role behaviour; the scope for individual interpretation of the role varies in each case but is on the whole very limited.

To define traffic as a system and traffic behaviour as role behaviour is to imply that traffic is based on teamwork or, in the sense of rational behaviour, co-operation. (Even if a road user finds himself temporarily alone on the road, his behaviour is still attuned continuously to encountering others, to uneventful moving along with and past each other, i.e. to co-operation.)

Now, in the social system of traffic co-operation does not pursue a really common aim, as other systems such as industrial concerns or the armed forces do. It could be said that co-operation in traffic is not a means to attain something positive, but to avoid something negative: every participant in the system attempts to attain his destination without friction. The common effort consists in avoiding accidents, incidents, obstacles, etc. *Communication* within the system is reduced to uniform behaviour (driving behind and beside each other) and to *symbolic signals* to transmit information, to prevent and indeed settle, conflicts (indicating the direction of travel, ceding the right of way by means of hand motions, using hooting or hand motions to warn of dangerous situations, shaking one's fists, tapping one's forehead with one's finger, etc.). Hence traffic is a system all its own; the less the participants come into contact with each other and are compelled to interaction, the better it works: a system defined and approved in the reality by a principle of *minimized contact*. Therefore I cannot agree with Claessens when he says, "As soon as someone climbs into a car, he may generally be assumed to have begun with this action a mode of conduct aimed at another person, several other persons or groups, organizations, associations, firms etc."[1] Yet the goals mentioned are precisely those that lie beyond the actual traffic action but have nothing to do with that action itself, other than determining its motivation and direction.

Criteria of Traffic Behaviour

Traffic behaviour is, as a rationally determined role behaviour, orientated quite concretely in each respective case to reaching a geographical destination or to connecting one place with another. In rational conduct (the more or less sportive motivations can be excluded from our considerations), getting to the destination occurs under at least three criteria grouped under the overall heading of rationality: *Speed, safety and economy*.

Speed should be understood as a time-relationship. The aim is to reach one's destination as soon as possible and one may choose a longer route if this allows the distance to be bridged more rapidly. We are therefore dealing with "economic", not real, distance.

Safety means the endeavour of the individual traffic participant to reach his destination as safely as possible, to avoid damage to people and objects.

Economy is the criteria of the lowest possible expenditure. The goal is to keep detours and wear and tear to a minimum.

Rationality of conduct demands constant *evaluation of the various criteria* according to the traffic situation, while driving. Hence safety may be improved at the expense of speed, economy be reduced for the sake of speed upon appropriate alterations in the objective situation. Basically one attempts to reach a *balance* that satisfies all the criteria. In view of these criteria of traffic behaviour, it becomes self-evident that rational individual conduct (a balance of the criteria) depends on co-operation, i.e. conduct attuned to partners. Also, the degree of co-operation must rise in proportion to the number of traffic participants, in other words with the traffic density, if rationality is to be maintained. From the individual traffic participant's point of view, this is a simple principle of mutual give-and-take. The simultaneous presence of many compels him to adjust himself to his fellows on the road, to conform as much as possible, to understand their intentions and express himself as unambiguously as possible by his use of signals and his driving method; all this not for personal, moral and like considerations, however, but for practical reasons, in order to "get on" himself. The amount of co-operation is surprising indeed, especially in the towns with the densest traffic. Kob rightly ascertains "that normal behaviour on the road with the instrument automobile . . ." could be described as "an interesting form of collective understanding and anonymous solidarity".[2]

Determinants of Traffic Behaviour

Both the rationality of individual conduct in traffic and the efficiency of the overall process rise markedly if all the objective factors of private traffic, that is, the motor car as a means of connecting A to B, the system of norms for collective behaviour and the structure of traffic facilities (the system of roads) as an "objective guidance system" ("objektives Leitsystem" — Claessens), are equipped for and directed towards helping the traffic participant to develop habitual behaviour. This is a basic premise. Habitual behaviour means the opportunity to perform driving functions as customarily, uniformly and as free of forced decisions as possible, with subconscious reactions and with the norms full internalized. If this conduct proceeds habitually as described only a trace of personal uncertainty, indecision and inability to master the unexpected will remain.

Both the road user's willingness and psychological constitution and the outer circumstances or objective conditions clearly contribute to his habituation of traffic conduct.

The objective conditions can equally be described as the *determinants of traffic as role behaviour* — The factors mentioned prove sociologically relevant.

Automobile

The motor car is one such relevant objective determinant, although for sociological purposes it must be considered in its uses as understood by the road user — that is, in his (subjective) consciousness. Only from this perspective does its character emerge as that of a factor which objectively determines behaviour.

Kob lists the following functions of the car for an individual, ". . . its function as an instrument, i.e. a transport-machine, its function as a consumer commodity, i.e. a means of luxury and sensations of pleasure and its function as a symbol of power, i.e. as a demonstration of both the social and technological superiority of the individual"[3]. These categories will be adopted and developed below.

The motor car is an *instrument*, a means of conveying people and things from house to house, a means of opening up not only preconceived routes but any areas chosen. This is the major advantage of the car, compared to collective means of transport.

The car is a *consumer commodity* in many respects. Firstly it is *a medium and symbol of freedom* and freedom of movement, its advantage being the principle of free choice of route and time of travel. Beyond this, the symbolic connotation of liberty must be taken into account in order to understand the extraordinary popularity of the car: the awareness of being able to go anywhere at any time in itself provides deep satisfaction. As Claessens rightly comments, the car moreover serves as an "escape from the demands of work, marital problems, unwished-for domesticity,"[4] and this too encourages the motorist's awareness of liberty. He is undeterred even by the paradox that when he ventures into the traffic with the help of this "liberty vehicle", he yields obediently and compliantly to one of the most strongly coercive social systems in existence today.

The car as a consumer commodity is a *symbol of status and prestige*: it represents the most visible proof of its owner's social position. In the public eye there is a hierarchy of car brands and types which corresponds to a prestige scale of social positions. Almost everyone tends to identify with their own car from the status angle, and to judge other people's in the same way, to rank them. This is more than confirmed by Claessen's observation, "We often find people who virtually apologize for their car, which measured by the social position is too 'small' or too 'large' "[5].

The consumer article "car" also serves as one's own portable, ever-available private sphere. The "monadic seclusion" it procures makes many prefer travelling in one's own car regardless of all the stress of long distances and commuter travel, because it offers the chance of being alone and avoiding the contact with strangers inevitable in public transport.[6]

Last not least, a car's shape, its lustre and the exhilarating experience of driving, which may rise to intoxicating heights, provides an emotional experience of a singular kind. With his poem *Der Knabe* (The Boy), Rainer Maria Rilke anticipated the motorist, aptly expressing this experience in poetic dream images:

> I would become as one of those
> That on wild horses journey through the night
> With torches which like undone hair
> Wave strongly in their chasing's wake
> I would stand up front, as in a boat
> Big and like a flag unfurled . . .
> And anyone is near and blasts a path for us
> With the trumpet which lightens and shouts
> And plays for us black loneliness
> Through which we race like a hasting dream:
> Behind us houses falling to their knees.
> The lanes twist oblique to meet us,
> The squares make way: but we take hold
> And our horses rush like pelting rain.

There is indeed something boyish in this exhilaration, made familiar to all by the motor car.

The car is an *instrument and symbol of power*, a perfect instrument for conflict. This extends from the sportsmanlike prowess of "commanding" (already we have the association with power) a relatively complex piece of machinery to real "power trials" in the shape of the struggles of overtaking, blocking another's rights of way and so on. Contests between brands are popular, too: the point is to "show" the driver of a different model what one's own is worth. Anybody driving a large Mercedes will soon see how quickly others on the autobahn make way for him; anyone intending to overtake him in a more modest car or a foreign model will just have to "wait their turn". In the first case, the prestige of a particular brand is crucial; in the second, power is matched against a less glamorous type of machine. Another typical power situation occurs when the driver of a powerful car is overtaken but "can't let that sort of thing happen" to him and prevents it happening again by stepping on the accelerator. It would be easy to continue the list of ways in which the car is used as a means of power over other traffic participants.

In comparing the functions of the motor car for the individual as sketched out above, the only function appearing to have a rational explanation seems to be that of an "instrument", while all other functions are emotional, even irrational qualities. They are no less important in the desire to own a motor car and may sometimes (the car as a means to power) have a negative effect on traffic conduct.

All these factors have led to the expanding number of motor cars hitherto; yet, for the individual, any further increase means a decrease in the effect of the functions mentioned. The appearance of cars *en masse* reduces the economic prestige and power value of each car. In other words, the rank of the motor car as determinant of traffic behaviour diminishes while massive occurrence and mass traffic make more rational and cooler handling of this instrument increasingly necessary. If our situation is compared with that of the United States, these claims are drastically confirmed. There the motor car has become a well nigh unnoticed fact of life; saturation point has been reached. In comparison we are still at the infant stage but we can expect similar developments.

The system of norms

As a determinant of traffic behaviour, the norm system belongs to the most intractable analytical and political problems of modern mass traffic. Firstly, there is an important difference between *formal* and *informal norms*. The former are the sum of the legally fixed regulations for conduct in traffic, the latter are "free" rules of the game of road conduct, continually formed and modified by the traffic situation as it develops, unwritten laws that make co-operation in traffic easier. Sociologically, these two kinds of convention interrelate in a peculiar, highly relevant, way.

The informal norms reveal themselves at first glance as a development of symbolic signs in the service of co-operation, representing a positive achievement without which smooth traffic would no longer be possible today. Kob observes, "The significance of so-called social signs that permit one to incorporate others into one's own behavioural system . . ., which make it possible to expect a certain pattern of conduct from them and at the same time demand one's own certain pattern of conduct to them, the significance of these social signs in automobile traffic has become nothing less than the foundation stone of optimal patterns of behaviour."[7]

Informal norms act as a complement or in extreme cases even as an opposite, as counter-conventions to the formal kind. Overtaking on the inside in single line traffic was an illegal counter convention for years and has only now on the decision of the federal court been absorbed into the formal code; inside overtaking outside a single line situation and on roads lacking lane markings is still an informal counter convention, with the added complication that this convention is not established in all towns.

In general, the informal code fills gaps in the formal code. They are always concomitant with the born of functional necessity and draw their legitimacy from it. They are flexible as they occur only when the situation requires. Their general purpose is to support and relieve the road user, but this they only partly do because they are *not compulsory*, offering no possibility of sanctions in case of transgression — and are therefore *unreliable*. In this sense they vex the motorist repeatedly; whereas they really do give him support, they also help to undermine his road conduct.

In all their complexity, the formal norms can be understood only in the light of the historical evolution of transport. With mounting traffic density the system of norms was elaborated more and more, attaining dimensions today that amount to a genuine burden on the participant, not least bacause traffic norms, except for statutory regulations, are always connected with direct information. The jungle of traffic signs in our cities is an eloquent example. It can be considered a godsend that the plethora of speed limits (and with them, signs in their thousands) have been replaced in towns by one limit of 50 km/h (whether that is the appropriate speed is another question), quite apart from the aid to habituation that such statutory regulations offer. Any new information amounts to an additional burden on the road user and distraction from his original purpose, prudent driving. Far from denying the need for norms and information, this justifies limiting them to the absolutely indispensable minimum. The *disproportionate burden of superfluous regulations and information* on the road user is the result of an historical process of constant growth in the system of norms. Another consequence is the system's *obscurity* for the participant, resulting from the inflexibility typical of all formal codes of norms; yet it is in situations like traffic, with its great dependence on individual reactions and decisions and therefore on the credibility of these regulations in any conceivable situation, its dependence, one might say, on plasticity, that obscurity leads at best to uncertainty in conduct and thus retarded habituation.

The precarious result of both phenomena, the excess and obscurity of formal norms, is that they are becoming effectively impossible to apply. This explains the recurrent transgressions against them, the continual deviations in road conduct: there is not a single road user who does not "sin" a thousandfold against the traffic laws.

This deviating behaviour is intensified still more by the absence of *ad-hoc* sanctions. Traffic is in a state of constant flux, the situation for the participant, the confrontations and constellations, vary continually; the "monadic insulation" in the motor car is a shield against defence reactions from the other participants and the opportunities for escape are relatively great. Such sanctions as do follow (if any) are usually late and lack the penetration to stop deviant behaviour effectively. Now it must be emphasized that the attitude of the authority that lays the rules down contributes significantly to the transgressions and escape attempts by its attitude of charging the traffic participants with the whole weight of responsibility for whatever happens to the traffic and basically acting as if all is well as long as the individual participant behaves properly. The truth of the matter is that the objective traffic situation frequently admits nothing other than norm-offending behaviour, erring reactions, and misjudgements. Naturally the legislator is aware of this, and the term "traffic offender" contains a hint that a person guilty of typical traffic omissions is not in fact a "criminal".

Another fallacy underlies the formal rules in that they call again and again upon personal conduct and moral qualities (considerations, decency, responsibility towards others and so on) where there is no possibility to sanction apersonal behaviour, no incentive to the individual for personal behaviour and most important of all, no objective support for such behaviour by the nature of the traffic system. In fact, only an anonymous role behaviour, stereotyped to the utmost and extensively objectified, can guarantee optimum traffic conditions. All these personal criteria are useless if the participant is unable to apply them to a relevant technical and therefore functional context which moreover assures him and his partners advantage of the best possible progress. Here too, the possibility of habituation of technical operations seems much more practical than vague, inappropriate and in the end impracticable criteria like so-called human qualities.

Hence we ascertain that the proliferation, the complexities and uncertainties of the formal code of rules, the chasmic rift between these and the informal norms and the insecurity this instils in the participant, all this makes the internalization of conventions into irrefutable and meaningful rules of conduct more difficult. The habituation of traffic conduct is hindered instead of being provided with a self-evident behavioural framework.

Structure of Traffic Facilities

The problem of habituation is particularly highlighted if the final objective determinant of traffic behaviour, the *structure of traffic facilities*, or as Claessens calls them, the objective guidance systems[8] are considered. Traffic facilities for individual traffic must be seen as systems of roads and signs which crucially determine the participant's behaviour by their respective structures. Here, closer examination reveals two different structural types of traffic facility. In practice they only rarely occur in a pure state; in towns even less so. Below, they will be considered in their ideal forms, i.e. their characteristic properties juxtaposed and their different effects on traffic behaviour illustrated.

I would term the two structural types *network system* and *circular system* (NS and CS below). The perfect model of the NS is a chequerboard, and that of CS a circuit; in practice, we find historically inherited urban road networks and country road systems, or urban environments and distributor networks in Buchanan's sense[9] and motorway systems. The NS is the historically *traditional type* with an irregular line pattern (not conceived with the motorist in mind), spread and accumulated by historical accidents.

The CS is the *rational type* formed by modern mass transport and designed for motor traffic. *The guidance system character* is negligible in the NS but optimal in the CS: not as absolute as a railway line, but it does "guide" the traffic participant with comparative certainty.

The NS is an *egalitarian system* knowing no privileged roads (priority or main roads), no road grading; crossings occur at one level and require mutual co-operation from the traffic participants who meet there. The CS is a *hierarchical system*, one of priorities with graded roads — motorways with access roads, A-class urban distributors, B-class local distributors and side-roads. There are no crossings at one level, hence there is no counter traffic; the participant only has to "thread" his way into the lane. The streets of the NS do have counter traffic, they admit participants of all kinds and do offer possibilities for stopping and parking. Except for the local side roads, the roads of the CS allow one-way traffic only and are made solely for motor cars; stopping and parking is only possible in the spaces provided (lateral lines and laybys).

The NS is *flexible* in its uses, particularly in cities; the motorist has a number of routes open to him to reach his destination and he can choose whichever is best at the time; the traffic in principle is distributed at the outset over the whole network. The CS is inflexible, the choice of route limited by the system of auxiliary and main roads: the A-class distributors are the busiest, followed by the B-class distributors and finally the side-roads. Thus the load on the system is never balanced, but distributed according to the functions of the various kinds of road. The NS knows no speed limits whereas the CS has lower and upper limits to assure traffic flow and reduce overtaking to a given level. As for the norms the NS requires *little or no formal* control or at most some general statutory regulations (right before left, certain signals, etc). Other than that, traffic manages with the informal rules which become necessary at given times. The CS possesses *traffic conduct controls that are inherent in the system*: the road complex itself takes on the task of regulating: encouraging the observance of formal but fewer, more readily understood and imple-mented norms.

How, then, do the two structural types affect traffic behaviour? The most important effect is that the system in the NS is unable to command and regulate behaviour and renders the motorist's adjustment to his fellows and his routinizing to driving conduct or the training of an appropriate driving style more difficult. In contrast, the CS's command and guidance of the participant aids his habituation. In the NS *individual conduct* is critical, the participants hardly depend on each other; the result is not organic, motorists accommodate themselves anew in each case. This makes personal decisions essential at all times; the road complex demands a high capacity for reaction. In the CS, the criterion for the flow of traffic is *collective behaviour*; those involved are interdependent to a high degree, the stream of traffic forms a framework in which there is little to force decisions on the individual. The traffic participant is in a sense led and borne along by the road system and the current of traffic. Driving in the NS is therefore much more diverse and complicated than in the CS, where it is reduced as far as possible to a few given operations; this is compensated for in the NS by greater variety and interest. Corresponding to the different normative potentials of the structural systems, *ad-hoc* sanctions are much harder to implement in the NS, with its great opportunities for flight, than in the CS, where the stream of traffic clogs and the transgressor stays there, trapped, or can be pursued easily if he should attempt to escape.

These are the inferences: the two types of structure are matched by *different modes of conduct* for the traffic user. This means that the motorist has to *internalize* both modes of conduct, but this is made extremely difficult for him because in practice the structural types, except for motorways, are mixed. Above all, in towns the motorist is led continually from one situation to another opposite one. Hence he is thoroughly overtaxed in his reflex power and scope of conduct. As in a confrontation with the system of norms then, unsure conduct and stress stand in place of habituation and relief.

The development of the mixed, i.e. unstructured, road patterns to be found generally in towns today can only be explained historically. The earlier system, which lasted for thousands of years, was the network. With the development of automobile transport, certain roads became through and main roads, networks were extended more and more. Not least because of the expense, genuine urban circular systems were only rarely built. This piecemeal, basically unsystematic, expansion required more and more commands, prohibitions and information and led to further and further softening of the network without any possibility arising to counter it with the only feasible equivalent, the circular system. So in practice, traffic facilities today present themselves to the user as an impenetrable chaos, an unstructured tangle.

Restructuring Traffic Facilities

Of the three objective determinants of traffic behaviour this one in theory offers the greatest scope, but it has to be admitted that the sociologist has no opportunity of visualizing how solutions might be implemented technically. Technically and socially the more efficient ideal type of traffic systems is without doubt the circular, but it would be utterly utopian to demand the introduction of the circular system as the exclusive traffic facility for towns; Buchanan's well considered studies have made that sufficiently clear. One rather more viable alternative would be to *realize* the two ideal types of net and circuit in towns as *purely as possible*. This may mean that two thoroughly different modes of conduct and reaction are forced upon the participant but this very difference makes them easier to apply properly than the unstructured and therefore unstable modes of behaviour in the usual mixed areas. The motorist has to be able to perceive very clearly whether he is on a network or a circuit; then he can attune his behaviour to the optimum. Cities are well supplied with networks; they would have to be turned into "pure" networks by abolishing priority roads. In principle the rule of priority from the right should apply. In view of the traffic density, however, this would not work without a very dense network of traffic lights. Traffic flow could be attained by green phases. It is probably not utopian to assume that photo cells installed in front of lights, circuits of lights controlled over television screens and radio receivers built into each individual car to give computor-transmitted motoring intructions (Burckhardt makes similar suggestions[10]) would be a successful means even in the network system to achieve relatively smooth traffic flows and above all optimal exploitation of the available road network. Possibly technical devices of this kind are less costly than gigantic infrastructure intended to provide circular systems. What is certain is that the cybernetic potential in the transport sector has not even begun to be tapped.

Traffic and Town Planning

To this comes the town planning aspect. Circular systems destroy both the structural and social substances of the existing fabric of a town, with the divisive effect of the traffic roads (exemplified by the enormous constructions in American towns). Networks maintain the substance with the greatest possible exploitation of the what is available while preserving what has been inherited.

It is only another step to *correlate the primary functions of a city and the types of traffic facility*. Thus network systems will suit areas where the work function predominates, such as industrial areas, areas with industries of the tertiary sector and within these, especially, industries with lively public traffic. Circular systems, except for the distributory roads, are ideal for residential areas. These should be planned as genuine "environments" in Buchanan's sense. In residential areas his concept of their minimal restructuring as environmental zones and in older, architecturally valuable districts his schemes for historic towns might serve as models.[11] Thus the mere deployment of traffic facilities as networks or circular systems would enable a conscious land use policy within a town.

Notes

1. Claessens, Dieter: Soziologische und sozialpsychologische Aspekte des Fahrens im Verkehrsfluß, in: *Zeitschr. für Verkehrssicherheit* 3/1965, p. 157.

2. Kob, Janpeter: Werkzeug, Konsumgut, Machtsymbol — Zur Soziologie des Automobils, in: *Hamburger Jahrbuch für Wirtschafts- und Gesellschaftspolitik*, 11th Year, 1966, p. 189.
3. Kob, p. 185.
4. Claessens, p. 157.
5. Claessens, p. 158.
6. See. Kob, p. 190.
7. Kob, p. 189.
8. Claessens, p. 157.
9. See Buchanan, Colin: *Verkehr in Städten*, Essen 1963, p. 39 ff.
10. See Burckhardt, Lucius: Stadtform, Lebensform und Urbanität, in: *Städtebauliche Beiträge*, publ: Institut für Städtebau und Wohnungswesen der Deutschen Akademie für Städtebau und Landesplanung, Munich, Issue 2/1964, p. 6 f.
11. See Buchanan.

Part III   Mobility or, Rather, the Lack of It

Introduction[1]

E. DE BOER

Two categories of problems are connected with mobility: problems caused by an over-measure of auto-mobility as discussed in the previous parts and problems caused by short measure in movement possibilities for the carless, the mobility-disadvantaged. This second category of problems, which in fact also find their origin in car use and implied increases in trip length, are the subject of this chapter. Mobility in general will not be treated, let alone behavioural modelling of travel demand, which anyhow is a subject belonging rather to a chapter on planning. It should be noted however that often the same factors setting bounds to the non- or less-mobile (like increasing spatial specialization or functional segregation) can serve as an explanation for car-use.

Transport Deprivation as a Social Problem

The basic question to be asked is whether different access to conveyance must, in conditions of great and increasing societal dependence on the motor car, lead to differences in freedom of movement, in accessibility, in opportunity for individual development and social integration.

Unequal access to transport is merely indicated by disparities in use and ownership of transport means. Availability and utility are the essential qualities: who can utilize specific means of transport at and during what time and for what purposes?

Questions like these probably have been explored best by Mayer Hillman *et al.* (1973, 1976). Problem categories are the poor, children, the aged, the handicapped, housewives and those without a driving licence. Limited transport opportunities for these categories represent a social problem only if they result in confined freedom of movement, in restricted accessibility and in reduced activity patterns.

Freedom of movement is the ability to travel at will. This is a problem especially for children depicted in Hillman's "Unfreedom road" (one of the papers selected) and for the handicapped (Ashford and Bell, 1978; Shepard 1978).

Accessibility is the ability to reach other people and activity-places. Important work in this field has been done by Moseley (1979) and — of a more analytical character — by Burns (1979)[2]. The title of the second study mentions "transportation, temporal and spatial components of accessibility". It elaborates on time-geography as originally developed by Hägerstrand in his "What about people . . ." (our first selection for this chapter). Time-geography seeks in fact to define the freedom of movement people have, within constraints set by time and space (Parkes and Thrift, 1980). Starting from the notion that the individual is neither omnipresent nor timeless and that he consequently never can be in two places at the same time, it explores the free action space left to the individual by his social obligations and the way these are patterned in space (locational structure) and in time.

Point in time, duration and cyclic recurrence (daily, weekly, annual) of activities both obligatory and voluntary set bounds to action space and to what could be done with remaining "free time". It is needed in part for transport, but less if transport is better.

Activity patterns. Vidakovic (1980) not surprisingly found that for people arriving home from work early (before 17.30 h) frequencies of evening out-of-home activities which were considerably higher than those of people arriving home later. Willmott investigated the incidence of car-ownership amongst different categories of the population and its predictive value for the variety of leisure activities people participated in. It proved to be surpassed as such only by age. In "The impact of transport on the quality of life" Hägerstrand (1973), using evidence from research of his "Lund-school", demonstrated that activity-patterns of non-car-users are comparatively constrained. The difference from those of car-users is so spectacular that he pleaded for a redistributive policy in transport, deemed even more necessary as employment and commercial services are gradually relocating to places accessible by car but hardly so by other means of transport.

Spatial processes like these are indeed aggravating the situation of the transport-disadvantaged. Concern for "transportation and poverty" in the USA during the early seventies stemmed from the consciousness that employment for unskilled or low-skilled labourers was shifting increasingly to the suburbs. The unemployed living in the inner city could not possibly follow due to lack of social housing in suburbia which moreover discriminated against their moving in. Transport had to bring relief similarly as it had to in racial segregation at school: the so-called "busing", bitterly resented by countless parents. Politics of this kind, intended partly to prevent social unrest like the violent riots in the Watts-district of Los Angeles, are bound to fail if they are not combined with other more fundamental measures[3]). Systematic treatment of spatial processes detrimental to non-car users is relatively rare. I tried to do this in 1976, in a contribution to a study on the future of Dutch transport. The result was only moderately satisfactory due to lack of much essential data, but it caused something of a public shock. Known facts combined in an unusual way yielded, at least for the Netherlands, a new, undeniable and most likely increasing problem (De Boer, 1976). Studies showing the pervasive impact of ongoing change have been done by Ellegård and Moline. Ellegård (1977) described how during one century technical change in the dairy industry and consequent concentration of productive capacity changed transport patterns and activity patterns of farmers and workers. Moline (1971) in his case-study of a small town in rural Illinois showed how, by the introduction of the automobile, an economically well-integrated community was denuded of nearly all its facilities in the course of 30 years (1900–1930)[4]. It is a phenomenon not uncommon to those remembering the variety of facilities the average village in Western Europe had before 1960.

Need

It may be reasonably concluded now that unequal access to transport and to activity places must be regarded as a considerable social problem. Yet, if distributive mobility-policies are to be designed, the factors contributing to the problem should be scrutinized in more detail. The transport-disadvantaged are labelled so because there is supposed to be a discrepancy between their transport-opportunities and their transport needs.

Transport-opportunities are determined by a number of factors:
— financial: income as compared to the cost of utilizing certain means of transport
— physical: validity as compared with requirements for vehicle-use
— mental: faculties and the call on these by transport means and traffic conditions
— legal: formal requirements concerning access to driving and riding vehicles and the degree to which the individual conforms to these
— social: the individual's role in the household (ranking his access to vehicle use) and his relations to the social environment deciding his chances for shared riding
— geographical: distance to lines of public transport
— temporal: point in time, duration and frequency at which certain means of transport can be used and the speed developed doing so.

Transport-necessity is caused by two broad categories of factors:
1. Space- and time-order of activity-places
   — spatial: distance to and pattern of activity-places
   — temporal: waiting- and opening-periods;
2. Activity-patterns, the number and variety of activities the individual is engaged in, to be distinguished according to the degree of:
   — necessity: meals, work, football
   — time-constraint: fixation in time, duration and frequency of activities

— spatial constraint: like that of time, decided by material conditions (presence of means of production for example) or by social conditions: teamwork and teamsport.

Assessing need. When transport-opportunities are limited activity-patterns will somehow be restricted. Thus, perceived patterns are no pure expression of need. The need for activities and consequently for transport can be assessed in different ways:

(a) *normative*: drafting a minimum activity-pattern and comparing it with real behaviour. This is likely to be socially undesirable and — by lack of knowledge — impossible in practice.

(b) *relative*: measuring differences between individuals with good transport opportunities and little necessity — as dictated by the space-time-order of society — on the one hand and comparable individuals with bad opportunities and great necessity on the other hand (Hillman, 1977). This however is likely to be sooner a measure of latent demand than of need. Knowledge of disparities is however essential for subsequent measurement strategies.

(c) *deprivational*: determining whether the "poorer" activity-patterns found affect individual well-being. They may in some cases be taken as a part of the bargain (accepted as a consequence of settling somewhere) and in other cases be sooner an expression of a specific "life-style". Wachs (1979) distinguished various life-styles in his study of travel needs of elderly people. Banister (1980) utilized a deprivational approach in his research of transport mobility in "inter-urban" South Oxfordshire. The report contains quite interesting reflections on defining transport needs (especially chapter 9, pp 132–161), suggesting one further strategy:

(d) *adaptational*: measuring the impact of conditional change on activity-patterns and on well-being. People adapt just as well to worsening circumstances as they do to improving circumstances, when latent demand is manifesting itself. People tend to make the best of it, accepting less satisfactory activity-patterns if they cannot act otherwise. Because in the end they tend to make a virtue of need, affected activity-patterns and consequently affected well-being had best be investigated in changing conditions. The 1981 Dutch before-and-after study of public transport withdrawal was undertaken with these conditions in mind (De Boer, 1982). It evidenced — like Oxley's survey (1982) — a decreased mobility especially for the elderly and a resented loss of freedom, qualities which proved to be enhanced by the volunteer-driven community bus (Kropman and Peters, 1982). Sophisticated treatment of travel need and (adaptive) travel behaviour can be found too in Paaswell (1979) and Jones (1980).

Now the fact that detailed research is desirable for effective mobility-policies, for supporting those most in need of transport, should not make us lose sight of the undeniable detrimental impact of continuous transport and spatial developments on the opportunities of non-car users. Spatial enlargement of scale and the car superseding other forms of transport or street-use should anyhow be reversed. Ideologies and policy-orientations in global transport planning are the subjects of Part IV.

Summaries

Hägerstrand's *What about people in regional science?* is no doubt the most renowned article selected. It is the classic beginning of the most fruitful branch of time-geography, the so-called "Lund school". Hägerstrand reproaches regional science — and he might just as well have chosen transport science as a victim — for neglect of individual behaviour and well-being. For reasons of social responsibility and of adequate behavioural modelling and prediction social organization and technology should be studied on the micro level. Most important is the notion that any location has for the individual not only space co-ordinates but time co-ordinates as well. His behaviour can be described as a time-space path covered during a day or some other period. Time is of essential importance when it comes to fitting people and things together for functioning in socio-economic systems. The socio-economic web on the micro level, i.e. the pattern of activities and relations, can be discovered in two different ways: firstly by collecting time-space paths and analysing these (with the risk of endless unstructured search) and secondly, more promisingly, by defining the mechanisms of constraints which determine how the paths are channelled or dammed up. Three categories of constraints present themselves: capability constraints, coupling and authority constraints. *Capability constraints* are those which limit the activities of the individual because of his biological construction and/or the tools he can command. Some of these are predominantly time oriented like sleeping and eating. Other ones are more specifically distance oriented, dividing the time-space surrounding the individual in "concentric" tubes or rings of accessibility. The three rings distinguished are those of physical (arm) reach, of communicative reach and of travel reach. The size of the island defined by a day's travel reach is tremendously different for walkers and motorists. Because of social obligations factual reach is much smaller and the influence of transport means all the more important. *Coupling constraints* decide where, when and for how long the individual must unite with other individuals in order to produce, consume and interact. The time- and space-order of these activities decide whether other activities are possible.

Authority constraints implying limited access to domains, "time-space entities within which things and events are under the control of a given individual or a given group". Domains vary from father's chair, via the premises of a firm, to a national state.

The three aggregations of constraints interact in many ways yielding an oppressive existence for less privileged members of society. Liveability of the time-space order and the ways in which it could be improved are research-objects of utmost importance.

"It seems that the main focus of our practical problems is moving away from the allocation of money towards the physical allocation of the uses of space and time".

Hillman in *Not a carborne democracy* accused transport planning as Hägerstrand similarly did regional science: it deals with the "needs" of vehicles, not people. This paper however is much less theoretical in character. After a general description of problems engendered by present-day car-use Hillman analyses a number of common misconceptions in transport planning, all detrimental to those without access to or with bad access to the car. Transport realities are depicted in a way that is colourful and unusually rich in argument. In the conclusions detailed scrutiny of travel needs and of the relationship of urban form, facility distribution and land use characteristics are deemed necessary for more adequate transport planning. The author however believes that transport and traffic conditions have been distorted to such an extent that immediate sharing-out of the available travel space should be exercised.

Mobility constraints of the carless is an American counterpart of Hillman's (British) article. *Koutsopoulos and Schmidt* present their treatment of travel needs differently however. Two broad categories of constraints are presented: trip-making constraints, related to individual characteristics and environmental or external constraints. Within these categories single constraints are grouped under six headings: physical, psychological and informational, socio-economic, locational, administrative and demand-response, thus putting part of the blame on planning. By its analytical nature this paper is somewhat less coherent than the preceding one, but in several of the paragraphs — especially the physical, the psychological and the demand-response ones — it goes into more and relevant detail. Yet, after so many general statements on facts, causes and effects of limited access to transport, one feels a need for fuller insight into the plight of at least one of the disadvantaged categories. An article on children's travel was selected because this is usually neglected, even in the literature on the subject. The children's particular lot should remind us that this problem affects the lives of all of us.

Unfreedom road, again by Hillman and this time his colleagues of the London Policy Studies Institute (PSI, at that time PEP) discusses part of the results of their five-area survey (Hillman a.o. 1973).

The main theme in the surveys of both teenagers and junior school-children was independence. It is a precondition of growth and maturity to be fostered in travel as well, since it makes unaccompanied visiting of facilities and places possible. Of the areas investigated, ranging from a high density inner London ward to a rural parish, the first one showed the most restrictions for children: more accompaniment, less bicycle-ownership, less permission to cross main roads. Twenty-two per cent of them could not even visit their friends on their own! The predictable conclusion: policies must be directed towards providing local ease of movement and access. "For these young people the freedom to walk around defines the limits of their world".

Notes

1. The text of this introduction has in greater part been adapted from the Summary and Conclusions of a report on mobility-deprivation which I made for the Dutch Department of Public Works: E. de Boer (1981), *Vervoersongelijkheid, relevantie en onderzoek-baarheid*, een verkenning van de internationale literatuur. Projectbureau Integrale Verkeers- en Vervoers-studies, Den Haag.
2. I have made an attempt to analyse the concept and to demonstrate its value, in: Bereikbaarheid, miskend planologisch kernbegrip (Accessibility an undervalued concept in planning), *Stedebouw en Volkshuisvesting*, **61**, No. 12, December 1980, pp. 637–642. S. Jones (1981) provided an excellent literature review of accessibility measures.
3. See J. F. Kain and J. R. Meyer (1970) Transportation and poverty, *The public interest*, number 18 (winter 1970), pp 75–88.
4. N. T. Moline (1971) *Mobility and the Small Town (1900–1930)* University of Chicago, Department of Geography, Chicago.

Literature

A. Ashford and W. G. Bell (eds. 1978) *Mobility for the elderly and the handicapped*, Proceedings of an international conference, Cambridge April 4–7, Loughborough University.

D. Banister (1980) *Transport mobility and deprivation in inter-urban areas*, Saxon House, Westmead, Farnborough (Hants.).

D. Banister (1983) Transport needs in rural areas: a review and proposal, *Transport Reviews* **3**, no. 1.

D. Banister (1985) *Rural transport and planning*, a bibliography with abstracts, Mansell.

E. de Boer (1976) Mobiel en niet-mobiel, een verkenning van de sociale betekenis van ons vervoer (Mobile and immobile, a survey of the social significance of transport), pp 47–78 in J. Overeem (ed.), *Stedelijk verkeer en vervoer langs nieuwe banen*? Stichting Toekomstbeeld der Techniek, publikatie 21, The Hague.

E. de Boer (1982) *De bus gemist* (Missing the bus), Summary report of a research project "Social consequences of curtailing rural transport", Provincial Government of Groningen.

A. Bonnafous a.o. (1981) *Mobilité et vie quotidienne*, Presses universitaires de Lyon.

T. Bracher and G. W. Heinze (eds. 1985) *Lebensbedingungen und Verkehrsmobilität*, Schriftenreihe des Instituts für Verkehrsplanung and Verkehrswegebau no 17. Technische Universität, Berlin.

L. D. Burns (1979) *Transportation, temporal, and spatial components of accessibility*, Lexington Books, Lexington (Mass.).

K. Ellegård (1977) *Utveckling av transportmonster vid forandred teknik*, en tidsgeografisk studie, Kulturgeografiska Institutionen Lunds Universitet.

E. Ericson, K. Libéus and L. Lindahl (1982) *Trafikens roll för välbefinnandet i tätortslivet* (The role of traffic for well-being in urban life), Stockholm University of Technology, Institute for Transport Planning.

S. M. Golant (1972) *The residential location and spatial behaviour of the elderly*, a Canadian example. University of Chicago, Dept. of Geography, research paper 193, Chicago.

T. Hägerstrand (1973) *The impact of transport on the quality of life*, Paper for the CEMT-conference "Transport in the 1980–1990 decade" in Athens, Paris.

M. Hillman, I. Henderson and A. Whalley (1973) *Personal mobility and transport policy*, Political and Economic Planning, **39**, broadsheet 542, London.

M. Hillman, J. Henderson and A. Whalley (1976) *Transport realities and planning policy*, Political and Economic Planning, **42**, broadsheet 567, London.

M. Hillman and A. Whalley (1977) *Fair play for all, a study of access to sport and informal recreation*, PEP, Broadsheet 571, London.

P. M. Jones a.o. (1980) *Understanding travel behaviour*, University of Oxford, Transport Studies Unit.

S. R. Jones (1981) *Accessibility measures: a literature review*, TRRL, LR 967, Crowthorne, Berkshire.

J. A. Kropman and H. A. J. Peters (1982) *De buurtbus: bijdrage aan de leefbaarheid in kleine kernen* (The community bus: contribution to liveability in small villages), Instituut voor Toegepaste Sociologie, Nijmegen.

B. Lenntorp (1976) *Paths in space-time environments*, a time geographic study of movement possibilities of individuals, Lund studies in geography Ser. B. Human Geography no. 44, Lund (Sweden).

M. J. Moseley (1979) *Accessibility, the rural challenge*, Methuen, London.

P. R. Oxley and R. Seaton (1980) *Mobility in rural areas*, Proceedings of a conference, Cranfield, Centre for Transport Studies.

P. R. Oxley (1982) *The effects of the withdrawal and reduction of rural bus services*, TRRL, SR 719, Crowthorne, Berkshire.

R. E. Paaswell and W. W. Recker (1978) *Problems of the carless*, Praeger, New York.

R. E. Paaswell (1979) *Travel and activity needs of the mobility limited*, Resource paper workshop 8, 4th International Conference on Behavioural Travel Modelling, Eibsee (Germany), Department of Civil Engineering, Buffalo (N.Y.).

D. Parkes and N. Thrift (1980) *Times, spaces and places*: a chroneographic perspective, Wiley, Chichester.

M. E. Shepard (1978) *Handicapped persons in the US and public transportation travel demand*, a literature review and annotated bibliography, Vance bibliographies no. 1552, Monticello (Ill).

P. A. Stanley and J. H. Farrington (1981) The need for rural public transport: a constraints-based case study, *Tijdschrift voor Economische en Sociale Geografie*, **72** (1981), no. 2, pp 62–.

S. W. Town (1980) *The social distribution of mobility and travel patterns*, TRRL, LR 948, Crowthorne, Berkshire.

V. Vidakovic (1980) *Mens-tijd-ruimte* (Man-time-space), uit de dagboeken van 1400 Amsterdammers, Dienst Ruimtelijke Ordening, City of Amsterdam.

M. Wachs (1979) *Transportation for the elderly*, Changing lifestyles, changing needs, University of California Press, Berkeley.

P. Willmott (1973) Car ownership in the London Metropolitan Region, *Greater London Council Intelligence Unit Quarterly Bulletin* no. 23, June 1973, pp. 5–19.

What about People in Regional Science?*

TORSTEN HÄGERSTRAND

Since this occasion is the first time in the annals of the Regional Science Association that the presidential address is being delivered at a congress in Europe, it seems appropriate to explore the past to see whether there has been a difference in emphasis or tone between the European and the North American meetings. I think there has been a difference although I am not prepared to show statistical evidence. When looking over the proceedings of the sixties, one gets the impression that participants in this part of the world have preferred to remain closer to issues of application rather than to issues of pure theory. We in Europe seem to have been looking at Regional Science primarily as one of the possible instruments with which to guide policy and planning. I have chosen to proceed along this line by suggesting that regional scientists take a closer look at a problem which is coming more and more to the forefront in discussions among planners, politicians, and street demonstrators, namely, the fate of the individual human being in an increasingly complicated environment or, if one prefers, questions as to the quality of life. The problem is a practical one and, therefore, for the builder of theoretical models, a "hard nut to crack."

Now, first of all, does the problem fall within the scope of Regional Science? I think it does. A forest economist remarked some time ago that, "forestry is people, not trees." How much more accurate it would be to say that Regional Science is about people and not just about locations. And this ought to be so, not only for reasons of application. Regional Science defines itself as a social science, thus its assumptions about people are also of scientific relevance. Regional scientists differ in their attitudes toward concepts related to the quality of life. In his presidential address of 1962 Ullman[10] concluded that the, "problem remains to design cities to take advantage of scale economies and the other advantages of concentration, and at the same time to provide optimum liveability." This formulation indicates a belief in "liveability" as a worthwhile problem for research and a goal for planning. In 1967 Lowry[6] sounded more skeptical, at least as far

*Papers of the Regional Science Association XXIV, 1970, pp. 7–21. Reprinted by permission of the Association.

as the idea of an optimum in physical planning was concerned. "People seem able to extract apparently equivalent values from diverse environments, so long as the mechanics of the environment are comprehensible, and so long as its responses to individual initiatives are predictable." However, the next sentence takes back some of the conviction of that statement by arguing that, "when our cities become too dismal for comfort, we retire to the suburbs and substitute the amenities of gardening for those of museums and bright lights."

One frequently notices that economists are very quick to suggest that we solve our problems by moving somewhere else. It is convenient in theory and often in reality, but the idea implies two things: first, that there is a worthwhile place to go to; and second, that it is of no relevance that some have to be left behind. To earn money and to find desirable things to spend it on is a basic part of liveability and Regional Science had a lot to say about that. But it is also important that there be easy access to schools, other educational facilities, universities, libraries, theaters and concert-halls, doctors and hospitals, security services, playgrounds, parks, even silence and clean air. One does not find much written in Regional Science publications on the location and dimensioning of such items in relation to the spatial distribution of needs. Perhaps the problems involved fit better into the more restricted framework of specialism or operations research. I do not feel that this is good research policy. The sum total of these items is regionally too important to make it reasonable to leave them entirely in the hands of people who view them predominantly from the inside.

I am not going to carry this point further and it is not my intention to remain on quite so practical a level. Let me instead raise a question as to what regional scientists assume about people at the level of first principles. Have the efforts to give spatial realism and generality to economic matters also brought human realism and generality to matters of spatial organization? It is hard to find an answer to this, since, as Isard and Reiner[4] have pointed out, "models of human behavior over space have been almost entirely oriented to mass probabilistic behavior." These models of large aggregates are often presented without explicit statements about the assumed social organization and technology that exist at the micro-level from which the individual tries to handle his situation.

It may well be that when a region is given a certain areal size, which is well above the daily range of the majority of its population, it does not matter very much (as far as the aggregate spatial outcome is concerned) what forms micro-arrangements have happened to take. Such possible insensitivity would, in itself, be a problem for analysis. Nothing truly general can be said about aggregate regularities until it has been made clear how far they remain invariant with organizational differences at the micro-level. As an illustration, let me refer to the great number of studies of consumer and commuter behavior. In one case only I found the straightforward statement to the effect that in, "the modal case, the male traverses the habitat to exchange labor for money, and the female traverses it to exchange this money for food and other objects of value." See Fox and Kumar[2]. It could be argued that a modal case of that kind is a particular solution, typical of a given culture area and of a given period of time. What about a model case where both man and wife exchange labor for money? Or what about doing away entirely with many of the retail trade establishments by equipping dwellings with refrigerators and storerooms beside the mailbox and having them filled from cruising delivery vehicles without the presence of the customer? Since we know that social roles can be redefined and that experts on physical distribution are working on new technical approaches, it would be rather interesting to determine to what extent variations in basic assumptions at the household level would affect the principles of Central Place Theory or those of traffic generation models.

In a different problem area it is unquestionable that there are fundamental direct links to be explored between the micro-situation of the individual and the large scale aggregate outcome. I am referring to migration. In spite of the intuitive feeling among all workers in the field that micro-environmental factors are important in the decision to move, nearly all models involve only the extrapolation of current aggregate behavior. These observations are sufficient to illustrate that there is a purely theoretical case for taking a closer look at the individual human being in his situational setting. To do so would improve our ability to relate the behavior of small scale elements and large scale aggregates. Failure in this respect is a common, fundamental weakness of all social sciences. To focus "on the locational dimension of human activities," as Isard and Reiner[4] have argued the regional scientist is obliged to do, should be a point of departure as promising as most others, or perhaps more so, for tackling the problem of establishing coherence between the two ends of the scale.

The initial task is, I think, to eliminate imprecise thought processes which conceptually deceive us into handling people as we handle money or goods once we commence the process of aggregation. In order to illustrate this I would like to relate an experience which can hardly be unique. When I was three or four years old my father tried to teach me the principles of banking and we trotted along to the local establishment to deposit what I had accumulated in my savings box, including a very shiny silver crown. The next day I insisted on walking back to the bank to make sure that the people had really guarded my money. The clerk was very understanding and showed me the correct mix of coins. But the shiny crown was not among them and it could not be produced. I decided that savings banks did not really save money.

It was primitive economics to assume that banks should worry about the identity of coins. Is it advanced or primitive social science to disregard the identity of people over time in the same fashion? This is what we do in most cases when we treat a population as a mass of particles, almost freely interchangeable and divisible. It is common to study all sorts of segments in the population mass, such as the labor force, commuters, migrants, shoppers, tourists, viewers of television, members of organizations, etc., each segment being analyzed very much in isolation from the others. As one of my students put it, "we regard the population as made up of 'dividuals' instead of individuals." Of course, we cannot focus on every single individual in the aggregate. We have to leave it to the historian to concern himself with biographies of sample individuals. But on the continuum between biography and aggregate statistics, there is a twilight zone to be explored, an area where the fundamental notion is that people retain their identity over time, where the life of an individual is his foremost project, and where aggregate behavior cannot escape these facts.

With a concern for the individual, it follows that we need to understand better what it means for a location to have not only space coordinates but also time coordinates. It might be quite reasonable to eliminate time by concealing it in costs of transportation and storage, as long as the handling of material is the main concern of locational analysis. But it is hardly reasonable to do so when the problems of people are brought in. When, for example, in a general equilibrium model, it is assumed that every individual performs a multitude of roles, it is also implicitly admitted that location in space cannot effectively be separated from the flow of time. Sometimes, of course, an individual plays several roles at the same moment. But more often the roles exclude each other. They have to be carried out within a given duration, at given times and places, and in conjunction with given groups of other individuals and pieces of equipment. They may have to be lined up in non-permutable sequences.

Of equal importance is the fact that time does not admit escape for the individual. He cannot be stored away for later use without complications for himself or society. As long as he is alive at all, he has to pass every point on the timescale. Every point in space does not demand the same of him; he need only be somewhere in an environment which grants at least minimum conditions for survival. But this "somewhere" is always critically tied to the "somewhere" of a moment earlier. Jumps of non-existence are not permitted. To argue that time had to be taken into account along with space does not necessarily mean that studies of change and of development trends should take precedence over examinations of equilibria and steady states. See Stewart[9]. It means primarily that time has a critical importance when it comes to fitting people and things together for functioning in socio-economic systems, whether these undergo long-term changes, or rest in something which could be defined as a steady state. What I have in mind is the introduction of a time-space concept which could help us to develop a kind of socio-economic web model. The model would be asked what sorts of web patterns are attainable if the threads in the web (i.e., the individuals) may not be stretched beyond agreed levels of "liveability." And when I speak of a web model, this is not just a metaphoric expression but a way of indicating what kind of mathematics one would need in order to handle it. Let me try to illustrate these ideas in an informal and surely very "half-baked" fashion. I will not be concerned with a research technique. I am stressing a point of view by indicating the outlines of a model presently under study. As you will see, the various traditional concepts will be tied up in only a few packets with new labels.

In time-space the individual describes a *path*, starting at the point of birth and ending at the point of death. (Inanimate things also follow time-space paths but the characteristics of these are excluded here although they are needed in the complete web model.) The concept of life path (or parts of it such as the day path, week path, etc.) can easily be shown graphically if we agree to collapse three-dimensional space into a two-dimensional plain or even a one-dimensional island, and use perpendicular direction to represent time. In a Garden of Eden in which life was so entertaining that we did not even feel the need for regular rest, with a continually pleasant climate, ubiquitous self-replacing fruits to consume, and no social responsibilities, the path could be a true time-space random walk. In a more earthly environment it cannot be so, even if some drop-outs would have us believe otherwise. Assuming that continued survival is the first choice of those who have already set out on their life path, then some sort of counter-randomness programming has to occur.

When Robinson Crusoe found himself alone on his island, he could make up his program without regard to pre-existing socio-economic system. The nature resources were all his to develop under his specific set of biological and technical constraints. An individual who migrates into an established society, either by being born into it or by moving into it from outside, is in a very different position. He will at once find that the set of potentially possible actions is severely restricted by the presence of other people and by a maze of cultural and legal rules. In this way, the life paths become captured within a net of constraints, some of which are imposed by physiological and physical necessities and some imposed by private and common decisions. Constraints can become imposed by society and interact against the will of the individual. See Vining[11]. An individual can never free himself from such constraints. To migrate during a pressing situation involves substituting a known pattern of constraints for one which is largely unknown. And, being a forward-looking animal, the individual probably tries to compare not just the prevailing situation but the anticipated situation in the life-perspective of himself and members of his family.

Several different ways of investigating the socio-economic web come to mind. One is to sample life paths. Biologists found this to be useful a long time ago when they invented the world-wide system of bird-banding. In countries with a continuously up-dated population register, it would be feasible (after computerization) to sample paths between dwellings on a very broad scale. Some experiments in that direction have already been made. See Jakobsson[5]. But it would be difficult to dig deeply enough to unveil the really critical events. Similarly, the short-term paths, days and weeks, can be sampled by observation or by some diary method. In either case, one risks becoming lost in a description of how aggregate behavior develops as a sum total of actual individual behavior, without arriving at essential clues toward an understanding of how the system works as a whole. It seems to be more promising to try to define the time-space mechanics of constraints which determine how the paths are channeled or dammed up. Some authors believe that the study of negative determinants might be the safest kind of social science. In the following pages, I am going to look at the matter entirely from the point of view of constraints.

Even if many constraints are formulated as general and abstract rules of behavior we can give them a "physical" shape in terms of location in space, areal extension, and duration in time. Even a universal rule such as "thou shalt not kill," means that a set of configurations of paths are not permitted, except in war and in traffic. It would be impossible to offer a comprehensive taxonomy of constraints seen as time-space phenomena. But three large aggregations of constraints immediately present themselves. The first of these could be tentatively described as "capability constraints," the second as "coupling constraints," and the third as "authority constraints."

"Capability constraints" are those which limit the activities of the individual because of his biological construction and/or the tools he can command. Some have a predominant time orientation, and two circumstances are of overwhelming importance in this connection: the necessity of sleeping a minimum number of hours at regular intervals and the necessity of eating, also with a rather high degree of regularity. Both needs determine the bounds of other activities as continuous operations. Other constraints are predominantly distance oriented, and as a consequence, enable the time-space surrounding of an individual to be divided up into a series of "concentric" tubes or rings of accessibility, the radii of which depend on his ability to move or communicate *and* on the conditions under which he is tied to a rest-place. The inner tube or ring covers the small volume which the individual can reach with his arms from a fixed place such as a position at a machine or desk. It follows him as a shadow when he moves. Two such tubes can never be brought to coincide completely but they have to be close to coincidence for procreation, nursing, and some kinds of playing and fighting. Handtools can enlarge this tube but normally not by very much. Food has somehow to be brought inside the tube at regular intervals.

The second tube is defined by the range of the voice and the eye as combined instruments of communication. The boundary is by no means sharp but it is clear that the convenient spatial size of this entity varies between the normal living room and the assembly hall or its outdoor counterpart, the agora of the Greek city, for example. Historically, this uninstrumented tube has had a tremendous significance for the chosen forms of social, political, military and industrial organization. It was only after the introduction of the loudspeaker that really big outdoor political rallies became practicable. I am sure that we are still far from understanding the locational implications of the next enlargement of the range of this tube (i.e., telecommunications), which have entirely broken up this once so narrow spatial boundary. One hears the most divergent opinions about future possiblities of having television screens substitute for face-to-face meetings around a table. The amount of traveling undertaken by functionaries these days indicates that a break-through in terms of new behavior patterns is still on the waiting list. The two kinds of time-space compartments just mentioned have, to a small extent, been systematically studied by biologists, psychologists, and sociologists. But mostly they have remained the practical concern of architects, engineers, and time-and-motion experts.

The next tube in the hierarchy brings us directly into the business of regional science. People need to have some kind of home base, if only temporary, at which they can rest at regular intervals, keep personal belongings and be reached for receiving messages. And once a place of this sort has been introduced, one can no longer avoid considering more closely how time mixes with space in a non-divisible time-space. Assume that each person needs a regular minimum number of hours a day for sleep and for attending to business at his home base. When he moves away from it, there exists a definite boundary line beyond which he cannot go if he has to return before a deadline. Thus, in his daily life everybody has to exist spatially on an island. Of course, the actual size of the island depends on the available means of transportation, but this does not alter the principle.

Improvements in transport technology have enlarged the size of the island considerably over the centuries. The difference in range between the walker and the motorist is tremendous. For the flyer the entity has been broken up into an archipelago of smaller islands around the airports which are within reach. While in the air, he is imprisoned in a narrow time-space tube without openings and he does not therefore effectively exist in the geographic locations over which he is flying. During the era of more primitive transport technology, the population was nearly homogenous with respect to daily range. Today differences between groups within the same area and differences between areas can be very great. On most days the effective size of an individual's island is much smaller than the potential size which is delineated by his ability to move. The purposes of movement from the home base include going to work, collecting goods, meeting other people, etc. If we look closer at the time-space volume within reach, it turns out to be not a cylinder but a prism. It not only has a geographical boundary; it has time-space walls on all sides. See Fig. 1. Depending on where the stops are located and how long they last, the walls of the prism might change from day to day. However, it is impossible for the individual to appear outside the walls. Every stay at some station means that the remaining prism is shrinking in a certain proportion to the length of the stay. A stay at a work place for eight hours might cause the remaining prism to disappear entirely if the stopping point lies at a maximum distance from the home base. A more normal situation for a week day in a Western society would be one in which the remaining prism breaks up into three portions, one in the morning before work, one at the lunch hour, and one in the evening after work.

Wherever the location and duration of stops inside the daily prism, the path of the individual will always form an unbroken line inside the prism without backward loops. He cannot pass a certain point in time-space more than once but he always has to be at some point. Over a lifetime he steers his path through a string of daily prisms, growing in radius during earlier years of his life and shrinking at an advanced age. Life becomes an astronomically large series of small events, most of which are routine and some of which represent very critical gates.

The path inside the daily prism is to a pronounced degree ruled by

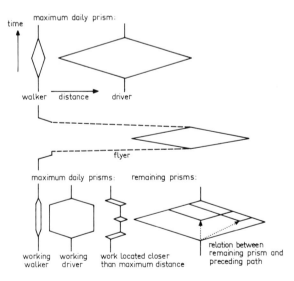

Fig. 1. Daily Prisms

"coupling constraints." These define where, when, and for how long, the individual has to join other individuals, tools, and materials in order to produce, consume and transact. Here, of course, the clock and the calendar are the supreme anti-disorder devices. We may refer to a grouping of several paths as a "bundle." See Fig. 2. In the factory, men, machines, and materials form bundles by which components are connected and disconnected. In the office, similar bundles connect and disconnect information and channel messages. In the shop, the salesmen and the customer form a bundle to transfer articles and in the classroom, students and teachers form a bundle to transfer information and ideas. Bundles are formed according to various principles. Many follow predetermined timetables, often the same, weekday after weekday. This principle, which exists in the factory and the school, generally operates over the head of the participating individual. His freedom lies in his choice of work or place of

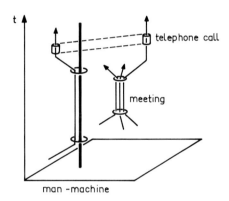

FIG. 2. Grouping of Several Paths

work. After that, he has to obey the choreography of his superior, as long as he wants to maintain this contractual arrangement. The schoolchild, however, does not have the freedom to select in most cases. And always, families have to adjust to compulsory timetables.

Shops, banks, doctors and barbers permit random access between given hours. In many functions, particularly the managerial ones in firms and organizations, bundles have to be formed and located some time in advance in a kind of trial-and-error fashion. Today, hoards of administrators and secretaries spend their regular working hours trying to get other people together for future meetings. The more principles of participation come into fashion, the more this business will expand. Appointments seem to be moving more and more into the future, indicating a growing congestion. A person, who wants great freedom to maneuver, now has to extend his programming ahead by a year to eighteen months. The bundles formed with family members and friends are subject to private administration during the time remaining after outside demands and associated transport requirements. Private administration does not mean that the bundles are entirely outside the general social and legal control.

The bundles tend to be closely interdependent because individuals, materials, and bits of information have to move from one to the other in an orderly way. (The principles of maximum packing would be an interesting area of research related to critical path analysis.) An individual, bound to his home base, can participate only in bundles which have both ends inside his daily prism and which are so located in space that he has time to move from the end of one to the beginning of the following one. This means, for example, that if a doctor holds his clinic during the working hours of his patient, the latter cannot see the doctor except by obtaining permission to be absent from work. It is also clear that the car-owner, because of his random access to transport, has a much greater freedom to combine distant bundles than the person who has to walk or travel by public transportation. The difference is not so much a matter of speed as one of loss of time at terminals and junctions. See Fig. 3.

A further kind of bundle deserves some passing comment. Telecommunication allows people to form bundles without (or nearly without) loss of time in transportation. Radio and television are of interest in this connection mostly because they take time from alternative activities. Everyone can jump on and off the bundle as he likes. But the telephone has a great significance from the point of view of social organization. It is true that a call may save much time, especially when it concerns the arrangement of future meetings. But at the same time, it is an outstanding instrument for breaking other activities. So one may sometimes wonder about the net outcome. In this regard, a world-wide dialing system seems to be a mixed blessing, since all too often people may forget differences in local time around the globe.

The third family of constraints, which I would like to discuss, relates to the time-space aspects of authority. The world is filled with a device which

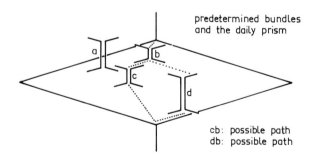

Fig. 3. Interaction of Constraints

we may call the "control area" or "domain". These words are essentially spatial. However, I would suggest that the concept of a domain be redefined to refer to a time-space entity within which things and events are under the control of a given individual or a given group. The purpose of domains (they are almost natural phenomena and many animals have them) seems to be to protect resources, natural as well as artificial, to hold down population density, and to form containers which protect an efficient arrangement of bundles, seen from the inside point of view of the principal. In time-space, domains appear as cylinders the insides of which are either not accessible at all or are accessible only upon invitation or after some kind of payment, ceremony, or fight. Some smaller domains are protected only through immediate power or custom, e.g., a favorite chair, a sand cave on the beach, or a place in a queue. Others, of varying size, have a strong legal status: the home, land property, the premises of a firm or institute, the township, county, state, and nation. Many of these have a long, almost permanent duration, such as nations, British universities, and Japanese companies. Others are only temporary such as a seat in the theater or a telephone booth at the roadside.

Thus, there exists a hierarchy of domains (see Fig. 4) and certain kinds are beyond escape. Those who have access to power in a superior domain frequently use this to restrict the set of possible actions which are permitted inside subordinate domains. Sometimes they can also oblige the subordinate domains to remove constraints or to arrange for certain activities against their will. Decision-makers in domains on equal or nearly equal levels cannot command each other. They have to influence each other by trading, by negotiation, or (in primitive cases) by invasion and warfare. Gaining access to power within a domain is a problem that may be solved in a variety of ways, of which only some are economic in the ordinary sense.

The three aggregations of constraints (i.e., capability, coupling, authority) interact in many ways; in direct obvious ways, and in indirect ways

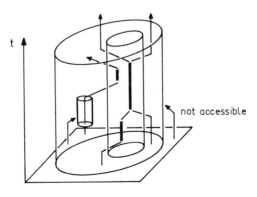

FIG. 4. Hierarchy of Domains

which are less easily detectable. See Fig. 4. A few cases are discussed as illustrations. It is obvious that a low-income job, compared to a higher income job, gives access to fewer or inferior domains. Inability to rent a dwelling close to a place of work may, in the first instance, directly lead to long commuting times but may also lead to more concealed repercussions such as incursions on the time available for other activities. It may well be that the low rate of participation in cultural activities by large groups of people has less to do with the lack of interest than the prohibitive time-space locations of dwelling, work, and cultural activities. Even in nations where medical care is free, considerable numbers of people do not get their intended share. The reasons for this could be similar.

Of special interest in terms of complicated interactions are the dependent members of families. The child has a small daily prism, unless a parent can spend a good deal of the day taking him from place to place. This means that the coverage and quality of the local training establishments and types of social contacts in the neighborhood will have very long-term effects on the life paths, since training as well as friendship ties provide the keys which open or close the gates to domains later in life. In all probability, the manner in which things are arranged for the child also affects the spatial structure of both the population composition and the labor market. Anderson[1] writing on location of residential neighborhoods, points out that, "if more satisfactory arrangements were devised for providing for the children of working mothers, then many larger families now suburban, might move into more central locations."

Important for interregional relations is the birth and death of jobs in relation to the effect of the life-path system on prism distance. First as Self[8] has observed, "It is false to think of regional balance simply in terms of numbers of jobs, when a better index is the *range* of jobs. . . ." Thus, if training and the spectrum of jobs do not match in a given time perspective then the need for migration inevitably arises. Migration, of course, is not necessarily a bad thing, unless it detracts from living standards in the exporting and/or importing areas. The timing of complementary events is also of importance here. One can find cases where there is a balance over the year in the number of new jobs available on one hand, and demand for jobs on the other, and still much out-migration occurs. Job opportunities may arise at times of the year other than exactly when a group of impatient young people are finishing school and are searching for jobs. Similar observations could be made with respect to dwellings. The influence of migration is not confined to the mover and his dependents: there is also an effect on the situation around him. An out-migrant partially breaks up an established network and removes some skills, information and purchasing power. This does not mean that the situation is always made worse by migration. It might improve the situation as would be the case when the remaining population has more elbow room in a formerly crowded rural area. Furthermore, the in-migrant may cause positive or negative external effects. There are surely cases where migration might assume forms which disorganize communities. We know very little, I suppose, about the convenient proportion between the stable and the moving parts of a population.

A society is not made up of a group of people which decides in common what to do a week ahead of time. It consists primarily of highly institutionalized power and activity systems. A majority of domains and bundles within them have a location in space, a duration over time, and a composition according to consciously or habitually preestablished programs of organization which are made up with no particular regard to the individuals who happen to enter these systems and play the needed roles for portions of their life-paths. A company, a university, and a government department are structured according to an arrangement which exists as a time-space pattern, even if the people are not there. The same is true of the multitude of barriers and channels formed by legislation, administration (e.g., taxation), entries to professions, maximum speeds on roads or building codes. In total, seen from the point of view of the individual, this is an enormous maze about which he personally can do very little. Of course, there is a slow response in the system to people's reactions and this means that the set of domains and bundles changes over long periods of time. One might perhaps say that technology, which changes the capability constraints, is the prime mover. Domains and bundles thus change position in time-space. New units are born, existing ones grow in size, dwindle, or die. However, because so many domains have a very strong legal status and consequently, a long life (as for example, units of land ownership or municipal boundaries) and because so much is constrained within buildings having typically long lives, reactions often seem (from a system-wide point of view) local and not very purposeful. It is sufficient to note that despite the new ranges created by improved transportation, local government units have tended to remain medieval in size. A farmstead attitude to the domain problem survives in political life, in strong contrast to the sophisticated conception of space which industry tends to possess.

Viewed in a time-space perspective, then, we have two diverse systems in interaction. One is the predominantly time-directed warp of individual life-paths, which make up the population of an area and the concomitant capability constraints. The other is the more space-oriented set of imposed constraints of domains and bundles to which the individual may or may not have access according to his needs and wants. The population forms a kind of traffic flow in a road net with generally rusty gates. Loose ends of life-paths either have to discover for themselves how to open new roads and domains, locally or after migration into more permissive regions, or they disappear. I think it is true to say that the system of domains is much better understood with respect to flows of goods and money than with respect to flows of people. Social scientists know very little about interactions of constraints, as seen from the point of the life-path of the individual. In the main, people are viewed as parts of activities to be performed within each domain in isolation, and not as entities who need to make sense out of their paths between and through domains. It may well be that the more we, as optimizers, estimate efficiency within domains in the use of bundles of people, machines, materials and information, the more loose ends, which do not know how to move on, will appear in the population flow. Extrapolated to the limits, the question of life-paths between domains has certain strange, even repulsive, aspects. If the transplantion of hearts becomes a standard surgical procedure, then a continued high rate of accidents in traffic and in industry will be necessary to maintain the balance.

When asked about the concept of liveability, people would express very different opinions. Nevertheless, I do not think it would be an entirely impossible task to make up a widely acceptable list of items which are fundamental for survival, comfort, and satisfaction. The individual who saw his life-path as an eighty year scheme, would need those items to be distributed along the time axis in characteristic ways. Thus, to consider the simplest items, it would be necessary or desirable, as the case may be, to have access: to air and a dwelling continuously, to food several times a day, to some daily and weekly recreation, to play and training during early years, to security of work and continuity of education at irregular intervals during a career, to assistance at an advanced age, and at all times random access to means of transportation, relevant information, and medical care. However, access involves much more than the simple juxtaposition of supplies in regions of arbitrary size. It involves a time-space location which really allows the life-path to make the required detours. It further involves the construction of barriers, physical, legal, economic and political, which serve to give to everyone his full share of the fundamental requirement listed. The study of liveability would need a large political science component, but one which does not hesitate to look into the micro-manifestations of power. In this latter area exist the direct links between the macro and micro realms, links which have been largely unexplored by regional scientists. As mentioned before, those who have access to power in domains use much of their energy within their area of competence to superimpose (or sometimes remove) constraints on activities in lower level domains. At least such upper echelons as national, regional, and municipal governments and sometimes big organizations tend to do this in a formalistic way without much understanding in terms of time-space interactions for the population involved. Therefore, even with the best of intentions, outcomes are often questionable.

Given the list of needs and their statistical biography, it would be the task of the analyst to try to find out how much of various kinds of liveability items would be simultaneously attainable under various assumptions of technical, economic and social organization. And since, once born, everybody has to be somewhere, everybody should be included in the picture, the child as well as the entrepreneur. This means, for example, that calculations of the demand for medical care must be seen as a function of the total population's state of health and not as a function of revealed demand. A time-space web model in the sense of a flow of life-paths, controlled by given capabilities and moving through a system of outside constraints which together yield certain probability distributions of situations for individuals, should, in principle, be applicable to all aspects of biology, from plants to animals to men. However, although some animals make buildings, defend domains, and believe in social rank, it is only man who can to a large extent choose between different constraints and, by restricting the number of offspring, even control the size of the population flow. The choice of constraints has always been a very piecemeal affair, more like a natural process than conscious planning. History and cultural anthropology show that it is possible to live under a tremendous variety of constraint systems, even if all have specific drawbacks, as seen from the viewpoint of individual survival and welfare.

The striking drawback of the so-called developed industrial society has been, and perhaps still is, the poverty problem, i.e., the fact that large groups of people have continued to live at the margin of famine or at least below what to people with a sense of fairness seems to be an acceptable standard. Systematic studies of poverty, started in Britain toward the end of the nineteenth century, eventually led to the concept of the Welfare State. Perhaps because of the initial limitations of their goals, even the best conceived versions of the Welfare State are not well prepared to cope with the new forms of poverty problems which are tending to affect everybody, e.g., ugly landscapes, simultaneous overcrowding and loneliness, alienation from crucial decision-making in work and society, etc. It seems that the main focus of our practical problems are moving away from the allocation of money towards the physical allocation of the uses of space and time.

Neurath[7] suggested some decades ago that we should be looking at, "markets and finance and at the whole reckoning in money as an institution like any other, such as funeral rites, golf, rowing, and hunting. To regard money as a historically given institution does not involve any objection to its use — though there may be such objections — but an objection to the application of arguments, valid in the field of higher bookkeeping, to the analysis of social problems and human happiness in general." Now, when looking at the other methodological extreme, we also do not get very far by running around and questioning people about their likes and dislikes. First of all, we need some way of finding out the workings of large socio-environmental mechanisms. To me, a physical approach involving the study of how events occur in a time-space framework is bound to yield results in this regard. In order to be realistic, our models would have to recognize the fact that the individual is indivisble and that his time is limited. Further, we would have to note that the individual in dealing with space not only considers distance, but also has a strong (and perhaps logically necessary) drive towards organizing space in sharply bounded territories.

It was said before that the choice of constraints has always been a piecemeal affair. Even in theoretical studies, social scientists have tended to take most of them for granted according to available experience. With a suitable technique for grouping constraints in time-space terms, one could perhaps hope to be able to boil down their seemingly tremendous variety into a tractable number. Simulation comes to mind as a way of analysis until more general mathematical tools become available. Reasonably good simulations should improve our ability to survey whole systems and help to reduce the considerable trial and error component in applications. A purely theoretical, even artistic, satisfaction for the regional scientist would then be the ability to invent entirely fictitious societies which were still founded on realistic first principles. The technological forecasts which edify us these days and often seem so promising, at least superficially, cry out for instruments which could help us to judge the impacts on social organization and thereby the impact on the ordinary day of the ordinary person.

Notes

1. T. R. Anderson (1962) Social and Economic Factors Affecting the Location of Residential Neighborhoods, *Papers and Proceedings of the Regional Science Association*, **9**, pp 161–170.
2. K. A. Fox and T. K. Kumar (1965) The Functional Economic Area: Delineation and Implications for Economic Analysis and Policy, *Papers of the Regional Science Association*, **15**, pp. 57–85.
3. B. Harris (1967) The City of the Future: the Problem of Optimal Design, *Papers of the Regional Science Association*, **19**, pp. 185–195.
4. W. Isard and T. A. Reiner (1966) Regional Science: Retrospect and Prospect, *Papers of the Regional Science Association*, **16**, pp 1–16.
5. A. Jakobsson (1969) Omflyttningen i Sverige 1950–1960, *Meddelanden från Lunds Universitets Geografiska Institution*, Avhandlingar 59.
6. I. S. Lowry (1967) Comments on Britton Harris [3], *Papers of the Regional Science Association*, **19**, pp 197–198.
7. O. Neurath (1944) Foundations of the Social Sciences, *International Encyclopedia of Unified Science*, **2**, No. 1. Chicago: University of Chicago Press.
8. P. Self (June 1968) "Regions: the Missing Link," *Town and Country Planning*, **36**, pp 282–283.
9. J. Q. Stewart (1958) Discussion: Population Projection by Means of Income Potential Models, *Papers and Proceedings of the Regional Science Association*, **4**, pp 153–154.
10. E. L. Ullman (1962) The Nature of Cities Reconsidered, *Papers and Proceedings of the Regional Science Association*, **9**, pp 7–23.
11. R. Vining (1964) An Outline of a Stochastic Model for the Study of the Spatial Structure and Development of a Human Population System, *Papers of the Regional Science Association*, **13**, pp 15–40.

Not a Carborne Democracy*

MAYER HILLMAN

There follows an edited and up-dated version of evidence given to the House of Commons Expenditure Committee (Environment and Home Office Sub-Committee) on Urban Transport Planning. The Committee wished to discover whether Government spending programmes are geared to achieving any particular balance between public transport and private car use in the larger conurbations; if so, whether the balance is the right one; and if not, how patterns of behaviour could be influenced to achieve the right balance. It heard evidence and cross-examined *inter alia* the Secretary of State for the Environment, DoE witnesses, planning chiefs in the conurbations, and professional consultants. (The Committee's report based on this evidence was published last year).

The social, physical and economic fabric of Britain has evolved substantially in the last quarter of a century, in response to the considerable increase in personal mobility that motor technology, transport planning and affluence have made possible.

The principal contributory cause has been the car, which has greatly widened its owner's freedom of choice of home and job location, and opportunities for leisure pursuits and holidays. At the same time, it has made possible the construction of dwellings in areas with poor public transport; industry has been able to draw upon labour from more extensive pools; and private and public facilities have been able to achieve economies of scale and provide greater choice and specialized functions by serving larger population catchments.

There is a growing understanding, however, of the implications of these changes, and an awareness of the high price that society has had to pay for them.

Indeed a causal relationship between the rise in traffic volumes and these concomitant unquantifiable costs can be recognized: the high incidence of road casualties (nearly one million people killed or seriously injured on British roads in the last 10 years); the pervasive disamenities of blight, noise and air pollution (the Road Research Laboratory calculated that, in 1970, 20 per cent of the population were exposed to undesirably high traffic

Built Environment, July, 1974, pp 342–44. Reprinted by permission of the publisher, Alexandrine Press.

noise); the increasing road congestion in off-peak as well as peak hours; the major rehousing programmes directly stemming from costly roadworks and motorway construction (and the consequential disruptive effects on communities); the impact of commuting on urban residential and working environments; the health hazards of a motorized society; the anti-social behaviour often associated with driving; the decline of the street as a functional locus for social interaction; and the incentive to devote a growing proportion of household expenditure for transport purposes (it is now over one and a half times what it was 10 years ago).

These considerations arise mainly from the construction and use of roads. But there are wider social issues concerned with personal mobility and accessibility; these latter aspects play a major role in determining an individual's field of opportunities. Increasing evidence shows them to have a strong influence on patterns of behaviour. This memorandum focuses on issues as they are likely to become more rather than less important with time, and as they are factors to which present planning policy and practice pay scant attention.

To some extent, difficulties in modern transport planning stem from historical circumstances. In earlier decades, when by present standards there was an abundance of road space for the traffic being carried, and when there was therefore less competition for that road space than there is today, transport planning was largely the concern of the highway engineer, whose preoccupations with cambers, roundabout diameters and vehicle flows were justified. As the volume of traffic on the roads rose and as the scale of the exercise in urban areas was recognized, so a switch had to be made from attempting to accommodate the unrestricted use of vehicles to distributing and regulating it. As a result, the more sophisticated approach of transportation studies evolved; the development of mathematical models for traffic prediction, of management measures (parking control and one-way systems), and of the application of technical innovations (computer controlled traffic flows, etc).

Now however too much is being asked of transportation planners; their goals and methods do not lend themselves to the adjudication of conflict, the judgement of environmental quality, or the solution of social problems. Indeed, they have been able to proceed with their work only by making the simplifying and distorting assumptions which pervade transport planning. These assumptions are examined under four headings:

(i)   the synonymity of the movement of people and vehicles
(ii)   the universality of car ownership
(iii) the availability of the household car to members of the household
(iv)   the existence of a balance between public and private transport.

The Synonymity Movement and Vehicles

Transportation studies have to date mainly ignored the needs of people to move about and have instead dealt with the movement of vehicles, focusing especially on traffic flows and road usage. The consequences of this are an allocation of resources between private and public transport consistently favouring the former; a disregard of pedestrian journeys and the resultant diminution of the quality and convenience of the pedestrian environment; a disinterest in methods of transport which provide alternative, and for most people critical, ways of getting around (between one-third and one-half of all journeys are made on foot). On this last point, when current planning proposals do include a degree of pedestrianization, they appear to remove walking from consideration as a method of travel, and accord it the function of a "trip end" to be enjoyed within the safety of a precinct which can only be conveniently reached by motorized means.

Universal Car Ownership

A futher assumption made by transport planners is that everyone has a car, or soon will have. Even if "everyone" is taken to mean every household, universal ownership is inconceivable (in the United States, 20 per cent of households are without cars). At the present time about 45 per cent of British households have no car. Moreover, ownership is very unevenly distributed being concentrated in the upper, middle and youthful social strata. Employers' households are more than twice as likely to be car-owning as skilled manual workers, which in turn are more than twice as likely to be car-owning as those of unskilled manual workers. Only about one in ten of elderly persons' households are car-owning[1].

If on the other hand "everyone" is taken to mean people, it is patently obvious that every person cannot have a car and, equally, that most people never will have one. This is simply because the optional use of a car is dependent upon three pre-requisites; adequate age and income and ability to hold a licence and run a car. As a result, the slight car-owning majority, in terms of housholds, becomes a small minority when individuals are considered. The number of persons with exclusive use of a car is less than a quarter of the total population. Official forecasts of future car ownership, of doubtful reliability in the face of current concerns on environmental road capacity and natural resource problems[2], show that by the year 2000, well over half the population will be without the optional use of a car.

The prevalence of this false belief in car ownership can be inferred from the following:

"Before very long, a majority of the electors in the country will be car-owners[3]."
"Without doubt, in 15 to 20 years time, the majority of the travelling public will want to use their own private transport[4]".
" . . . to devise an urban structure which . . . needs to be extendable to accommodate almost universal car ownership[5]."
"In the 40s, planners saw no reason to believe that the motor-car would become the universal possession[6]."

"We have a generation growing up which will expect, in the majority of cases, to have private cars and they will want to use private cars . . .[7]".

Household Car Use

Even in a car-owning household it cannot be assumed that the car meets the mobility needs of all its members. This assumption is often implicit in transportation planning practice, though several studies throw considerable doubt on it. Firstly, only some members of a car-owning household have access to the family car for their own use. Those with driving licences are, in theory, all members over 17 years, but in practice is usually the male householder; 60 per cent of men have driving licences, compared with only 20 per cent of women. For other members a licence-holder must act as chauffeur. Secondly, by means of data on car occupancy rates, the extent to which the mobility needs of household members overlap can be seen. For leisure purposes, the average occupancy rate is less than two people compared to the average household size of three. The third and most important source of information is survey data on the extent of car use by members of car-owning households. A survey in Stevenage recorded that about half the trips in one-car households and a quarter of trips in two-car households were made by bus or on foot, and moreover, 90 per cent of teenagers' trips were made unaccompanied by another member of their household[8]. A survey in Sunderland showed that only a fifth of the housewives in car-owning households used the car for shopping[9]. The dependence of car-owning households on means other than the car is also demonstrated by data in the Family Expenditure Survey which shows that expenditure on bus fares is about half that in non car-owning households.

Thus people in households live fairly independent lives, and although this varies with social class, the household acts as a unit for a relatively small number of the total journeys made by its members. There is clearly a continuing necessity to provide public transport for people, in both non car-owning and car-owning households, for those who cannot conveniently walk to their destinations.

The pervasiveness of this particular myth, of household car use can be seen in the following quotations:

"The automobile has freed the family . . .[10]".
"Public transport must be provided for the people unable to use cars, although they are relatively few in number.[11]".
"Britain will be a nation of car owners with about eight families out of ten running at least one vehicle[12]."

Although current transportation planning appears to be based on these mistaken assumptions, it must yet be shown that their acceptance has resulted in bad planning, for it is quite possible to arrive at the right answer for the wrong reasons. The use of these assumptions in arriving at both the concept of "balance" between private and public transport and its effectuation clearly demonstrates however that distorting planning decisions are made.

Balance between Public and Private Transport

The assumption of balance does not, like those above, have to do with people and how they get about, but with the characteristics of travel methods, and their interactive effects upon one another. Planners have recognized that public transport vehicles and private cars make different and inherently conflicting demands on urban structure and that techniques must be developed to resolve this conflict. But it has been presumed that the spending of sufficient money can resolve the differences between them in a "balanced way". It would appear from current proposals that such a solution is based on assumptions which favour the car. Insufficient account is taken of the dependence of the majority of the population on a public transport system which is declining in convenience as fast as its fares are rising. For instance, as the number of cars on urban streets has increased, and congestion has slowed traffic speeds on bus routes, the efficiency and economic viability of the bus system has been reduced. Furthermore, the existence of pedestrians has been ignored except when, by reason of their numbers, they interfere with traffic flows.

The long-term influence of rising vehicle use on cycle and pedestrian movement, and management measures to cope with the conflct between these and the motor may not be appreciated, for people's use of them is rarely admitted. The fact is overlooked that everyone capable of getting about is partly a pedestrian, and that even excluding the "trip ends" of motorized journeys, about half of all trips are made on foot. Consequently the amenity and convenience of the pedestrian movement system has diminished. The pedestrian is exposed to more noise and pollution, and roads are more difficult and dangerous to cross.

Thus, through the interactive effects of one mode on another, a steadily widening gap has been created between the level of mobility of those with and without access to a car. The assumption that a balance can be achieved is reinforced by the mistaken yet pervasive belief in political and planning circles, that people can exercise a choice as to whether they travel by car or public transport. In fact, for those with a car there is no real choice, as the car is, in the absence of restraints, preferable to other modes[13]. Indeed, it is thought that conductors would have to hand out money to persuade car owners to travel by public transport. For those without a car there is no choice except for distances of about a mile when there may be a realistic choice between public transport and walking.

Everyone is affected by the present situation. For instance, 20 years ago children could usually cycle around and explore as far as they wished or their energies permitted. Nowadays few parents will allow children to use their bicycles on the roads. As a result their journeys are much more circumscribed largely for reasons of safety[14]. A recent survey in the Outer Metropolitan Area has found that about half the mothers of primary schoolchildren accompany them to and from school every morning and afternoon of the school term[15]. Constraints on adolescents typically growing up in postwar low density suburbs are also increasing since their preference for leading lives separate from their parents makes them largely dependent upon expensive public transport services operating infrequently outside the rush hour. Housewives without their own car are also dependent on these services: those that have the use of a car often find that much of their time is spent as a chauffeur for other members of the family. The behaviour of elderly persons is particularly sensitive to the quality of both public transport and pedestrian environment as their capabilities decline and considerations of comfort and cost loom larger. People in low income households are, of course, the most deprived for their constraints are compounded by concern for the cost of travel. Their low level of mobility can combine with and reinforce their other disadvantages.

Apart from these consequences, further disruption to the urban environment can occur through the creation of road hierarchies, environmental areas and pedestrian precincts which once again stem from a preoccupation with traffic volumes[16]. For instance, Colin Buchanan stated in *Traffic in Towns* that "the amount of traffic to be planned for . . . (is) likely to be controlled *not* by what might be needed within the area itself, but by what could be practically contrived in the way of a network to bring traffic to and from the area". Whilst one cannot show that these changes will have disastrous social consequences, the fact that he recommended the sizes and shapes of environmental areas to be delineated *solely* according to traffic considerations suggests that the social impact would be unforeseen and unplanned for.

In addition to the interactive effect of one mode on another, the assumption of balance does not really come to grips with the fact that an urban form suitable for cars directly conflicts with that suited for a public transport service. The car-orientated form of the new city of Milton Keynes is characterized[17] by the dispersal of facilities through a low density grid-network, while the public transport form requires a large measure of centralization of facilities combined with higher densities. With the car as the focus of attention, the separation of facilities occurs and decreasing residential densities render local facilities inefficient or uneconomic, and their provision within walking distance impractical. Indeed the debate on hypermarkets has raised the issue of the repercussions of their operation on town centres and corner shops more accessible to non car-owners[18]. Their development has put additional demands on the transport system, induced people with cars to use them more frequently and further aggravated the problems of accessibility of those without cars.

Most transportation plans have thus dealt with problems of personal mobility on the basis of a number of untenable assumptions about transport realities and thus made predictions about future levels of traffic. But these too are open to question, as population forecasts for Britain for the year 2000 have dropped by 12.6 million in the last 9 years! Moreover, techniques for predicting car ownership and usage rest on the propensity of individuals to acquire cars at various future income levels, whilst not taking account of the fact that approximately half the new cars registered are bought by companies[19]. Thus the propensity of companies to buy cars is of equal importance; but it is quite possible that the substantial tax concessions enjoyed by the users of company cars may be withdrawn, or the law tightened to preclude this growing influence.

Perhaps the most disturbing aspect of transportation planners' methods is that their techniques are focused on the problems caused by peak hour traffic. The determination of a modal split is as a function of the existing capacity of the road network, and the adequacy of funds to increase it so as to accommodate with the minimum of restraint the projected traffic of the next 10 to 15 years. It could be observed that the primary problems in transport are to reduce road accidents dramatically, and to enable people with difficulties in mobility, mothers with young children, elderly and disabled people, to get around more easily.

In the cost-benefit techniques employed for analysing alternative transport strategies, social costs are measured within a narrow framework, and an inegalitarian policy is adopted whereby different values of time are assigned to different travellers. Bus users' travel time is valued at half that of car users', and pedestrians' at half that of vehicle occupants, children's time is valued at a third that of adults', while the latter's working time is given six times the value of their non-working time[20]. In addition compensation for injurious disturbance due to road building varies according to the rateable value of the affected property and thereby according to the socio-economic circumstances of the affected household.

Children are generally not recognized as people with perhaps independent lives to lead. The DoE has instructed Local Authorities not to include children below secondary school age in traffic counts taken to establish the need for pedestrian crossings, and one of the grounds on which a previous GLC administration objected to the extension of a reduced fares policy for schoolchildren travelling by bus was that it would encourage them to use an already overloaded system.

It is not surprising that, with these questionable methods and techniques for assessing transport proposals the outcome is distorted in favour of car-orientated solutions involving ever-increasing investment in road construction and so-called road improvements. This is all the more disturbing as these solutions are short-term with present transport policies, as demand catches up with and eventually exceeds the capacity of most roads built to accommodate it. At the same time, the increased capacity generates additional traffic and compounds the problem.

Conclusions

The achievement of a correct balance in transport planning is unlikely to come about, without a reappraisal of goals and objectives. In future, the field must be dominated by social considerations, with the issue of road accident prevention paramount, for the daily deaths and injuries of men, women and children are sufficient indictment in themselves of present transport policies. Next the scarce resources of space and funds according to principles of equity and economic efficiency, for while it is impossible to achieve a technical balance between modes and urban forms, it is both possible and necessary for a social balance to be achieved between people and their need for travel. It is essential that, in the long term, planning measures are devised to solve these problems, which are both political and technical.

Transport planning, therefore, should be concerned not with traffic needs but with movement needs. It should aim at how best these can be met in the public interest, and include analyses of the effects of alternative plans on the ability of everyone to get around. This requires the development of new techniques for transport planning: the examination of the travel needs of all household members irrespective of age; the inclusion of all movement irrespective of method; and the coverage of all journey purposes irrespective of impact on the road system. Additionally, the relationship of urban form, facility distribution and land use characteristics, and the relationship of scale to the generation of motorized traffic must be the subject of equally detailed investigations, for transport is not an end in itself but principally the connection between different land uses.

In the short term, however, the principles of equity and economic efficiency may be immediately applied in the sharing out of the available travel space. Such a solution requires: priority to be given to pedestrians; preference to be given to cyclists and public transport in the use of road space; transport planning to be integrated with land use planning in such a way that the need and incentive for travel by car is deliberately reduced. These principles are intended only as guidelines, for much more research into the social reality associated with accessibility and transport must be undertaken to provide clearer goals for future transport planning.

Nevertheless, the suggestions outlined above already serve the postulated principles. They have the advantage in requiring only a reallocation of present road space and not the massive expenditure and social costs

involved in major urban road construction. They provide further economies by virtue of the fact that public transport is flexible while investment
in roads is not. They do not depend on romantic visions of a new and
expensive technology for intra-urban transport and they result in accident
reduction. Finally, they minimize the differences between the attractions
of the different methods of travel and thereby reduce the polarization of
opportunities stemming from the widening gap between individuals'
personal mobility.

But their implementations requires a considerable political initiative.

Postscript

Since the above memorandum was written, my colleagues at PEP, Irwin Henderson, Anne
Whalley and I have been egaged in further research on personal mobility and accessibility.
Some of this work was published in *Personal Mobility and Transport Policy* (Political and
Economic Planning, 1973), and final report being prepared for publication. We interpret the
surveys which we have carried out over the last two years as reinforcing the conclusions of the
memorandum.

Notes

1. Unpublished data from the *National Travel Survey*. 1972–73.
2. A. H. Tulpule (1973). *Forecasts of Vehicles and Traffic in Great Britain*. 1972 Revision,
   DoE: Road Research Laboratory Report LR 543, p. 6.
3. Report of Steering Group (1963). *Traffic in Towns*. HMSO, para 9.
4. Ministry of Transport (1967). *Public Transport and Traffic*. Cmnd 3481, HMSO, p. 113.
5. Clifford Culpin and Partners (1968). *Mosbrough Master Plan: Interim Report*. Sheffield
   City Council.
6. Greater London Council (c1969). *Tomorrow's London*. p. 63.
7. J. D. W. Janes, Minutes of evidence taken before the Expenditure Committtee, para 49,
   29/1/72.
8. Mayer Hillman (1970). *Mobility in New Towns*. PhD dissertation, University of
   Edinburgh.
9. Sunderland Corporation (1971). *The Sunderland Hypermarket Survey*. p. 11.
10. Alan Vorhees (1962). Factors affecting growth in American cities, in T. H. Williams and
    D. Munby (ed). *Urban Survival and Traffic: Economics of City Traffic*. E & M Spon.
11. Arthur Ling and Associates (1967). *Runcorn New Town*. Runcorn Development
    Corporation.
12. A. J. Flowerdew (1969). *International Road Traffic Conference*.
13. Mayer Hillman, Irwin Henderson and Anne Whalley (1973). *Personal Mobility and
    Transport Policy*. Political and Economic Planning Broadsheet No. 542, Chapter 2.
14. Mayer Hillman, Irwin Henderson and Anne Whalley (May 1973). Unfreedom road,
    New Society. pp. 75–77.
15. As yet unpublished findings of travel surveys carried out by Political and Economic
    Planning (PEP).
16. Mayer Hillman and Irwing Henderson (12 July 1973). Towards a better kind of
    environmental area, *New Society*. pp. 75–77.
17. Mayer Hillman and Anne Whalley (August 1973). The disadvantaged of Milton Keynes.
    Architectural Design. pp. 540–41.
18. Mayer Hillman (February 1973). The Social Costs of Hypermarket Developments, *Built
    Environment*. pp. 89–91.

19. Greater London Council: Letter from Joint Director of Surveys of National Population, 12/1a.
20. R. F. F. Dawson (1969). *The Value of Time Saving in Transport Investment.* unpublished Technical Note 3.

Mobility Constraints of the Carless*

K. C. KOUTSOPOULOS and C. G. SCHMIDT

This article examines the urban mobility needs of carless households as a distinct population subgroup. Underlying this discussion is the belief that effective transportation policies can be derived by directing research investigations toward the study of this population grouping, which is homogeneous according to one or more structural or functional characteristics. While there is disagreement as to whether the carless represent a distinct minority group, it is clear that despite their diversity, the majority of carless households do possess common mobility attributes and mobility problems. This study provides some insight into the nature of the vehicular-environmental interaction of the carless population; that is, the relationship between carless urban residents and the various mobility constraints presented by the metropolitan environment. Although much attention has been directed toward the needs of the poor and the ghetto resident, little research is available concerning the policy implications of the mobility needs of carless households.

The Carless Population

Many transportation planners have noted that cities in all parts of the world are struggling to achieve some acceptable standard of mobility. Even where automobile ownership is low, modern and traditional means of transportation combine to create chaos and congestion not unlike that familiar to the American commuter.[1] Yet, while the commuter crisis may not be uniquely American, there are transportation problems that occur in a specifically American form, reflecting the particular American experience with race, poverty, and limited access to an automobile.

Since the end of World War II, the predominance of the private automobile as the preferred means of travel and the growth of suburbia as a preferred dwelling pattern have resulted in the concentration of low-income, elderly, and other carless households in the core areas of the

*Traffic Quarterly, 1975, pp 67–84. Reprinted by permission of the Eno Foundation for Transportation, Inc.

nation's cities. At the same time a growing trend toward dispersal of employment opportunities, particularly in the unskilled and semiskilled categories, is contributing to a special mismatch of carless residential areas and location of available jobs. In addition, recreational, educational, and cultural activities have increasingly dispersed to follow the residential population.

Barriers resulting from the increasing distances between carless inner city residents and decentralizing recreational, shopping and workplace locations have created a severe mobility problem. For these people urban transportation represents a tremendous obstacle:

> The person who for a variety of reasons has no car is increasingly barred . . . from what the city has to offer. Because urban growth assumes the availability of private cars, everything becomes increasingly difficult to reach by other means. . . . While there are many people who depend on transit for their mobility, they are too few to support a transit system extensive enough to provide anything approaching the mobility that other members of the community have.[2]

The members of the metropolitan community who do not have access to an automobile, because of social, economic, and physical constraints, are defined here as the urban carless population. This group of people who are totally dependent on others for transportation includes (1) the elderly who cannot or choose not to drive; (2) the young who are not of age or do not have access to private transportation; (3) the poor who cannot afford an automobile; and (4) the handicapped who do not possess the physical capabilities necessary to operate a vehicle. The factors that affect the travel behavior of the carless are numerous, complex, and interrelated. Yet it is imperative that they be identified and understood.

Within an urban transportation setting there are two inter-dependent and conflicting sources of travel variability, people and their environment, that operate simultaneously in forming what is called *travel behavior*. Accordingly, if all factors that contribute to the observed variations in travel behaviour of the carless groups are to be accounted for, the barriers imposed by both sources should be analyzed in detail.

It was noted that the carless household, defined by the lack of access to the automobile, can be best described in terms of their mobility constraints. Consequently all constraints associated with the carless groups themselves and their environments must be identified and evaluated. Despite the shortcoming encountered in any classification system, a simple classification scheme is proposed here in order to account for the major constraints impeding mobility in the carless population. Mobility constraints can be divided into two major categories: trip-making and environmental constraints.

Trip-making Constraints

Millions of Americans suffer from one or a combination of several physical or mental disabilities, as well as socioeconomic restrictions, that adversely influence their spatial behavior. In addition to limiting employment, social, educational, and recreational opportunities, such constraints restrict the extent to which these persons are able to be productive members of society. Trip-making constraints are those physical, mental, and socioeconomic limitations that relate to the carless population's inability to generate a vehicular trip, by prohibiting a household from owning or operating an automobile and restricting their use of mass services (see Fig. 1).

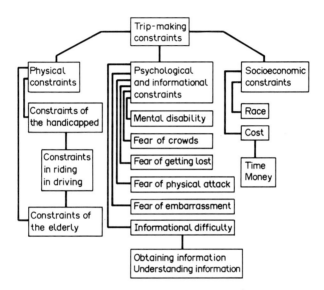

FIG. 1. Trip-making constraints for the carless

Physical Constraints

Physical constraints greatly affect the travel and transportation behavior of two groups of the carless population — the handicapped and the elderly. As defined by the Urban Mass Transportation Act of 1964, a handicapped person is "any individual who, by reason of illness, injury, age, congenital malfunction, or other permanent or temporary incapacity or disability, is unable without special facilities or special planning or design to utilize transportation facilities as effectively as persons who are not so affected."[3] The elderly are defined as individuals 65 years of age or older.

Physical conditions that are likely to reduce mobility and affect automobile and transit usage for these persons can be grouped under three major categories.

1. *Ambulatory limitations* have to do with the impairment or limitations that reduce or preclude walking and standing.

2. *Vision and hearing limitations* have to do with the impairment or loss of vision and hearing that hinder communication and prevent perception of visual and auditory cues essential to automobile and transit usage.

3. *Motor limitations* have to do with impairment or loss of motor skills.

The average person has sufficient difficulty traveling in urban areas to create a problem commanding national attention. How much greater must be the difficulty of the handicapped. Consider the range of mobility problems for those with physical disabilities, such as the arthritic, the blind, those confined in wheelchairs, and those utilizing prosthetic limbs or mechanical walking aids. For these people, one of the greatest impediments to mobility is the prevalence of stairs and steps. Our urban environment has a strong vertical component to which most people adapt easily. For those with physical disabilities, the environment is inherently horizontal. In short, urban environments are designed with little attention to people with handicaps, and as a result their mobility is severely restricted.

One or a combination of physical limitations prevents many handicapped persons from driving an automobile. But even an individual who can obtain a driver's license faces yet another constraint. Commercial shopping or health centers often are large and sprawling, covering many acres. Their parking lots, at considerable distance from the centers' activities, can represent a severe problem to the driver who has ambulatory difficulties. This is because the individual must cover a considerable distance between the parked car and the actual destination.

Not all handicapped persons are unable to use buses. But the inability to perform one or more of the required physical operations prevents a large group from riding them, and difficulty in meeting the physical requirements makes bus travel laborious for an even larger group. Furthermore, using a bus is more complicated during inclement weather or when mechanical aids must be utilized.

Transportation services are important to all population groups, but in the case of the elderly, lack of adequate transportation can have a more deleterious effect than the loss of the transportation service alone.

> Transportation has a . . . "multiplier" effect. With it, a couple or single person can more easily cope with adjustments or hardships that come with age. Without it, they may enter into what has been described as a "syndrome of deprivation."[5]

In recent years there has been considerable testimony that in many urban areas, poor transportation service has had an important adverse effect on the quality of life for the elderly. It has led to social isolation and has kept some persons from regular access to even minimal life-sustaining functions. Recently the Special Committee on Aging of the US Senate declared that the transportation difficulties encountered by many elderly citizens have already reached the crisis stage.[6]

Advanced age is often accompanied by lessened sensory capacity, coordination difficulties, and a more selective perception of the environment, making the reaction or response time of elderly drivers slower. For these reasons the elderly may lose confidence in their ability to drive and therefore may limit their driving to certain times of the day or may avoid driving altogether.

The elderly, like the handicapped who depend on public transportation, must endure certain other difficulties. In nonrush-hour traffic periods, when transit service is severely limited, long waits can expose the elderly to weather conditions that may endanger their health. If they wish to travel during the rush hours, they must endure pushing or crowding and the constant stop-and-go lurching of the vehicle. Moreover, many elderly persons have difficulty in utilizing transit services because of the unfavorable design of transit vehicles.

Psychological and Informational Constraints

Mental disabilities are responsible for the institutionalization of millions of persons and are serious mobility barriers for others who are not in institutions but are unable to travel alone. Mild mental limitations may prohibit individuals from owning or operating an automobile and force them to rely on mass transit or vehicles operated by others. Serious mental disabilities affect even the capacity to perform the simple actions required for mass transit usage.

Carless people often face perceptual barriers that inhibit their use of mass transit. Anxiety, apprehension, fear — these emotions act as constraints on mass transit use and cause many carless persons to avoid travel altogether. The following are among the most important perceptual constraints.

1. Fear of crowds affects many carless persons. Some are made nervous by crowds or are anxious about the rudeness sometimes demonstrated by crowds. The handicapped are fearful because crowds force them to function faster than their comfortable rate.

2. Fear of getting lost is a serious mobility constraint for the young, elderly, and handicapped because they lack confidence in themselves. But this problem affects all transit riders when the exact location of the destination is unknown.

3. Fear of physical attack while waiting for or riding in public transportation vehicles has been noted in many surveys as a serious concern of bus riders. This fear makes carless persons avoid using mass transit, particularly at night.

4. Fear of embarrassment stemming from the impatience of other riders is not a significant barrier to most transit riders, but some individuals are

disturbed about the actions and attitudes of other passengers toward them.[7]

Carless potential transit passengers may also have difficulty in unraveling the macrostructure of the public transit service. Their notion of the complexity or simplicity of the transit system is related to their perception of "how difficult it is to use the system".[8] One kind of difficult system requires persons to transfer frequently and/or inconveniently.

Carless persons often have difficulty in obtaining information about public transportation, and as a result many avoid mass transit use. The most frequently used informational sources are bus drivers and telephone information services. However, complaints are common about difficulty in obtaining a telephone response as well as in obtaining information from drivers. Moreover, certain of the handicapped, elderly, and illiterate are unable to make themselves understood well enough to solicit information.

Maps are widely used to illustrate routes and schedules, but they may be too complex for many people to read and understand. Signs are not the same in every transportation district and may not be standardized even within the same district. What is more, signs may not have sufficient information or may not be posted at every stop, which adds barriers for mass transit users.

Socioeconomic Constraints

Geographers, economists, and planners have noted the conflict between suburban and central transportation needs:

> When, for understandable reasons, the rest of us — the nation's suburban majority — decide to improve transportation facilities into, outside, and within the city, it further displaces the already displaced; makes less secure those already insecure; further depletes the already depleted housing supply; further inflates the already inflated cost of shelter; further diminishes the already diminishing tax base; makes easier the exodus of those fortunate who already have too easy an escape; further breaks up neighborhoods already disrupted; drives out businesses, the small shops and services that are already operating too close to the margin.[9]

The socioeconomically disadvantaged groups must attempt to utilize transportation systems built in response to the needs of the urban and suburban majorities. Because of the limitations imposed on them by their inability to afford better transportation and housing, they are forced to use expensive private transportation in emergencies and to severely limit their travel behavior at other times. These socioeconomic limitations represent major mobility constraints for the poor, elderly and handicapped.

Mobility constraints of any journey within a metropolitan area can be measured in terms of travel costs. But the cost of travel is itself complex, involving monetary expenditure, time, inconvenience, discomfort, effort, and exposure.

Commuting time clearly must be considered part of the working day or part of shopping expenses. But the travel time of the carless is longer than that of car owners. Myers, in comparing the time requirements for buses and automobiles, wrote: "Even when bus users are traveling in the same direction as the mainstream of traffic, they must spend just about twice as much time going between the same two points as auto users."[10] In a recent study by Federico, user costs were estimated to be $2.82 per hour.[11] Even at this low rate, a transit rider who travels for most of an hour at a cost under half a dollar has paid far more in time than in money for the trip. Even for the carless, to whom dollar cost may be considerably more important, this situation is very likely to restrict their travel activities.

An analysis undertaken by the Federal Highway Administration found that the income of carless families and individuals is roughly three-fifths the income of car owners.[12] In addition, testimony during Senate hearings in 1971 revealed that the income of older families is approximately half that of their younger counterparts.[13] The same picture emerged when income comparisons were made between blacks and whites and between those who are handicapped and those who are not. Furthermore, it was reported that transportation takes an average of 9 cents out of every dollar of income and is the third highest expense for elderly Americans.[14] Analogous figures have been presented for handicapped, blacks, and other carless groups. Clearly, there is considerable evidence that carless households and individuals experience high transportation costs which, when coupled with low incomes, represents yet another considerable economic and mobility constraint.

The role of public transportation has been changing in the United States over the last 60 years. What was once an essential public service has increasingly become a mode for poor and carless people in an automobile-oriented age. As a result, public transportation planning today in many urban areas involves certain welfare considerations that were not present 60 years ago. The question with regard to racial discrimination is not just whether fares, service levels, or costs along routes are equal for black and white neighborhoods.[15] Rather, it should relate to whether minority groups, the poor, the elderly, the handicapped, and others who depend on public transportation have adequate service: "is the present in-kind income transfer of public transit sufficient to meet society's view of a minimum level of mobility?"[16]

Environmental Constraints

A transportation problem exists when a person is available to work or needs to undertake a shopping, health, or recreational trip but the external or environmental difficulties are so great that they prevent the activity–customer linkage from taking place. Environmental constraints are limitations imposed upon the carless by the physical and social environment in which they live (see Fig. 2).

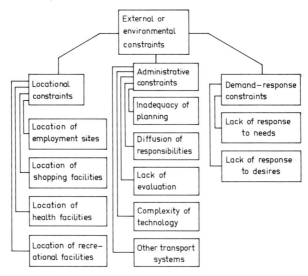

FIG. 2. Environmental constraints for the carless

Locational Constraints

The quality of a location in relation to jobs, or any other element of urban life, is measured in terms of opportunities available. If opportunities are not present in a certain location, or the means to reach them are not provided, barriers to the mobility of its residents are evident. These constraints have to do with a carless household's location and are therefore termed locational constraints.

In most metropolitan areas, the existing transportation network, both highway and mass transit, tends to be radially oriented, focusing on the central business district (CBD). Despite what has been said about the effects of congestion on the speed of movement into and out of the CBD or about the lack of comfort and convenience of mass transit services, the fact remains that transportation improvements have been oriented toward better accessibility to the CBD. This emphasis on access to CBD has allowed only minimal recognition of the appreciable proportion of new manufacturing plants and retail trade centers being constructed in the suburbs. The CBD and its contiguous zones are declining, in relative and absolute importance, as a source of trade and manufacturing employment.

This change in the spatial distribution of employment sites has given rise to new requirements for movement. Two significant types of work trips associated with the new locational patterns are emerging as important constraints for the carless population — reverse commuting and lateral or circumferential movement. Neither the travel demands from central areas to the periphery nor the pattern of lateral movement is adequately served by existing transport facilities in metropolitan areas. As a result while travel to central locations is to some extent possible for the carless group, the transportation services offered virtually preclude reverse commuting or lateral movement.

Urban transportation systems should provide all city residents with adequate mobility or access not only to employment sites but also to shopping, health and recreational facilities. On this basis the major transit difficulty confronting the carless may be conceptualized in terms of the absence of public transit not merely to employment opportunities but to the other important urban facilities as well.[17]

Since World War II a continual shift has occurred in the pattern of retail business location in US cities. Chain supermarkets, large shopping centers, and discount stores (the main sources of consumer goods) have followed the population to the suburbs. Because they lack private automobiles and public transportation to these retail establishments, carless households are left with two choices: (1) to utilize expensive transportation (usually taxi) to reach these establishments or (2) to do their shopping at the small neighborhood independent stores, which tend to have higher prices than the supermarkets and discount stores. Such alternatives represent costly locational constraints for the carless.

Adequate transit for medical trips as with transit for employment is essential for maintaining a reasonable standard of living in any community and for any household. The carless health service user suffers inordinately from the uneven distribution and poor accessibility of health services. Maldistribution of health services in areas such as the inner city and physician avoidance of urban low-income, nonwhite areas have been demonstrated for such cities as Los Angeles,[18] Chicago,[19] Washington,[20] and Cleveland.[21]

A typical case of the constraints imposed on the carless by the location of health facilities can be seen in Los Angeles. The south and southwest districts of the health department are composed mainly of the Watts and Willowbrook sections, which are typical carless areas. The main source of primary medical care for these areas is the 3,000-bed Los Angeles County University of Southern California Medical Center (about 12 miles away). Thus an inadequate and unreliable transportation system puts the center 2 hours and $1.75 away from the carless areas.[22] Obviously accessibility is a problem for these residents. During night-time hours and emergencies these mobility constraints can put their lives in jeopardy.

In the case of recreational facilities, city parks are usually accessible by transit, but a small percentage of the people who use them actually arrive by bus. The inconvenience, energy, time, and money requirements of such a trip by public transportation often exceed the desire to visit the facility. This results in limited use of available recreational facilities by the carless population. The most serious problems are encountered when the carless wish to use state and federal parks, which are remote from their residences and from public transportation. As Myers pointed out, "Even for the poor, the car is an important pleasure vehicle."[23]

Administrative Constraints

Urban transportation plans involve consideration of a variety of objectives and the reconciliation of conflicting goals:

> For the city planner, urban transportation is a tool for shaping or creating a city with certain desired characteristics. For local businessmen and property owners, urban transportation is a force that creates or modifies real estate values and business potentials. For the engineer, urban transportation is a challenge to design facilities to meet the needs of the community while remaining within budgetary constraints. For the economist, it is a bit of all of these plus a problem in public finance.[24]

Clearly metropolitan transportation planning focuses on movement requirements for the whole metropolitan area, and in this approach it may be financially and politically expedient to overlook the requirements of some user populations. This is why carless groups as a small subsection of the metropolitan population commonly do not receive the attention they deserve, nor do they have a voice in the transportation planning process. Further, responsibility for each form of transportation is often divided among different agencies within the central city and among the various units of government that share transportation responsibilities in the metropolitan area. Broad general mandates and descriptions of responsibilities at these levels prompt agencies to develop transportation plans that are not coordinated with other agencies working on related problems. The most devastating constraint that carless people are facing in improving their mobility is the virtual absence of communication between those concerned with the needs of the carless and those concerned with providing transportation services.

Obsolete transit vehicles, poor ventilation, inadequate headways, inconvenient schedules, and overcrowding are added reasons for reduced mobility of the carless groups. Today the difference between public and private transportation is often the difference between a modern automobile and antiquated transit equipment. There is need for new or improved technology and new ways of offering public transportation service. Those types of public transport facilities that offer considerable potential for serving masses of riders and therefore stand a chance of competing with the automobile (in terms of service as well as cost to the user) receive far too little attention from planners and decision makers. Martin Wohl was among the first to point out this neglect when he noted:

> One, work on newer flexible and/or high service types of technologies or operations (such as dial-a-bus or dual-mode) seems to receive scant effort rather than the level consistent with their potential. Two, the public taxi — a service regarded by some as "the transit system of the future" because of its higher service features (which increasingly are

desired by a society of growing affluence), and because of its immediate high potential both for large masses and for the poor, aged, and handicapped — seems to be excluded from the domain of public transportation services generally considered to be eligible for government study and funding.[25]

Demand-Response Constraints

Existing transportation services are often the result of discrete, isolated decisions. These decisions have supplied needed services to automobile owners and have created conditions unresponsive to the needs and desires of carless groups. Most transport services fulfill a particular need when they are instituted, but they ignore changes in users' needs.

Public transportation services seem to be particularly slow in responding to new demands of a changing urban environment. One sees evidence of transportation services oriented to yesterday's needs and desires being offered to today's users. Bus operations in urban areas are an interesting example. Buses have considerable potential flexibility in routing, in service frequency, in pricing, and in other aspects of operation. Many innovations have been suggested in recent years to develop a system more responsive to the carless group's needs. Nonetheless, there is little evidence that bus operations are substantially different from those of 30 years ago, or that the potential of bus systems is being fully exploited.

Transportation investment is one of the tools available to public agencies for upgrading the quality of urban environments and counteracting opportunity imbalances. Given the locational separation of activities and the nature of a family's activity options, there is a growing demand for those with public responsibilities to increase and improve the overall level of mobility for the carless group.

In order to improve the urban environment for the carless population, activities must be made much more accessible than the minimum required to meet essential needs. It is important to have a range of choice, even if that choice is deferred or infrequently exercised.

Concluding Remarks

The link between mobility and social goals is much stronger than many people acknowledge and more complicated than transportation experts would like to believe. Certainly there is no one-to-one relationship between social problems and transportation solutions, and deficient mobility is admittedly not the most pressing burden that the carless must bear. However much more than transportation to employment opportunities must be provided if the carless are to achieve acceptable levels of mobility.

The mobility difficulties of the carless population stem from a host of constraints that range from physical and mental limitations to the inability of administrators and planners to meet the needs of the disadvantaged. Mobility of the carless can be improved when the mobility constraints outlined in this article are given more consideration in urban transportation planning. To accomplish this, the travel patterns of the elderly, the poor, and the handicapped must be investigated in detail. What are the work, shopping, health, and recreation travel patterns of the carless? What specific trip-making and environmental constraints have the greatest influence on their travel behavior? How can transportation planners and transit services alleviate these mobility constraints? Finding the answers to these questions could benefit the carless and also provide valuable information on the behavior of other transportation users relative to modal choice.

Notes

1. Wilfred Owen (1966) *The Metropolitan Transportation Problems*, New York: Double-day Anchor Books, p. 7.
2. Sumner Myers (January–February 1968) "The Soft Revolution," *Architectural Forum* 128: 87.
3. Public Law 88–365, Urban Mass Transportation Act of 1964, Section 16(c).
4. US Department of Transportation, Transportation Systems Center, *The Handicapped and Elderly Market for Urban Mass Transit* (Washington: Government Printing Office, 1970).
5. US Congress, Senate, Special Committee on Aging (1970) *Older Americans and Transportation: A Crisis in Mobility*, Washington: Government Printing Office, pp. 1–12.
6. *Ibid.*, p. 10.
7. See Battle Mark and Associates (1973) *Transportation for the Elderly and Handicapped*, New York: National Urban League, p. 47.
8. Carnegie-Mellon University Transportation Research Institute (1970) "Latent Demand for Urban Transportation," *National Technical Quarterly* 23, no. 2, 10–25.
9. Paul Ylvisaker (March 2–5, 1969) "The Resident Looks at Community Values," in *Transportation and Community Values*, report of a conference held at Warrenton, Va.
10. Sumner Myers (April 1970) "Personal Transportation for the Poor," *Traffic Quarterly* 24, no. 2, 193.
11. R. C. Federico (1969) "Total Transportation as a Social Concept", *Proceedings of the 1968 Transportation Engineering Conference on Defining Transportation Requirements*, Washington: American Society of Mechanical Engineers, p. 192.
12. US Department of Transportation, Federal Highway Administration (July 1972) *Availability of Public Transportation and Shopping Characteristics of S.M.S.A. Households*, Nationwide Personal Transportation Study, Report No. 5, Washington: Government Printing Office.
13. US, Congress, *Older Americans and Transportation*, pp 1–2.
14. *Ibid.*, p. 37.
15. Damian Kulash and William Silverman (1974) *Discrimination in Mass Transit*, Urban Institute Report 712–10–1, Washington.
16. *Ibid.*, p. 46.
17. Edward Kalachek (June 1968) "Ghetto Dwellers, Transportation and Employment," Paper presented at the Conference on Transportation and Poverty, American Academy of Arts and Sciences, Boston.
18. J. C. Norman (1969) *Medicine in the Ghetto*, New York: McGraw-Hill, p. 75.
19. L. A. Ferguson, "What Has Been Accomplished in Chicago," in *ibid.*, pp. 88–90.
20. Gary W. Shannon and G. E. Alan Dever (1974) *Health Care Delivery*, New York: McGraw-Hill, p. 64.

21. R. L. Bashshur, G. W. Shannon, and C. A. Metzner (September–October 1970) "Application of Three Dimensional Analogue Models to the Distribution of Medical Care Facilities," *Medical Care* 8, no. 5: 404.
22. Norman, *Medicine in the Ghetto*, p. 193.
23. Myers, *The Soft Revolution*, p. 193.
24. John Mayer (1968) "Urban Transportation: Problems and Perspectives," in *Metropolitan Enigma*, ed. James Q. Wilson, Cambridge: Harvard University Press, p. 42.

Unfreedom Road*

MAYER HILLMAN, IRWIN HENDERSON and ANN WHALLEY

In view of the considerable effort and sums of money which have been invested in planning and transport research in the past decade, it is difficult to understand why no comprehensive studies of the travel needs of children and teenagers have been made. These two groups constitute over a quarter of the total population: and they are the main groups in society that can never have the optional use of a car. Indeed their existence contradicts the notion of universal car ownership, that tarnished fantasy of planning in the 1960s. It was for this reason that in planning our mobility research study at Political and Economic Planning, we considered it was at least as important to survey them as their elders.

A child's life is usually thought to revolve around his home, school, and playground, and the siting of these places governs the possible need for special transport. Some research has been carried out in this field: Anthea Holme and Peter Massie studied, in *Children's Play*, factors affecting the use of 152 playgrounds. P. H. Levin and A. J. Bruce studied the journeys by schoolchildren to 34 primary schools in two local authorities. The Department of the Environment's recently published *Children at Play* reported the effects of differing characteristics of the built environment on patterns of play.

Transport associated with particular teenager activities has also been examined, though not by planners. The Newsom report highlighted the essential function which public transport has when the switch is made from primary to secondary education, which usually involved a longer journey to school. The Crowther report and Michael Schofield's work showed a marked increase during teenage years in joining social clubs and other recreation. Pearl Jephcott in her west Scotland study showed the strong influence on adolescent activities of cheap and convenient bus services.

These studies suggest that the personal mobility of young people plays a major role in their activities. Some travel is obviously done with parents, but as children grow older they wish to assert their rights and establish an identity apart from the family. In our survey, therefore, we made a general appraisal of the trips made by 630 children and 415 teenagers.

New Society, 3 May 1973, pp. 234–36. Reprinted by permission.

We carried out the surveys of both teenagers and junior schoolchildren in conjunction with an adult survey in five areas. The areas ranged from a high density inner London ward to a rural parish, and included a sector of a small town of 30,000 people, a new town neighbourhood, and an outer suburb of a large provincial city. The teenagers were surveyed at the same time as the adults, at their home addresses. The primary schoolchildren were surveyed in their schools: in each area four classes were selected — one class from each school year.

The main theme running through the surveys of both teenagers and children was that of independence. This was because, firstly, it would provide essential data for planning policy. If it can be seen that teenagers and children make a great majority of their trips with other members of their household, then one can assume that, in providing for adult needs, those of children will also be met. If, on the other hand, their trips are made independently, it would be possible to see how their special needs can be better served in planning. Secondly, independence is a pre-condition of various aspects of growth and maturity. These aspects have been recognized for many years as important by educationists and psychologists in the planning of school curricula. It would be ironic if attempts to foster freedom and independence inside the school were matched by an increasingly inappropriate outside environment.

Yet childhood memories of the freedom to walk and cycle anywhere with few parental restrictions or cautions, point to this being the case. During the 1960s, traffic levels almost doubled, and while the rate for adult pedestrian fatalities or serious injuries increased by 9 per cent, the rate for those below 17 rose by 52 per cent, with 12,000 victims last year.

The ways in which the two questionnaires investigated independence differed. Primary schoolchildren were asked about the journey to school, the places they could go to by themselves, the restrictions (if any) placed on their getting around, and the places they went to with their parents. A similar trip record to the adult one was obtained from the teenagers, plus details of the journeys made on their own, accompanied by parents, or by others.

In the urban areas studied, 75 per cent to 95 per cent of primary schoolchildren went to school on foot. Only in the rural area did any come by school bus, and even there 50 per cent walked; in the inner London area, 6 per cent used public transport. The highest proportion travelling to school by car was 23 per cent, and this was in the area of highest car ownership. However, more than half of those taken by car in the morning walked home. This implies that some adult accompaniment in the morning is due to the coincidence of the child's journey to school and the parent's journey to work, rather than concern over safety.

A more reliable reflection of this concern is provided by the number of parents who accompany their child home *from* school on foot in the afternoon. (Levin and Bruce reported that, among those respondents who did accompany children home, over 80 per cent mentioned some sort of danger as the reason.) Home-bound accompaniment was highest in inner London, where the risk from traffic is also highest — 25 per cent of children were taken home by an adult. It was the lowest in the new town and in the town with 30,000 people.

In spite of the fact that virtually none of the children cycled to school, the majority did own a bicycle. In the total sample, ownership was 65 per cent — the proportion varying from 50 per cent in the provincial city suburb and inner London, to 80 per cent in the rural area and small town. However, our survey shows that extensive restrictions are placed on the use of bicycles to get to leisure or social activities. In fact, the survey would seem to point to their being more a toy than a method of travel, for Table 1 shows that although ownership was highest among the youngest children, these children used bicycles least for getting to places.

Bicycles were used to get to only a third of all the places visited by children owning them. Their use increases with age, as independence is asserted and parental restrictions are lifted. As far as travel to different places is concerned, cycle use is nowhere higher than about 50 per cent, even among children owning bicycles, and variations are still closely related to age for any particular type of place. But there are also strong differences between the places, as shown in Table 2. The fact that the

TABLE 1. *Bicycle ownership among primary schoolchildren and use for all leisure activities*

	1st year %	2nd year %	3rd year %	4th year %	all %
cycle ownership	71	65	61	60	65
cycle used as transport	34	35	45	49	35
(No. in sample)					(630)

TABLE 2. *Places visited by bicycle by cycle owners*

	%
shops	50
play areas	50
visiting friends	52
entertainment	16
library and clubs	26
(No. in sample)	(407)

lowest usage was to town centres or areas with high volumes of traffic, suggests again that traffic hazards affect the opportunities for cycling. In addition to the journey to school, other indications of the extent of the children's ability to get around by themselves are provided by restriction on crossing main roads, and on using public transport.

The proportion allowed to cross main roads by themselves varied greatly: in the rural area and the provincial city suburb, 84 per cent were allowed to do so; in the new town 79 per cent; and in the small town and inner London area, 61 per cent and 47 per cent respectively. These figures are as indicative of traffic volumes in the different areas as of parental anxiety over the safety of children. At the same time, they also show widely varying areas of activity available to children. In the rural area, only the road through the village can be termed "main", and even this has very little traffic. In the new town, and the provincial city suburb, heavily trafficked roads are separated by distances of about a mile. Towards the centre of the small town, radial and orbital roads occur at more frequent intervals. In inner London, a major thoroughfare is reached within a quarter of a mile in any direction and the minor roads are dangerous for children because of their relatively large amount of traffic. It is in this inner London area, in particular, that the risk to children, and the restriction on their crossing roads, deprives them of creative opportunities which the school is trying to provide.

The proportion of children in each area allowed to use the public transport system by themselves reflects the areas' different characteristics. In the rural area where bus destinations are the neighbouring towns — at least four miles away — about 30 per cent of the children were allowed to travel by themselves. The proportion was the same in inner London, where there is a lot of traffic on the way to the bus stop, and the transport system is complex. In the three other areas, however, about 60 per cent were allowed to go on the buses by themselves. Over all the areas, the average age when children were allowed to ride the buses on their own was nine to nine and a half.

The questionnaire also included a list of facilities and places which the children could get to unaccompanied. The list included a park or children's playground, friends or relatives, shops, and places of entertainment ("places where you pay to get in"). Table 3 shows the percentages of children in each area who could make these different trips by themselves.

The most accessible place was the shops, where with the exception of the small town, over 90 per cent could go on their own. But between 8 per cent and 22 per cent reported that they could not visit their friends on their own. The proportion was highest in inner London — which had the smallest area of opportunity open to children, due to the number of main roads in the area. Least accessible were the places of entertainment, probably due to their widespread locations — from puppet shows to football.

TABLE 3. *Children allowed to travel unaccompanied to selected destinations in five areas*

	park/ playground %	visiting friends %	shops %	entertainment %
rural parish	89	86	90	47
small town	84	85	88	45
new town	90	82	96	68
provincial city suburb	94	92	99	77
inner London	89	78	97	71
(No. in sample)				(630)

The extent to which parents in the different areas went out with their children was gauged by a checklist in the questionnaire: the children were asked to tick places to which they had been taken at the previous weekend. The results of this show that more than 70 per cent of the children had been somewhere with their parents, and children whose households had a car were more likely to be taken somewhere.

The survey of 415 teenagers, like that of the younger children, was designed particularly to throw light on the question of independence. In view of the smaller numbers of teenagers in the survey — those aged 13 to 18 years — the five areas have been grouped together. The sample was evenly balanced between the sexes, and two-thirds of the respondents were still at school. Access to means of independent movement was considered first. As teenagers under 17 years are ineligible to hold licences, not surprisingly only 6 per cent had motorized transport of their own: 4 per cent with motor scooters and 2 per cent with cars. However, 11 per cent reported that they held a licence — either a motorcycle or a full or provisional car licence, while 40 per cent said that they had a bicycle. Although bicycles were, in fact, used infrequently, this may be because of the social influence of contemporaries or the unsuitability of bicycles for journeys due to traffic danger. In total, 54 per cent reported that they had no means of independent mechanized movement — relying either on walking, the public transport system, or lifts from parents or others old enough to drive. The proportion of trips, other than for work or school (that is, social, leisure and shopping) by each method are shown in Table 4.

Nearly two-thirds of the teenagers' trips were made on foot or by public transport, and less than one in ten by bicycle. Other modes accounted for less than 4 per cent of trips. Household car-ownership makes some difference; but, perhaps more significantly, there was little difference in the proportion of trips made on foot. The extent to which trips were made accompanied was also investigated. The results are shown in Table 5.

TABLE 4. *Social, leisure and shopping journeys by teenagers, according to method of travel*

	walk %	cycle %	car %	bus %	other %
no car	45	8	13	31	2
one car	45	10	24	16	6
two cars	42	5	36	14	4
(No. of trips)					(1,754)

TABLE 5. *Teenager trips by type of accompaniment and household car ownership*

	alone %	parents %	others %
no car	45	10	46
one car	36	21	43
two cars	34	18	48
(No. of trips)			(1,491)

What conclusions can be drawn from this look at the personal mobility of children and teenagers? Have transport planners been right to ignore them and include their needs amongst those of their household? Or do their needs merit special attention?

Firstly, it seems that these two groups have been among the losers as more people use cars. Traffic volumes have increased both the danger to children and the restrictions placed on them, while teenagers have been hit by decreasing services and increasing fares on public transport (full fares are still mandatory at 14 although school leaving age is now 16).

The surveys show that children's ability to get around on their own is most severely curtailed in urban areas with heavy traffic. The inner London area was the one with the greatest restrictions. But the fact that in no area did any significant number of children ride bicycles to school points to a more widespread limitation on their independent mobility. Planners must recognize that traffic danger is a major cause of this restriction and that the resulting "area of confinement" may be very small.

It would be unfair, however, to say that children's safety has not been a concern of those responsible for traffic and environment: school crossing patrols, cycle proficiency tests and reminders to observe road crossing practice are all employed in the campaign to reduce accidents. Yet transport planners' concern to maintain vehicle flows, in the face of rising numbers of vehicles, works against any real efforts to reduce child accident rates by reducing the amount of traffic. For example, in 1967, the Ministry of Transport warned that it would be unduly optimistic to expect a significant reduction in road casualties, while in 1972 the Department of the Environment is reported to have instructed local authorities to ignore children in pedestrian and vehicle counts taken to establish the need for pedestrian crossings.

Teenagers also require to be considered apart from their households, according to their needs and limitations. Only a minority of their trips are made with parents, and a significant proportion by public transport. This should be reflected in more attention being given to the quality of the public transport service, its fares and hours of operation. A service geared only to peak-hour journeys to work does not meet their needs for social and leisure travel during evenings and weekends, and for those still at school during the twelve week holiday period.

For both children and teenagers, it is obvious that the local environment must be the focus of the planners' concern. Unless policies are directed towards providing local ease of movement and access, the curtailment of their independent activity might well be increased. Sir Colin Buchanan has said that the freedom to walk around is a guide to the civilized quality of an urban area. But for these young people the freedom to walk around defines the limits of their world.

Literature

Anthea Holme and Peter Massie, *Children's Play* (Michael Joseph, 1970).

P. H. Levin and A. J. Bruce, The location of primary schools, *Journal of the Town Planning Institute*, **54**, No. 2, 1968.

Department of the Environment, *Children at Play* (HMSO, 1973).

John H. Newsom *et al., Half Our Future* (HMSO, 1963).

G. Crowther *et al., Out of School* (HMSO, 1959).

Michael Schofield, *Sexual Behaviour of Young People* (Longmans, 1965).

Pearl Jephcott, Time of one's own, *Social and Economic Studies Occasional Paper* No. 7, (University of Glasgow, 1967).

Part IV   Ideology

Introduction

E. DE BOER

This chapter is on the role of ideology, of guiding principles relating to transport policy. In spite of my neutral definition, the concept of ideology may arouse suspicion. It usually has a negative, emotional context with associations such as revolutionary, impractical, over-complicated and anti-metaphysical[1]. Indeed, a history of ideas on transport is likely to be a history of misconceptions. Transport planning cannot even do without assumptions about reality, views of its problems and visions of future development.

Transport is interwoven so much with other societal phenomena, both conditioning these and being moulded by them, that explicit ideology is a prerequisite for functional planning. Alas, political ideologies have never worried much about transport: it has been perceived as politically neutral and left to technicians, who, in recent times, have been accused of being technocrats and of arousing public opposition. Colcord compared urban transportation and political ideology in Sweden and the United States, concluding that "although urban transportation issues are rarely debated ideologically in either country, their contrasting ideologies with respect to (a) planning versus free enterprise and (b) collectivism versus individualism are clearly reflected in their urban land use and housing as well as transportation patterns."[2]. Of course this implies that different policies are less a matter of ideology than of tradition and culture.

Explicit ideology has flowered with exceptional richness in oppositional literature. The anti-car and anti-highway literature dating predominantly from the first half of the seventies and appearing in practically every Western country is an insufficiently tapped source of ideas[3]. Ideas, beliefs and misconceptions are quite varied. There is belief and disbelief in technological progress (US Department of HUD (1968), Bendixson (1974), Appleyard (1971)), in restraint policies, in single but sweeping measures like "free transit" (Bohley (1973), Domencich and Kraft (1970), Van Hulten (1972)). Deep public resentment of motorized traffic was shown in actions for carless Sundays, a truly draconic measure, in, for instance, The Netherlands and Switzerland[4].

The history of ideas in transport is still waiting for its author. It is modern history, with the inherent risk of insufficient objectivity due to proximity to its subject, but a few general outlines can still be given. In

1975 I attempted it in a paper "From traffic policy to mobility policy" under the headings "From underestimated growth . . ., through accepted growth . . ., to despised growth" (in car use)[5].

Fundamentally different ways of thinking about the automobile as a conspicuous factor in change, alternated in rapid succession. Increasing car-ownership and -use was denied at first as unthinkable. Thoenig and Despicht have analysed the French case[6]. Once acknowledged, growth was often truly embraced resulting in extensive highway schemes — like the Dutch one of 1966, which was nearly halved in 1975 — and large scale urban reconstruction. The Buchanan Report marks the (dawn of a) turning point in official thinking about reconstruction (1963), the "highway revolts" occurring at various places marking the actual change. Steiner described several of these conflicts, analysing their backgrounds (Steiner (1978)). The famous Boston case is introduced in *Rites of way* by Lupo, Colcord and Fowler (1971)[7].

Ideas often succeeded each other at such a pace that planners were only just facing up to the previous problem. In practice the only choices open seemed to be inertia (a moratorium on plans) or perseverance to the bitter end — for either of the parties involved. A way out can only be found in balanced ideology — taking account of spatial, social, economic and environmental functions and implications of transport (Gakenheimer (1978) e.g.) and in fundamentally different planning practices.

Summaries

Taebel and Cornehls have sought in their *Ideological and policy perspectives of urban transportation* to classify current normative approaches to urban transportation. The outcome is satisfying order in the apparent chaos of transport literature from which the authors were suffering severely in their introduction. Most urban transportation questions — they notice — have a "decidedly ideological basis even though there is often an exaggerated show of objectivity". Seven ideological approaches are described remarkably true to life. Three of these are favourable to an automobile society: 1. the *automobile monopolists* who are whole-hearted supporters (and are tellingly characterized), 2. the *automobile-apologists* subscribing to the need for some public transportation for the carless and to relieve centre-city congestion, 3. the *social engineers*, concerned with immediate benefits for the needy and seeming "to have tacitly accepted the automobile monopolists' belief that affluent Americans will not give up the automobile". The (highway) *trust-busters* 4. are solely anti-automobile in their orientation. This category has yielded substantive literature with eloquent titles like "The pavers and the paved". The *transit technicians* 5. "prefer a total mass transit society. This view is not expressed in journals and books". Therefore it is a less convincing category, though there are no doubt transit enthusiasts with blinkers on. The *balancers* 6. "would seldom insist that there should be complete parity between the automobile and public transportation. Each serves an important purpose and there should be an appropriate mix". Being related to the *ecologists* 7. who the authors sympathize with, they are (not entirely inadequately) depicted in fact as half-hearted and opportunistic. The ecological perspective sees transportation as an urban subsystem exercising a profound influence on the design and function of the city itself. It is "total in scope, holistic in content, and heuristic in design . . . The magnitude of this approach frequently leads one to immobilization and paralysis. Indeed this frustration has led many to a total rejection of the current urban system".

Frank's Mass transport and class struggle is a rare application on transport of another encompassing ideology rejecting the current social system: marxism. It was written in 1969/70 in the heyday of German student-activism during which marxist theorizing was revived. The quest for free transit — a main theme in the article — was typical of the era. This is not to say that it was written fashionably, nor that it is consequently outmoded. The author has assured me that his argument would not be very different today. In a rather difficult introduction, with some inevitable jargon, it is explained that the fundamental transport problem is not public versus private transport but a collision of planning for maximizing individual profits with the interests of the masses. Minimizing transport is essential for production (uniting production factors) and reproduction: recreation of the labour force. Yet commuting distances are increasing, thereby in fact increasing production-costs. Being unproductive costs, these are passed on to the workers and to government. The inherent contradiction between capitalism and the state becomes manifest when the increasing division of labour requires more investments in infrastructure than the state can afford. From here on the text is increasingly attractive. Growing use of the motor-car, Frank points out, cannot be stopped easily: the "Volkswagenidee" is functional in enhancing a false middle-class consciousness amongst workers and, moreover, the car is an important instrument of capitalist exploitation. So over-production of cars is reinterpreted as under-production of road-space. A catalogue of frequently proposed measures for tackling traffic problems are shown to be ineffective or inapplicable, predominantly for economic reasons. Large scale expansion of public transport on a social welfare base is the only viable solution. To attract sufficient numbers of car-users, transit should be free. Actions aimed at bringing about free fares (like the transport strike) are excellent in awaking class-consciousness. Hitherto the students organizing the actions were neither theoretically nor organizationally prepared for this process. They are trying to improve this. But, as Frank states in 1985, "my belief in the better organizing of political activities has yielded to deep scepticism". It cannot be denied, however, that transport planning has in the meantime organized its political activities much better.

Notes

1. B. A. G. M. Tromp (1981) De onstaansgeschiedenis van het woord ideologie (the origin of the concept of ideology), *Sociologische Gids*, **28**, pp 498–515.
2. Altshuler in his summary (p. XI) of F. C. Colcord's contribution (pp 3–15) to A. Altshuler (ed. 1979), *Current issues in transportation policy*, Lexington Books, Lexington (Mass.).
3. Bakker en Bierman (1972), Hultgren (1977), Independent Commission on Transport (1974), Linder a.o. (1975), Sauvy (1970), Schneider (1971).
4. Public experience of carless Sundays during the oil-crisis of 1973/1974 was reported in: Nederlandse Stichting voor Statistiek (1974), *De autoloze zondag, reacties van inwoners van de Haagse agglomeratie op het zondagse rijverbod*, The Hague, 2 volumes. The study of the Sociaal en Cultureel Planbureau (1976) was reluctantly undertaken by the Dutch national government after receiving a public petition. Research done in 1974 showed that 26 per cent of the Dutch population thought that it was necessary to have at least a number of carless Sundays a year.
5. Tijdschrift voor Vervoerswetenschap, 1975, number 5, pp 261–271.
6. J. C. Thoenig and N. Despicht (1973), pp 390–423 in: J. Hayward and M. Watson (eds.), *Planning, politics and public policy, the British French and Italian experience*, Cambridge U.P., London.
7. Further references are given in: Gakenheimer (1976) and Sloan (1975). *Citizen participation in transportation planning: the Boston experience*, Ballinger, Cambridge (Mass.).

Literature

J. Adams (1981) *Transport planning — vision and practice*, Routledge and Kegan Paul, Henley-on-Thames, Oxon.

A. Altshuler a.o. (1980) *The urban transportation system*, politics and policy innovation, M.I.T. Press, Cambridge (Mass.).

D. Appleyard (1971) *Social and environmental policies for transportation*, Working paper 161, Department of City and Regional Planning, Berkeley (Cal.).

H. Bakker and M. Bierman (1972) *Steden, wegen, ruimte, op weg naar de bermbeschaving* (Towns, roads, space, en route to a hard-shoulder-society), Van Gennep, Amsterdam.

T. Bendixson (1974) *Instead of cars*, Temple Smith, London.

P. Bohley (1973) Der Nulltarif im Nahverkehr, Antrittsvorlesung Universität Zürich, *Kyklos* **26**, pp 113–142.

C. Buchanan (1963) *Traffic in towns*, HMSO, London.

M. Buchanan a.o. (1980) *Transport planning for greater London*, Saxon House Westmead, Farnborough.

T. A. Domencich and G. Kraft (1970) *Free transit*, Lexington Books, Lexington (Mass.).

R. Gakenheimer (ed.) (1978) *The automobile and the environment*, an international perspective (prepared by the OECD), M.I.T. Press, Cambridge (Mass.).

M. van Hulten (1972) *Gratis openbaar vervoer* (free transit), Kluwer, Deventer.

K. Hultgren (1977) *Människan och bilsamhället* (man and car-society), PAN, Norstedt.

The Independent Commission on Transport (1974) *Changing directions*, Coronet books, London.

Institution of Civil Engineers (1975) *Transport for Society*, London.

J. F. Kain, J. R. Meyer and M. Wohl (1965) *The urban transportation problem*, Harvard University Press, Cambridge (Mass.).

T. Krämer-Badoni, H. Grymer and M. Rodenstock, *Zur sozio-ökonomischen Bedeutung des Automobils*, Suhrkamp, Frankfurt am Main.

W. Linder a.o. (1975) *Erzwungene Mobilität* (enforced mobility), Alternativen zur Raumordnung, Stadtentwicklung und Verkehrspolitik, Köln.

A. Lupo, F. C. Colcord and E. P. Fowler (1971) *Rites of Way*, the politics of transportation in Boston and the US city, Little & Brown, Boston.

L. Mumford (1960) *The highway and the city*, Harcourt and Brace, New York.

W. Plowden (1971) *The Motor Car and Politics*, 1896–1970, Bodley Head, London.

H. W. Rittel (1973) Gesellschaftliche Alternativen im Berufsverkehr, (societal alternatives in work traffic), pp 76–108 in G. Friedrichs ed., *Aufgabe Zukunft, Qualität des Lebens, Band 3, Verkehr*, Frankfurt am Main.

A. Sauvy (1970) *Les quatre roues de la fortune*, essai sur l'automobile, Flammarion, Paris.

K. H. Schaeffer and E. Sclar (1975) *Access for all*, Transportation and Urban Growth, Penguin, Harmondsworth.

K. R. Schneider (1971) *Autokind versus mankind*, an analysis of tyranny, a proposal for rebellion, a plan for reconstruction, Norton, New York.

Sociaal en Cultureel Planbureau (1976) *Autogebruiksbeperking*, mogelijkheden en aanvaardbaarheid (Restraining car-use, possibilities and acceptability), Rijswijk (the Netherlands).

D. Starkie (1982) *The motorway age:* road and traffic policies in post-war Britain, Pergamon Urban and Regional Planning Series, Vol. 28. Oxford.

H. M. Steiner (1978) *Conflict in urban transportation*, Lexington Books, Lexington (Mass.).

E. Sylven (ed.) (1978) *Trafik i nordisk tätort*, en framtidsstudie med tonvikt på kollektivtrafiken i medelstora tätorter, Resultat från Nordkoltprojektet (traffic in the nordic towns), Nordiska Ministerrådets sekretariat, Oslo.

J. M. Thomson (1977) *Great cities and their traffic*, Victor Gollancz, London.

P. M. Townroe (1974) *Social and political consequences of the motor car*, David & Charles, Newton Abbot.

US Department of Housing and Urban Development (1968) *Tomorrow's transportation*, new systems for the urban future, Washington D.C.

Ideological and
Policy Perspectives
of Urban Transportation*

DELBERT A. TAEBEL and JAMES V. CORNEHLS

In the past several years, a large number of articles and books have been written about the problems of urban transportation.[1] The literature is extensive and far reaching in its thrust but tends to be rather chaotic. Urban transportation researchers represent a wide variety of disciplinary and professional practitioners, including traffic engineers, political scientists, urban planners, sociologists, economists, and environmentalists. Because transportation systems in cities so obviously affect virtually every other facet of urban life, there has been much crossing of disciplinary lines by these analysts, thereby contributing to the somewhat disorganized nature of the body of urban transportation literature. However, this literature has been beneficial in at least two ways: first, since many people are interested in the urban transportation problem, a large amount of knowledge is being generated that may bear on its resolution; and, second, the literature now covers almost every detail of urban transportation.

Yet there is at least one important caveat: The available literature tends to be so extensive and so detailed that it is almost impossible to uncover any focus, theme, or common ground for discussion of the issues. Indeed, the issues themselves are difficult to distinguish. While this is no doubt a reflection of a transitional stage in the analysis of urban transportation, it creates a perplexing dilemma: there seems to be no appropriate place to begin and to end. Some overall organizational scheme or set of foci is needed that would enable the sorting out and interpretation of urban transportation research and policy. Otherwise, one may be overwhelmed by more information than can be digested or put to skillful use.

This article represents an attempt to develop a framework for understanding the various approaches taken by scholars and practitioners who have been concerned with urban transportation, even though it is recognized that any classification scheme that is posited can only be tentative. As the study of urban transportation matures, classification

*_Traffic Quarterly_, 1975, pp. 541–54. Reprinted by permission of the Eno Foundation for Transportation, Inc.

schemes will become more complex and more sophisticated, and they will differ in kind from the one suggested here. But the need for organizational and evaluative premises will become increasingly acute in the future.

Although there are many possible bases for developing a classification system, it is believed that one of the most useful is the identification and definition of the normative orientation of transportation research and policy analysis. Accordingly, the classification scheme adopted here can best be described as ideological.[2] Most urban transportation questions have a decidedly ideological basis even though there is often an exaggerated show of objectivity. In fact, it would be surprising if this were not the case since the issues surrounding urban transit are critically important policy matters and, as such, are contested in the arena of politics.

The Seven Ideological Dimensions

An analysis of the current literature reveals seven identifiable ideological approaches or analytic dimensions. Of these seven approaches three are favorable to an automobile society; one is solely antiautomobile in its orientation; one is devoted exclusively to the expansion of mass transit; one stresses the concept of "balanced transportation," while a final, somewhat heterogeneous category may be referred to as the ecological approach. These approaches tend to overlap, of course, but for the most part each has certain clearly distinguishable characteristics. These approaches are designated as: (1) the automobile monopolists, (2) the automobile apologists, (3) the social engineers, (4) the trust-busters, (5) the transit technicians, (6) the balancers, and (7) the ecologists.

1. The Automobile Monopolists

Many of the proponents of this approach are associated with economic organizations directly involved in the production of automobiles and petroleum. They are buttressed by the construction and trucking industries. The highway lobby is the most articulate exponent of this viewpoint. Although not every automobile monopolist may swear allegiance to the highway lobby's views, its position is effectively communicated through a variety of channels — public meetings, professional associations, newspaper articles, advertising, and professional presence at hearings before legislative bodies that have under consideration measures affecting the lobby's interests.

The principle values of those who are extremists in this approach are quite straightforward. In the first place, they consider the automobile to be almost synonymous with the existence of industrial society. In their opinion, the great era of industrial expansion was linked with the emergence of an automotive society. Those adhering to this point of view have as implicit (and sometimes explicit) goals for the nation two cars in every garage, a gasoline station on every corner, and cities devoted overwhelmingly to streets, parking lots, and maintenance facilities for the automobile. To them, progress is measured by car ownership and by highway and street mileage.

Many automobile monopolists believe that the automotive industry is virtually indispensable to the continued prosperity of the United States — and if not indispensable, it is a very desirable component of a healthy, prosperous economy. Since nearly 20 percent of the gross national product is linked to the automotive industry,[3] they believe that far too many jobs are at stake and that the shock waves sent through the economy by the demise of the automobile and truck as the dominant surface transport mode would be politically unacceptable; industrial might would be severely crippled; and the enormous capital loss along with new investment requirements involved in the transition to a new system would be foolish and unattainable.

The idea of free choice in transport mode is upheld by many automobile monopolists as the only tenable democratic desideratum; and they are convinced that, even if safe, efficient and pleasant transportation alternatives were available, the average American still would choose the automobile.

Automobile monopolists tend to believe that the automobile is of great intrinsic value to society and epitomizes the way of life of Americans: free men and women freely choosing that most individual and uninhibited way of getting about, the private automobile; all brought about by the interplay of market forces in the free enterprise system; a populace unbeholden to any "public" authority that might dictate when one could go and by what route. This outlook is expressed in the advertising slogan:

> Driving in your car,
>   It's all there in your hands,
> You've got room to go,
>   And the whole wide world to see;
>
> There's something in the feeling,
>   Of a really fine machine,
> That turns you loose,
>   That really sets you free.
>
> It's a better way,
>   It's a better feeling,
> When the wheel belongs to you,
>   The road goes anywhere you say;
>
> It's a better way,
>   It's the feel of freedom . . .[4]

The slogan suggests that the automobile is peculiarly well suited to American lifestyles. It is true that the suburban, spread-city development coincides with America's rural roots and its space-loving, open style of life. Footloose, mobile Americans want to feel free to spread all over the landscape, to move frequently, to be able to go, on a moment's notice, anywhere within a reasonable distance from their front doors for work, play, or shopping.

Because of this lifestyle the automobile is championed by the ardent automobile monopolist as having the capability of providing the best possible service. This explains its almost universal domination of the transportation field. It is instantly available to go anywhere, allowing flexibility in choice of living location and work site. It provides individual service at the least apparent cost. And even if it does not minimize costs, Americans are generally affluent and have the ability to pay for the convenience afforded by personalized transportation.

Finally, many automobile monopolists believe that Americans simply will not accept anything other than a personalized form of transportation. The evidence offered for this is the past decline in bus ridership, the phenomenal growth in automobile ownership, and the defeat of legislative proposals that would in some way curtail automobile use. These facts are taken as dicta that preclude the serious consideration of alternatives: what exists is what Americans want; if they had wanted something else, the market would have provided it.[5]

It should be pointed out that many advocates of the automobile society are not opposed to public transit, but believe that it should be self-supporting through the farebox. Public transportation's inability to pay for itself is taken as evidence that it is not sufficiently wanted.

2. The Automobile Apologists

Although this approach is similar to the one described above there are some significant variations that entitle it to be considered separately. The automobile is seen as socially desirable because it epitomizes free choice and hence consumer welfare. Yet there is some recognition accorded to the need for public transportation. Many proponents of this approach recognize some of the limitations of the automobile, especially external diseconomies, and believe that public transportation would be beneficial for the city.

Three specific factors set this approach apart from that of the automobile monopolists: (1) Although automobile apologists generally see transportation primarily as an economic good in which the journey-to-work is paramount, they understand that the costs of owning an automobile may be beyond the financial capability of some urban residents and that the size of this carless group may not be large enough to support a useful public transportation network — thus some form of public transit subsidy may be required. (2) They recognize that motor-vehicle-related industry may need unskilled labor for many of its jobs and hence could provide employment for those who might otherwise end up as welfare recipients, necessitating even greater public outlays. (3) They also recognize a need to relieve center-city congestion. With downtowns dying and office space moving to suburban locations, and with increasing demands for higher air-quality standards, some form of public transportation is accepted as inevitable.

Of critical importance to the automobile apologists is the quantity and form the public transportation is to take. Only the amount that is absolutely necessary, requires a minimum of subsidy (or preferably no subsidy at all), and does not necessitate large public capital outlays is regarded as desirable. The apologists, with limited cognizance of public needs and private wants, usually subscribe to a motorized, highway-oriented transit system, principally buses.

Proponents of this approach are those who realize that the day of uncontrolled growth of private automobile ownership and use may be coming to an end. To them, if changes are to be made in the urban transportation systems, it would seem prudent to support motorized public transportation. After all, buses can be thought of as large automobiles, and they certainly run on roads and highways. The preservation of the street and road network is of transcendental importance to many automobile apologists — as long as streets and highways are available it is always possible for automobiles to travel along them.

The apologists enjoy considerable support from certain segments of the academic community. These sophisticated spokesmen for this approach are generally transportation engineers or economists by training, whose own values tend to accord with those of the automobile apologists. For the most part, however, their expertise is used with the cold, hard logic of their mathematical models to knock down the arguments of those who support rapid mass transit. Like the automobile monopolists, the apologists' prime weapon is the density argument, and through cost-benefit models (which often avoid any but measurable economic costs and benefits) they are persuasive proponents of a motorized public transit system.[6]

3. The Social Engineers

The social engineers adopt the dictum: In the long run we are all dead. Short-run goals are the only important considerations. The only immediate changes that can be made with respect to the delivery of transportation services lie within the existing transport system. Long-range changes in the system may be intrinsically desirable, but the overriding concern of the social engineers is immediate benefits for the needy. The social engineers see the automobile and other motorized transportation as a means for improving the lot of the elderly, the handicapped, and the poor in the urban community who are either ill-served or not served at all by the present transportation system.[7] In a sense, the social engineers are humanistic automobile monopolists.

Economic realities are of utmost importance for the social engineers. The lack of adequate transportation is seen by them as the major barrier in securing employment; and, although they may realize that automobiles could have undesirable impacts on the city, they see the transportation needs of the poor and under-privileged as so compelling that immediate remedial action is necessary.

Perhaps the social engineers take much the same perspective as those who advocate the redistribution of income but are skeptical of the possibilities for meaningful income redistribution. Some social engineers would like to redistribute transportation to the poor by means of a system in which government would provide the poor with cars.[8] Still others would like to see increased use of taxis and jitneys,[9] with the possibility in some cases that public transportation service would be provided free of charge to the user.[10]

Proponents of this perspective are drawn mainly from the academic community, although officials from various social welfare agencies are also spokesmen for the approach. The social engineers seem to have tacitly accepted the automobile monopolists' belief that affluent Americans will not give up the automobile. They also tend to see the city in terms of the haves and the have-nots, and to see transportation as one of the key means of ensuring that everyone is a part of the haves. Though many social engineers would object to such a characterization, their perspective on transportation is analogous to that of the proponents of minority capitalism who advocate a piece of the action for the disadvantaged. Providing transportation for the poor, the elderly, and so forth can then be thought of as a holding operation pending the entry of many of these groups into the mainstream of economic life — and the few who can never be expected to enter will still be enabled to get about much like everyone else.

4. The Trust-busters

Although trust-busting refers primarily to the efforts of those who would like to dismantle the Highway Trust Fund, the term symbolizes an approach that is much broader in its orientation and negative in its thrust. In principle, trust-busters are those who for one reason or another oppose the primacy of the private automobile. Before any real progress in altering transportation priorities can be realized, the trust-buster generally argues that the self-perpetuating nature of automotive taxes must be halted — society cannot afford the resources already going into automobile transportation plus those required for mass transit.

In general, the trust-busters view the automobile as the prime culprit in downgrading the American city. They view urban sprawl, suburban isolation, noise pollution, air pollution, visual pollution, disparities in job opportunities, and the isolation of subgroups such as minorities, the elderly, and the handicapped as direct consequences of the automobile society. While they may recognize that a modified highway transportation system is necessary, the highway lobby and the highway engineer are held up as the immediate enemies, and the first and only task is the total defeat of the highway lobby. Numerous articles and books in recent years reflect this viewpoint, such as Leavitt's *Superhighway-Superhoax*[11] and Mowbray's *Road to Ruin*.[12] In addition, many articles recounting the efforts of local citizen groups to block highway development exemplify this approach.[13]

Trust-busters come from a variety of groups and organizations. Environmentalists have become some of the more vociferous opponents of the automobile society at the national and local levels. Neighbourhood groups have largely confined their activities to specific highway projects that threaten their area.[14] Yet the movement has gained considerable support. Indeed, the Highway Action Coalition serves as a lobby for this viewpoint in Washington and even publishes its own journal, *The Concrete Opposition*.

5. *The Transit Technicians*

The transit technicians have at least one similarity to the automobile monopolists — they favor a transportation monopoly. Rather than having a total automobile society, however, they prefer a total mass transit society. This view is not articulated in journals and books, of course, but it prevails at the meetings of various trade groups in the mass transit industry.

Many hard core "mass transporters" are the operators of local transit systems. They take pride in being hard-headed businessmen who see problems of mass transportation from a parochial viewpoint. Their conferences are devoted to such matters as marketing, schedules, maintenance problems, fiscal arrangements, and more efficient equipment. Although they may be sensitive to urban problems such as the environment, minorities, and urban desgn, many transit operators are more concerned with the day-to-day problems which center on the revenue box and the operational status of their equipment.

A large segment of transit operators, the bus companies, occupy an uneasy position. Although they represent mass transit, their functions are paradoxically tied to the continuation of the automobile. Buses are considered mass transit, but they run over roadways that would undoubtedly not have been built were it not for the automobile. Notwithstanding, in the face of increasing transit deficits and forced municipal takeovers the perspective of many in this group is still firmly fixed on the goal of smooth, quiet, air-conditioned, attractive buses generating a new wave of public use. To them, the dreams of city planners and scholars for improving the transportation system in the urban community are almost seen as diversionary ploys. The real problem for the transit technician in this case is to make sure that the buses are operable and on time.

6. The Balancers

The idea of a balanced transportation system for our cities is enjoying a considerable vogue in journals and public meetings. Obviously, the terminology invoked is of some importance in itself since the opposite of balance is imbalance, and it would be preposterous to advocate an imbalanced anything. Of course, balance — like beauty — may to some extent reside in the eye of the beholder. Unless the idea of balance is accompanied by criteria for determining when it occurs, it may be a spurious and diversionary idea devoid of any real content.

The balancers are, ideologically speaking, in the same philosophical camp as the advocates of the mixed economic system. They tend to give preference to the private sector (automobiles), while simultaneously maintaining a keen perception of the need for public provision of facilities the private sector either cannot or will not produce. Why, they seem to say, can't we have our cake and eat it too? Like the automobile monopolists, they are enamored of the lofty ideal of free choice, but at the same time they are willing to concede that free choice may not work well in practice. The balancers, ever attuned to acceptability, have the further advantage of appearing to agree with everyone. As is the case with all compromise approaches, their appeal is to reasonableness and the avoidance of conflict.

In principle, the advocates of balanced transportation would like to see the city's reliance on the automobile curtailed somewhat and the role of public transportation expanded. Although they speak of balance, this group would seldom insist that there should be complete parity between the automobile and public transportation. Each serves an important purpose, and there should be an appropriate mix.

Among the advocates of this approach will be found numerous political scientists and liberal economists who are aware of the sophisticated externalities arguments.[15] Because the costs of social diseconomies cannot be internalized to private producers and users of transportation, only public authority can compensate the losers. These advocates provide a part of the analytic rationale for the professional city and regional planners, whose conception of the physical plan for the city coincides with the balanced system.

Even though most city planners view balanced transportation as a more viable means for restructuring the city, there are other constraints implicit in their endeavors. In the first place, the city planner is stuck with the city in which he finds himself, and the historical development of that city serves as a major constraint on his plans. Second, the planner is wed to a highly rational model. Although comprehensive planning receives the same adulation as a balanced transportation system, planning as it now operates in most cities is incremental in nature and hardly comprehensive.

7. The Ecologists

The final approach, which is of some importance in the study of urban transportation, is the most amorphous and for its proponents the most frustrating. Although the term "ecology" is employed, it should be acknowledged at the outset that this approach does not refer to the environmentalists and conservationists who have attained a good deal of recent popularity, though many environmentalists and conservationists may also be advocates of this approach.

Ecologists see the transportation system as extending far beyond the narrow objectives of moving people and goods, or of efficient and well-integrated transportation networks, or even, for that matter, of urban design. The ecologists tend to see transportation as only one subsystem in the urban environment, but one that is capable of exercising a profound influence on the design and function of the city itself, one that is capable of affecting the physical environment and the wise use of land and natural resources to preserve beauty and life. Generally, they believe that the costs of transportation are reflected far beyond the transit, fare box, traffic congestion, right-of-way acquisitions, and capital outlays; and that the benefits of transportation may be realized in the diversity and pleasantness of neighborhoods and landscapes, in the impact on political representation, in the attractiveness of the city to new residents, and in the diminution of current social problems such as crime and racism.

The ecological perspective is total in scope, holistic in content, and heuristic in design. It seeks to encompass all the other major subsystems operative in the urban community, to examine all the effects of transportation on the interrelated parts of the system, and to foster an open systems model for analysis that is capable of including each new discovery.

The magnitude of this approach frequently leads one to immobilization and paralysis. Indeed, this frustration has led many to a total rejection of the current urban system. In this sense, the ecologists may be likened to the trust-busters, but whereas the trust-busters reject only an automobile society, some ecologists argue that the automobile society is merely one manifestation of what is wrong in such diverse areas of American urban life as housing, health care, and education.[16] For others the solution is not quite so clear and hardly so simple —if there are basic flaws in the various subsystems that make up the urban community, the task is to identify these flaws and try to postulate the kind of systems that would overcome these flaws.

For the ecologists the benefits from transportation occur collectively, not individually. One person can benefit by having everyone else use public transit while that person alone uses the now uncluttered roadways to drive a private automobile. Ecologists therefore believe that only groups, through democratic action — as in the control of contagious disease, for example — can be relied on to obtain the maximum social benefits of transportation. The ecologists would have us avoid the trap of believing that freedom in choice of transportation includes the right to inflict great social harm, however unwitting and unintended.

Conclusion

The large mass of literature on urban transportation is unorganized, and some organizing principles for the study of this literature are needed. It is proposed that an understanding of the attitudes of those who influence urban transportation research, policy, and development may be an appropriate means of organizing this study.

Seven general approaches or analytical dimensions for the study of urban transportation have been discussed in this article. The seven categories are not meant to be exhaustive or complete in their treatment, and there is some overlap between them. (Whenever one classifies, one tends to isolate and generalize — that is the nature of any organized study.)

The understanding of the seven approaches found in the urban transportation literature may serve only as a starting point and therefore should be considered primarily as a tool for the organization of urban transportation study. It is hoped, however, that this article's rudimentary framework of approaches will give the student of urban transportation a better understanding of the information that may be found in the masses of data, articles, and books on the subject.

Notes

1. A sampling is contained in a bibliography by the authors entitled *Urban Transportation: The Social Dimensions: An Annotated Bibliography* (Monticello, Ill.: Council of Planning Librarians, August 1973).
2. The concept of ideology has a long history with blighted overtones, and no rigorous definition will be offered here. For an extensive analysis of this concept, see Willard A. Mullins, On the Concept of Ideology in Political Science, *The American Political Review*. **66**, no. 2 (June 1972): 498–510.
3. The figure is an estimate derived by the authors from input-output data. Certain parts of the steel industry, petroleum industry, etc., are linked to the automobile industry through interindustry demand; hence a part of their output is linked to automobile production.
4. An advertising jingle developed for General Motors Corporation and quoted with permission.

5. An interesting, informative and amusing assessment of the logic of this position is contained in an article by Ezra J. Mishan, Pangloss on Pollution, *Swedish Journal of Economics.* **71**, no. 1 (March 1971): 113–120.

6. Some illustrations of these views may be found in papers delivered at a Symposium on Urban Transportation jointly sponsored by Southern Methodist University's Urban Institute and the Dallas Central Business District Association at the Statler-Hilton Hotel, Dallas, Texas, October 26, 1972.

7. Papers that epitomize this approach are found in the American Academy of Arts and Sciences, *Conference on Poverty and Transportation.* (Springfield, Va.: National Technical Information Service, 1968).

8. Sumner Myers, Personal Transportation for the Poor, in *Conference on Poverty and Transportation.*

9. Cordell K. Ballard, Transportation Dependents, *Traffic Quarterly.* 21, no. 1 (January 1967): 83–90.

10. Gerald Kraft and Thomas A. Domencich, Free Transit, in *Conference on Poverty and Transportation.*

11. Helen Leavitt, *Superhighway-Superhoax.* (Garden City, N.Y.: Doubleday, 1970).

12. A. Q. Mowbray, *Road to Ruin.* (Philadelphia: J. B. Lippincott, 1968).

13. See, for example, Delbert A. Taebel, Citizen Groups, Public Policy, and Urban Transportation, *Traffic Quarterly.* **27**, no. 4 (October 1973): 503–515. Also see Ben Kelley, *The Pavers and the Paved.* (New York: Donald W. Brown, 1971).

14. See, for example, William B. Furlong, Profile of an Alienated Voter, *Saturday Review of the Society.* **55**, no. 31 (July 1972): 48–51.

15. An interesting and useful exposition of the main features of the externalities problem is contained in an article by Ralph Turvey, Side Effects of Resource Use, in *Environmental Quality in a Growing Economy.* ed. Henry Jarrett (Baltimore, Md.: Johns Hopkins, 1966).

16. See, for example, Robert Goodman, *After the Planners.* (New York: Simon and Schuster, 1971).

Mass Transport and Class Struggle*

HARMUT FRANK

In the late summer of 1969 two events, hitherto rare in the Federal Republic of Germany, almost coincided. The wave of "wildcat" strikes showed the grand coalition of Christian and Social Democrats the limitations of its so-called concerted action of government, industry and unions and reminded the union leaders, who had declared the class struggle to be a phenomenon of the nineteenth century, that the workers had still not quite forgotten how to safeguard their interests. At about the same time large populations in Hannover, Heidelberg and other cities resisted price rises in public transport. The "Red Spot" campaigns, the blockades of tram lines, protest meetings and mostly reformistic demands not only heightened discussion on the problems of mass transport but also questions the effectiveness of such actions to transform existing society.[1]

The fact that these transport campaigns happened immediately after the first great wave of strikes in postwar Germany raises the supposition that they cannot be explained as a problem of transport alone but should be analysed in their relationship to the sphere of production in general. The popular demand for free fares transformed the debate on public transport. For the first time economic considerations played a part, whereas before only alternative technical measures had been discussed. It became evident that the real problem was neither "public" nor "individual" transport, but that a mode of planning obviously orientated to guarantee a maximum of private profits must necessarily collide with the interests of the masses. The demand for free travel to work showed that the means of local transport whether public or private cannot be freely chosen, but that on the contrary, compulsion to sell one's own labour necessarily dictates transport from home to one's place of work.

Types of Transport

All the usual classifications of different types of transport in the

---

*"Massenverkehr und Klassenkampf," Bauen und Wohnen 25, Jahrgang, Heft VI, Juni, 1971. Reprinted by permission.

bourgeois economy — in particular of passenger transport to and from work — into fundamentally separate types serve in the end only to hide the connection between transport and the division of labour, and its function in the circulation of capital. Basically one distinguishes between transport of passengers and of goods; passenger transport is then further subdivided according to the purpose of the journey, i.e. transport to and from work, for shopping and for leisure. The distribution and exchange of products in the market are prerequisites for realizing the surplus value contained in the goods. It is paramount for the capital which has been converted into merchandise to shorten the time taken by distribution. Shortening the duration that capital is tied up in the merchandise reduces the costs of capital realization as a whole.[2]

The goal of traffic planning generally is the reduction of the costs of circulation, or as Marx says, the "destruction of space by time".[3] The level of development of the transport industry thus becomes the direct precondition for the maintenance of a given rate of profit.

Further, if the transport industry's product is consumed individually i.e. the transport of people is involved, the cost of transport appears on one hand as the costs of reproduction of labour (leisure and shopping transport) and on the other as the cost of transporting the commodity of labour from its place of reproduction to that of its productive application (transport of passengers to and from work) and the latter expenses are more crucial to capital than the former. Here a contradiction comes to light, because transport to work place increases the price of labour, without it becoming any more exploitable in the process. Its exchange value at the place of work is higher than its utility value at the place of reproduction. The latter is expressed solely in the cost of reproduction, whereas expenses accruing only from the alteration of the commodity's form, i.e., with no change in the content, obey the laws of circulation cost and add no value to the commodity, so that the capital invested in the expenses belongs to the lost expenses of capitalist production that have to be regained from surplus production; that is, they form a deduction from surplus value.[4,5]

The individual consumption of transport services consequently proves unproblematic for capital as long as it does not involve the problem of procuring labour. Leisure traffic, like every other kind of individual consumption, remains a source of profit, whereas transporting people to and from work results in unprofitable expenditure. It directly raises the cost of production, representing fixed and not variable capital, if it cannot be transferred. So the capitalist argument aims naturally to declare the cost of travel to work as "necessary consumption expenditure" for each and every worker. However, the bourgeois economy does not hesitate to admit in its debates on the commuter problem that these expenses are basically costs of production.

"Any expansion in commuter travel as well as any rise in the cost of commuter transport, means . . . a lowering of the economy's productivity . . . (because) the rising costs of commuting increase the costs of production but not automatically the volume of production."[6]

The class character of bourgeois scientific thinking is here clearly revealed: connections recognized at a general level are veiled at the specific level in the interests of power. The costs of production that arise from supplying labour are styled as "consumption" of the individual worker under the laws of a market which trades in equivalents. The limits to which expenses for this system can be transferred on to the worker are set by that portion of his wage which he was left for his other reproductive needs after the deduction of travel expenses. If the proportion deducted rises to any degree, the worker's potential for reproduction decreases (in 1969 an average of about 5 per cent of wages were used for travel).

The constant expansion of commuter travel results from the disentangling of functions in towns and agglomerations that is the declared objective of the spatial planning policies in all the industrial nations. The increasing commuting time, as well as the constant deterioration of mass transport facilities caused by increased so-called private traffic, stretch the standard eight-hour day to such an extent that the worker's physical potential for reproduction, which it is meant to guarantee, is seriously reduced.[7] This development, the threatening of the productive power of the individual worker by no means favour the capitalist. In times of full employment, the level of commuting costs becomes a serious supply problem when purchasing labour. These problems may under certain conditions force large-scale industries to build up their own transport systems for workers; for example works buses.

In principle, however, a measure of this kind is, in the capital context, an additional expense to be borne like other so-called non-productive costs by the state. The state covers these expenses either by waiver to revenue (deductability of travel expenses from income tax) or by subsidies to public transport concerns, and by increasing spending on road construction, etc.

The significance of transport for the reproduction of the community of labour is reflected in state intercessions of this kind. Even projects geared solely to the reproductive needs of the masses become possible. But they are only implemented if they serve the interests of capital, i.e. reproductive needs are only satisfied to the extent that seems necessary to maintain the given levels of exploitation. Once this limit is disregarded, the contradiction between the individual capitalist and the state then becomes evident — a contradiction already all too apparent in traffic, where constantly multiplying traffic needs are brought about by increasing division of labour and have to be satisfied to sustain production while the investments thus necessitated cannot be raised in the long term without still worse problems of capital realization in other sectors of the economy.

Volkswagen Concept

The still increasing importance of so-called private traffic and the replacement of rail by road, simultaneously represent an immense increase in the price of commuting in general. At the same time the ever-growing importance of the private car bears little relation to its economic value if, for example, its rationality and economy as a means of transport are considered. That its usefulness does in many aspects surpass that of most other means of public transport, especially over middle distances, remains undisputed; but this superiority in no way explains the extraordinary discrepancy in the way the populace of capitalist industrial states evaluate this compared with other means of transport.

"The passenger car is not a means of transport designed for rationality and economy. The passenger car is the vehicle of the class-indifferent personality cult, the individual means of transport par excellence".[8]

It was thought that supporting the passenger car rather than mass transport might kill two birds with one stone. Firstly, a means akin to the "owning one's own home" ideology it was meant to instill an ideology of property so that the unpropertied masses should at last forget ideas of the genuine distribution of property. Second, through encouraging the ownership of private cars, the number of which is still popular as a means of measuring wealth, a gigantic industry was created which skimmed off the economic surplus to a hitherto unanticipated degree.

"If one reflects that the automobile industry includes not only the factories that gave it its name but also engine manufacturers, works for car bodies, trailers, containers, etc., and then again the manufacturers of parts and accessories and others, then every ninth West German now earns his living from the motor car."[9] The significance of the automobile industry is further intensified for industrial nations if one includes the interdependence of the automobile and road-building industries.

The combination of the private production of the means of transport with public planning and financing of the complementary infrastructure has proved to be altogether more profitable than the private financing of both parts, as happened with railway construction in the nineteenth century. The requirements of today's crisis management of monopoly capitalism will only in exceptional cases admit direct intervention by capital in this sphere. This restriction, however, applies only to direct intervention. Indirectly, it is particularly the automobile and crude oil industries that employ a number of means of intervention and manipulation.

An essential instrument of their pressure on public funds to force building schemes is the proclamation of the dire state of traffic. In this, the overproduction of cars is conveniently interpreted as an underproduction of traffic space. Traffic forecasts by Shell and Esso paint a gloomy picture of the future; the automobile industry is demanding special budgets to be set up for road building to be administrated solely by the transport users. "The Association of Automobile Manufacturers calls for urgent elimination of the ascertainable economic restraints and better augmentation of policy decisions on road construction with analyses and forecasts to ascertain regional traffic needs".[10]

"A particular difficulty in traffic planning where an optimal housing structure is concerned arises from the interaction between private and public local traffic. For instance the growth of private local traffic is largely unaffected by planning measures, where it should be noted particularly that only adaptation of supply to demand in individual transport services by improvement in traffic routes and parking areas can stimulate this demand in the first place".[11]

Here predictions are turned into unchangeable planning foundations; their use secures the profits of the very people who have so altruistically pointed out the dilemma with which traffic is beset.

"The claim of a crisis will persist as an inherent component of automobile speculation, just as the *scarcity* of land persists in building construction; or, expressed in the terminology of goods traffic, its supply problem. This reveals the peculiar coincidence of a commodity flourishing commercially with alleged difficulties in circulation".[13]

Planning Measures

Meanwhile some people have had stirrings of anxiety, they sense dangers of a new kind. "Today as many as sixty per cent of passenger car buyers are wage earners . . . their proportion will rise higher still. But will not these private car owners who have often acquired their cars by making great sacrifices, going without other desirable things and subjecting themselves to restraint, feel that they are the deceived, the betrayed, if in the future they can drive only under great difficulties — if at all? We can expect an army of millions of discontented and angry people."[12]

There is method in this argument. The car crisis, produced by making great sacrifices, exacts even greater sacrifices for its ostensible solution — or more precisely, its perpetuation. Thus two pages later the same author promptly claims that only more road construction can help.[13]

A long catalogue of town planning measures plays down the traffic problems of the moment, and creates new ones by suggesting first, "disentangling" the types of traffic and then separating urban functions. The first demand is usually the redevelopment and architectural opening up of the town centres. "In areas of new construction and clearance, flyovers or underpasses and their link roads will be easy to integrate. A succession of roads at a second level can even lead to an improved townscape especially in clearance areas. In this case the simultaneous redevelopment of the traffic and architecture of an area should be aimed for."[14]

The "accent on traffic" also determines the second demand, "building up areas of urban expansion to make a structured, airy town interspersed with green."[15]

The third measure, which produces even more traffic, is the proposal to construct satellite towns because "the differentiation of functions made possible in a modern economy by the division of labour has resulted in ever growing manifold traffic relationships."[16]

The division of labour and with it the division of functions, far from being recognized as the cause of the dilemma, is offered as its remedy. The contrast between town and country is reduced to transport problems and consequently is overcome by transport.

The proportion of the social product given to traffic expenditure at present fluctuates between fifteen and twenty per cent. So the wiser traffic strategists are worried about whether all these fine technical proposals for expanding the road network can be implemented. The extra growth that such construction plans might still induce in the economy and therefore in taxes would hardly suffice to cover the budget deficits caused by financing them. The consequence would be an inflation in which the automobile and building industries would be the only ones to profit.

But how can the workers' cars be taken away from them again now that they need them so much as an expression of their self-awareness now that they have grown accustomed to their convenience and comfort? No patent prescription has yet been found to solve this dilemma, but the objective is clearly defined. The trend to own a vehicle is to be maintained for economic reasons, but at the same time traffic is to be reduced for equally general economic reasons, to avoid the need for further expansion in road building. So people are supposed to continue buying cars, but they are not supposed to drive around in them too much!

Journey to work traffic is notorious as the cause of "peak traffic" so it is first on the list for being reduced. An EMNID survey (Institute for Opinion Polls in Bielefeld) in September/October 1964[17] showed that seventy-eight per cent of car owners in the Federal Republic drive their cars to work, sixty-five per cent with the explicit justification that they are forced to do so by the poor state of public transport during the rush hour.

The routine planning approach to combat peak traffic is of an organizational nature. Firms are called upon to stagger their working hours in such a way that not all their staff drive home at the same time. As it is just this coincidence of trade and working hours that is being sought, such an appeal to the employers is surely bound to fall on deaf ears.

Another organizational proposal is to decentralize works with a large labour force by means of spatial reorganization; at least to redistribute them in such a way that the lines of traffic no longer have to cross the town centres.

Capitalism sets narrow limits to any effective town-planning policy. Everywhere it meets with the barrier of privately owned land and the middle-class interest groups associated with it. A further barrier can be seen in the lack of power of the planners to execute at any time planning measures other than those which are in the interests of the monopolies. "It would be futile and senseless to demand of the town planner that he change the urban disorder which the car has stimulated because the changes needed now cannot be brought about by action in town planning alone, but only by political changes in the conditions of production and transport."[18] Hence all their efforts to decentralize or otherwise rationalize will in the end achieve no more than perpetuation of the class differences and dilemmas resulting from the present conditions of production, or to shift them to and fro. In the short term the de-individualization of journeys to and from work does seem more promising than town planning because those affected do not appear to possess the power to defend themselves effectively against such measures, at least not at present.

The way for this "de-individualization" is being prepared by curtailing parking space or increasing its price. This strategy of impoverishment towards motorists in town centres simply leaves responsibility for the construction of car parks to "private enterprise." "The concept of an unlimited right of use of public roads for parking is irreconcilable with today's conditions and even less with the further great increases to be expected in the number of motor vehicles."[19] That is why those who can hardly afford their own car anyway are going to be the first to have to leave it at home.

So that it should not occur to them to sell their car altogether, however, parking space is made scarce only in the town centres and near their places of work. At the edge of the town centre, generous car parks are laid out. Then the car owner drives from home as far as the car park at the underground terminus, there to step into the collective means of mass transport which will take him to his work place. This so-called park-and-ride system is the most ingenious solution yet for the objective set out above. It does however, encounter vehement opposition from traders in the urban centres who can see shopping traffic being reduced and are afraid of competition from the supermarkets erected beside the peripheral car parks.

A much sought after complementary strategy is to raise car prices through higher automobile or petrol taxes, accompanied by the abolition of favourable tax allowances for travel expenses. Until now this has been prevented successfully in the Federal German Republic by the automobile industry and the oil companies — although such proposals regularly occur when there is still a lot of time before the next election.

Measures like these would be appropriate and justifiable only after improving public transport enterprises. Otherwise the only result would be a lowering of the standard of living for large sections of the population. Consideration is only grudgingly given to ways in which comprehensive improvements in public transport might provide a substitute for work journeys in dense industrial areas. The main reason for this probably lies with the bourgeois planners who face the difficulty of giving up their "exclusion principle" when it comes to public transport. The principle is that everyone has to pay for any service to the extent that they take advantage of it, so the other amenities can be clearly recognized as publicly financed social welfare.

They are the captives of an ideology which can measure goods only by their exchange value. What such people would like most would be to make the use of roads, as scarce economic commodities, depend on payment. The usage fees for motorways and bridges in some countries are first tentative steps in this direction. However, everyone is now beginning to recognize the financial impossibility of plans which fit the needs of the motor car, at least "not in this generation," so "The only choice we have . . . whether we like it or not, is to support public transport."[20] There is no way out: fare increases proved to be a dead-end that led only to an accelerated loss of custom.

In view of the limits to capacities for road construction nobody now dares to claim that the effect of subsidies to public transport leads to "the hindrance of structural reorganization vital to growth"[21] and that such subsidies "could therefore be justified only in exceptional cases."

Now that the effects of the shortcomings in transport planning are seriously threatening to draw other areas of the economy into difficulty, people are prepared to jettison the ballast. "For this we must remove the one unfortunate shackle which has restricted optimum expansion especially in mass transport in a downright oppressive way. That is, the constricting obligation that a traffic route planned for construction should be economically viable or at least cover its running costs".[22]

"The . . . economic aspects (must) however be considered in the context of the economic potential of urban transport as a whole; then they acquire a different emphasis."[23] Or according to Walter Möller, former transport officer of the city of Frankfurt and then its Lord Mayor, "The profitability of transport industries (can) no longer be judged for the enterprise in isolation, but must be seen in the overall context of their use to the economy and the duties of sound spatial planning."[24]

Transport Strike

The modest subsidies so far commonly granted to public transport have not even been enough to keep the number of passengers reasonably constant. Instead, the only attempt has been to keep the subsidies relatively constant by raising the fares and reducing staff. This policy resulted in the demand already described to at least collectivize journeys to work.

As transport planners nevertheless face the need to increase the number of passengers in order to counter the road and car parks-building dilemma, some of them are tentatively considering "free fares" so vehemently denounced by the so-called pragmatists when demonstrators in Hanover, Heidelberg, Bremen and Saarbrücken made it their demand.

"To give public transport over to free use would certainly be preferable to forcing already cramped conurbations to cope with the mounting streams of traffic without sufficient preparation."[25] This realization has even percolated to the daily press: "According to traffic experts, free fares are in sight, especially in conurbations . . . In years to come the outlay for the ticket system will have lost all relation to the revenue, and furthermore the aims of regional and urban development also swing the balance for free fares . . . but it will still be a long way before we get there; probably not before 1980.[26]

Those resisting free fares fear that once workers have been granted such concessions in the consumption sphere, they might cast doubt on the functioning and necessity of the wage-price spiral. The workers' wage battle could be aggravated by added demands for low rents, cheap staple foods and so on. This worry is an important reason for politicians to act against a possible process of awakening of consciousness in the workers and to let the timely introduction of measures like non-cost-covering transport fares develop an image of the benevolent welfare state whose sole aim is the well-being of its citizens. If steps like this are taken at the right time and without prior pressure from the masses, they are admirably suited to whitewash the capitalist state as a public service organization.

This is not at all the case if such measures are taken to pacify an obvious class-struggle situation. Then it is not the caring paternal state in action, but for all those affected quite visibly the state as the advocate of capital, forced to divert a troublesome conflict. A transport strike is a very troublesome case of conflict indeed. "The circumstances of tramway blockades differ fundamentally from those of other campaigns within the consumption sphere. Tram fare increases do not affect individuals at diferent times and places and this alone makes it easier to organize resistance. This resistance must take place in the street and is much more easily legitimized in the street than, say, a protest action against increases in the price of butter. But if economic weapons (effective boycott) and political protest (street demonstrations) look to and depend on one other, then the immediate aims of the battle for reduced fares are also much more easily transmitted through the class war at work than in other campaigns in the consumption sphere, because there is decidedly nothing luxurious about travelling by tram and everyone knows that one only uses it because one has got to work and because one needs work in order to live. So it is very easy to point out that those who should pay for the tram should be those who profit from labour, the capitalists . . ."[27]

Concerted action by all the agents of state, not only the police but especially the planning authorities, the unions and the "state supporting" press, becomes necessary to prevent the masses from realizing that the transport issue manifests the basic contradiction of capitalist methods of production, the contradiction between wage-earning labour and capital. The masses are exposed to this contradiction in its most acute form at their work places every day, and the realization that only its elimination will clear the way for effectively combating all the ancillary contradictions would have the power to explode the ruling system.

In the case of a transport strike, therefore, the powers that be having failed to recognize and avert it in time must isolate it from any general social implications and reduce it to economic problems. The tools to this end are public debate on the financial position and functional economics of the transport enterprise in question and haggling between the unions and established parties on the extent of subsidies necessary. At the same time, the press is charged with the task of "de-ideologizing": anti-capitalist class struggle has to become a show of "public spiritedness". In Hanover the *Bild Zeitung* recognizes the "contradiction of anti-capitalist argumentation and Red Spot transport put to the service of capitalist every day life,"[28] and proceeds to print its own red spots for the windscreens of its readers' cars.

Red Spot transport saw to the maintenance of production while demands like "free travel to work" and "pay for the trams from industrialists' profits" remained isolated slogans which were all the easier to defuse as no class conscious organization was in a position to establish the connection necessary between the spheres of consumption and production. The absence of a socialist strategy quashed hopes of these campaigns opening prospects of overall social change, hopes which might also have made effective change in the transport problem seem possible. As it was, self-help campaigns merely reflected traces of collective modes of behaviour and a faint intimation of the real power of the masses to bring about changes.

The students and schoolchildren who prepared and at first executed the campaigns in Hanover, Heidelberg and elsewhere on their own initiative, were neither theoretically nor organizationally prepared for the process of gaining support (*Solidarisierung*) for which they were agitating.

Their argument was based on criticism of superstructural phenomena such as the manipulation of information by the mass media and on equality of opportunity in our education system. They sought the immediate liberation of the individual from the tyranny of consumption in the "affluent society" and to fulfil their aims in spontaneous campaigns. Their ideology was moulded by the theories of the "New Left", the writings of Marcuse, Baran, Gortz, Sweezy and the Frankfurt school. They mistook the momentarily stunted class consciousness of the German workers for an insight into objective circumstances, that is, they did not know how to separate the years of influence of fascist and anti-communist propaganda on the workers' consciousness from the objective economic situation in which these workers found themselves.

In brief, these campaigns, programmes and objectives did not distinguish between classes. They hinged upon the disparity thesis of the Frankfurt school[29], which had them believe that all population groups were affected equally by flaws in the infrastructural sphere in particular and that it would only require a certain optimization of information and democratizing of planning to eliminate these disparities. The means to this improved information on the actual economic potential of our system was to be "public relations" (which definitely includes the transport strikes discussed here). The foundation thus laid would then "automatically" get more and more extensive demands, more and more fundamental reforms through, so that one fine day by democratic methods, socialism might at last be achieved.[30]

But the quickly accumulated successes of these campaigns were not as grand. It may be true that fare increases were withdrawn, that "progressive" planners now publicly called for free fares and that citizen participation in planning was sought, but the masses have not organized themselves, are placing no more penetrating claims.

The groups involved in these and similar campaigns have recognized their mistakes and acknowledged the need for better organization in order to achieve education of the masses — an education to establish the inevitable connections between the spheres of consumption and production, an education that will grant some prospect of gain to the proletariat in the class struggle; an education that will show how all reformism of some sectors of capitalist production amounts to curing only the symptoms and simply contributes to the perpetuation of the existing situation.[31]

Notes

1. See Hüfner, Peter, Schütt, (1969) *Aktion Roter Punkt*, Munich.
2. See Marx (1969) *Das Kapital*, II, MEW 24, Berlin, p. 60.
3. Marx (1939) *Outlines of the Critique of Political Economy* p. 438, Moscow.
4. See Marx *Das Kapital* II, p. 150 ff.
5. See Mandel (1960) *Marxistische Wirtschaftstheorie*, pp 207, 221, Frankfurt am Main.
6. Voigt (1968) *Arbeitsstätte, Wohnstätte, Nahverkehr*, p. 191, Hamburg.
7. See *Frankfurt Rundschau* of 27th June 1970, Pendler mit Zwölfstundentag.
8. Janssen (1965) Der Personenkraftwagen, *Die Sonde*, 1, Bonn.
9. *Frankfurter Rundschau*, 14th May, 1970, In der Bundesrepublik lebt gegenwärtig jeder neunte vom Auto.
10. *Frankfurt Rundschau* of 29th April 1970, Autoindustrie; Straßenbau in eine Hand.
11. Voight, p. 23.
12. Janssen, *op. cit.*
13. Lambert, Städtischer Massenverkehr und Kraftfahrzeugverkehr in Zukunft, p. 90 *Beiträge zum Generalverkehrsplan*, Stuttgart 1963.

14. Federal Government Paper: *Bericht der Sachverständigen-kommission über eine Untersuchung von Maßnahmen zur Verbesserung der Verkehrsverhältnisse der Gemeinden*, p. 157, Bonn/Bad Godesberg 1964.
15. Lambert, p. 93.
16. Federal Government Paper, p. 29.
17. Quoted in Prigge, p. 21.
18. Helms, Die Stadt — Medium der Ausbeutung, historische Perspektiven des Städtebaus, in: Helms/Janssen (eds) *Kapitalistischer Städtebau* p. 10, Neuwied/Berlin 1970.
19. Federal Government Paper, p. 130.
20. Lambert, p. 94.
21. Nicolaison (1968) *Regionalpolitisch orientierte Verkehrsplanung im Ballungsraum*, p. 25, Göttingen.
22. Voight, p. 182.
23. Federal Government Paper, p. 97.
24. Nulltarif: Subventionierter Schlendrian?, *Der Volkswirt* no. 1, 13th March, 1970, p. 24.
25. Voight, p. 201.
26. Engel, Nulltarif: Das Auto soll am Stadtrand bleiben, *Frankfurter Rundschau* of 21st May 1970.
27. "Rote-Punkt-Aktion in Heidelberg", *Rote Pressekorrespondenz 19* of 27th June, 1969, p. 22.
28. "Rote-Punkt-Aktion in Heidelberg", p. 30.
29. Offe (1969) Politischer Herrschaft und Klassenstrukturen, *Politwissenschaft*, Frankfurt am Main.
    Offe (1969) Sachzwang und Entscheidungsspielraum, *Stadtbauwelt* 38, Berlin.
30. Faßbinder (1969/1970) "Zur politökonomischen Analyse der Demokratisierung infrastruktureller Planung" unpublished university diploma dissertation, Technische Universität Berlin, Winter semester.
31. Barnbrook, Frank, Große, Hamann, Joeres, Stirnemann, "Zur Analyse der Planung im Spätkapitalismus", unpublished MS for the European Cultural Foundation, Amsterdam.

Index

Other Titles in the Series

CHADWICK, G. F.
A Systems View of Planning, 2nd Edition (Volume 1)

BLUNDEN, W. R.
The Land Use Transport System (Volume 2)

GOODALL, B.
The Economics of Urban Areas (Volume 3)

LEE, C.
Models in Planning: An Introduction to the Use of Quantitative Models in Planning (Volume 4)

FALUDI, A. K. F.
A Reader in Planning Theory (Volume 5)

COWLING, T. M. & STEELEY, G. C.
Sub-regional Planning Studies: An Evaluation (Volume 6)

FALUDI, A. K. F.
Planning Theory (Volume 7)

SOLESBURY, W.
Policy in Urban Planning Structure Plans, Programmes and Local Plans (Volume 8)

MOSELEY, M. J.
Growth Centres in Spatial Planning (Volume 9)

LICHFIELD, N. et al.
Evaluation in the Planning Process (Volume 10)

SANT, M. E. C.
Industrial Movement and Regional Development: The British Case (Volume 11)

HART, D. A.
Strategic Planning in London: The Rise and Fall of the Primary Road Network (Volume 12)

STARKIE, D. N. M.
Transportation Planning, Policy and Analysis (Volume 13)

HEALEY, P.
Local Plans in British Land-Use Planning (Volume 31)

COPE, D., HILLS, P. & JAMES, P.
Energy Policy and Land-Use Planning: An International Perspective (Volume 32)

BANDMAN, M.
Regional Development in the USSR: Modelling the Formation of Soviet Territorial-Production Complexes (Volume 33)

BROMLEY, R.
Planning for Small Enterprises in Third World Cities (Volume 34)

The terms of our inspection copy service apply to all the above books. A complete catalogue of all books in the Pergamon International Library is available on request. The Publisher will be pleased to consider suggestions for revised editions and new titles.